Roll Over Adorno

D1715979

THE SUNY SERIES IN
POSTMODERN CULTURE

Joseph Natoli, *Editor*

Roll Over Adorno

*Critical Theory, Popular Culture,
Audiovisual Media*

Robert Miklitsch

State University of New York Press

Cover photo: Action Portrait of Chuck Berry. Frank Driggs Collection/Hulton Archive/ Getty Images. Used by permission.

Published by
State University of New York Press, Albany

For information, address State University of New York Press,
194 Washington Avenue, Suite 305, Albany, NY 12210-2384

Production by Marilyn P. Semerad
Marketing by Fran Keneston

Library of Congress Cataloging-in Publication Data

Miklitsch, Robert, 1953–
    Roll over Adorno : critical theory, popular culture, audiovisual media / Robert Miklitsch.
        p. cm. — (SUNY series in postmodern culture)
    Includes bibliographical references and index.
    ISBN 0-7914-6733-3 (hardcover : alk. paper) — ISBN 0-7914-6734-1 (pbk. : alk. paper)
    1. Television broadcasting—Social aspects—United States. 2. Motion pictures—Social aspects—United States. 3. Popular music—Social aspects—United States. 4. Popular culture—United States. I. Title. II. Series.

PN1992.6.M49 2006
302.23—dc22

                                                        2005015254

ISBN-13: 978-0-7914-6733-6 (hardcover : alk. paper)
ISBN-13: 978-0-7914-6734-3 (pbk. : alk. paper)

10 9 8 7 6 5 4 3 2 1

It is peculiar to the bourgeois Utopia that it is not yet able to conceive an image of perfect joy without that of the person excluded from it. . . . we can understand why the "problem of the Ninth Symphony" was insoluble. In the fairytale Utopia, too, the stepmother who must dance in burning shoes or is stuffed into a barrel spiked with nails is an inescapable part of the glorious wedding.

—Theodor Adorno, *Beethoven*

On August 20th, 1977, as part of the US bicentennial celebrations, a Voyager spacecraft left Cape Canaveral with a message to other life forms in our universe and beyond. On board was a recording of the 5th Movement from Beethoven's String Quartet in B Flat, Number 13, Opus 130; also, a piece of rock and roll music called Johnny B. Goode by Chuck Berry.

Contents

Illustrations

Acknowledgments

When Keith Richards was once asked how he came up with the world-historical chords for "Satisfaction," he responded by saying that he had dreamed them: he got up one morning and, bam!, there they were on the tape recorder. "In dreams begin responsibilities . . ."

I invoke Delmore Schwarz because, to accentuate the obvious, books incur responsibilities, not least to one's dreamwork. Although the following debts are rather more familiar and less strange, none of the people acknowledged is in any way responsible for whatever errors of fact or fantasy remain uncorrected in this book.

First off, I'm enormously grateful to James Peltz, Interim Director at State University of New York Press, as well as to the editor of the Postmodern Series at SUNY Press, Joe Natoli, for their steadfast encouragement and unstinting support. I'm also grateful to Margaret Copeley for her painstaking copyediting of the manuscript, and to Marilyn Semerad, for scrupulously overseeing its production.

I owe debts, both large and small, to numerous people at Ohio University: Leslie Flemming, the Dean of Arts and Sciences, for time off to work on this book; Ken "The Kinks" Daley, for being an unusually solicitous and good-natured chair while I was going down the long and winding road of actually completing the manuscript; Joe McLaughlin, our new chair, for cheerfully working to remunerate me for the illustrations and, together with Howard Dewald, Associate Dean of the College of Arts and Sciences, for the cover image of Chuck Berry; my colleagues in the English Department for their day-to-day, week-to-week, quarter-to-quarter collegiality (no mean thing these days); Gerri Lux, for graciously greenlighting miniprojects and generally being a super-fun person; Barb Grueser, for being unfailingly helpful and cheerful about assisting me in all manner of tasks; Todd Gardner, for regularly coming to my aid, with alacrity and nary a complaint, in the electronic preparation of the manuscript; Richard Comfort, for assiduously assembling the index; Cara DiBlasi, for diligently compiling the bibliography; and last but by no means least, the graduate and undergraduate students in my Literary Theory and Popular Culture classes—especially the "Buffy" gang (Grant Allen, Katherine Furler, Christina Pedersen)—who, like good Socratic fellows, sparked me while I endeavored to think and feel my way, sometimes blindly, through various texts and ideas.

As a number of these chapters have appeared, albeit in slightly different form, in journals, I'm much obliged to the following editors: for chapter 1, "Rock 'n' Theory," Lisa Brawley and Stuart Moulthrop at *Postmodern Culture*; for chapter 4, "Audiophilia," John Caughie and Simon Frith at *Screen*; for chapter 5, "Gen-X TV," Stephen Tropiano at the *Journal of Film and Video*; and for chapter 6, "Shot/Countershot," Warren Buckland at *New Studies in Film and Television*. A tip of the hat goes, in addition, to Matthew Byrnie, for offering some early, prescient suggestions about the final shape of the book; and to Michael Bérubé, fellow drummer and rock music fan, who provided the perfect response to the call of the book's title (and the conclusion to the introduction): "Roll over Adorno and tell Horkheimer the news."

Other debts closer to home include my erstwhile compatriots in Athens (and, now, Columbus): Kasia Marciniak, who over the years has proved to be an especially probing interlocutor; Elizabeth Renker, with whom I shared, over red wine and dinner, mutually sympathetic conversations about the labors of book-making; Whitney Huber, who despite my occasionally indiscriminate fondness for the ephemera of pop culture, has impressed upon me the importance of feminism and the very real pleasures of counter-cinema (not to mention the enduring musical virtues of PJ Harvey and Sonic Youth); and David Lazar, with whom over music and the more than occasional martini (not shaken or stirred, but poured straight from the freezer), I've discussed virtually everything under the sun—from Art Deco to Hitchcock, Houdini's Box to The Really Big Questions (Kelly vs. Astaire).

Merci to Jayne "Jessica" Burchard, who not only put up with me in the most pleasant manner imaginable during the time in which I composed the very last parts of this book but has continually reminded me that Prada and progressive politics, NOW and Cat Power, though by no means identical, are not mutually exclusive either.

Since intellectual work can seem pretty hollow without the support of family, however one chooses to define it, a special shout-out to my nephew, Ray, for instructing me about new music ("I'm slippin, I'm fallin, I can't get up / I'm slippin, I'm fallin, I can't get up / I'm slippin, I'm fallin, I gotta get up . . ."); a heartfelt thank you to my sibs—Cathy,

David, Teresa, and Rose—who have been there for me more than they know; a very special thank you to my sister, Fran Fran Fran, for taking time from the kids, Cai and Zhen-Hua, to design the cover; and, finally, perennial thanksgiving to my parents, Robert Senior and Catherine Berry, who are very proud of me even if they don't always understand what exactly I'm talking about.

I leave off, reluctantly, with these not so disenchanting lines from "I've Seen It All," performed by Thom Yorke and Björk—who knows a thing or two about hi and lo, good and Bad Taste ("Beethoven and Bach bollocks")—in Lars von Trier's *Dancer in the Dark*: "You've never been to Niagara Falls?" / "I have seen water, it's water, that's all . . ."

Script

We're messing around, the three of us, getting
ready to go home and rubbishing each other's five
best side one track ones of all time (mine: "Janie
Jones," the Clash, from *The Clash*; "Thunder Road,"
Bruce Springsteen, from *Born to Run*; "Smells Like
Teen Spirit," Nirvana, from *Nevermind*; "Let's Get It
On," Marvin Gaye, from *Let's Get It On*; "Return of
the Grevious Angel," Gram Parsons, from *Grevious
Angel*). Barry: "Couldn't you make it more obvious
than that? What about the Beatles? What about
the Rolling Stones? What about the fucking . . . the
fucking . . . Beethoven?

—Nick Hornby, *High Fidelity*

This book is composed of a series of essayis-
tic encounters, the first and foremost being
between Chuck Berry and Ludwig van
Beethoven, the duck-walking, Gibson-guitar-wielding rocker from St.
Louis and the definitive Western icon of musical genius. Although the
not so "vanishing mediator" of this discursive encounter is Theodor
Adorno, the title of the book is intended to recollect not only Berry's great
rock anthem, "Roll Over Beethoven" (1956), but the rebellious spirit of
early rock 'n' roll and American popular culture itself. In other words, if
Adorno stands for European high culture and all things classical, including and especially music (Beethoven being, for Adorno, the consummate
figure of artistic expression), Chuck Berry—the de facto king of rock 'n'
roll—signifies American popular culture in all its iconoclastic energy.

Before I turn to a more formal, chapter-by-chapter synopsis of the
book, I might mention that part of my attraction to popular culture stems,
like my interest in fantasy, from a wish to engage politically fraught
topics. One corollary of this wish has been a strong desire to attend to the
intricacies of the aesthetic register, the kinks and quirks of individual
texts, to maintain a high or, if you will, hi-lo fidelity to what Adorno in a
letter to Walter Benjamin calls the "objectivity of phantasmagoria."

Part 1, "Popular Music: Hi-Lo Fidelity," examines the role of popular music in American culture from early rock 'n' roll to recent debates, in the wake of MP3 and P2P technologies, about the death of the music industry. Chapter 1, "Rock 'n' Theory: Cultural Studies, Autobiography, and the Death of Rock," starts by turning back the clock to the rock-around-the-clock 1950s. This '50s tack is mirrored in the musical form of the chapter, which is structured like a 45 record. On the "A" side, called "Memory Train" (after Elvis Presley's "Mystery Train"), I present a brief sketch of the birth of rock 'n' roll in the context of some of the more memorable popular-musical moments in my life. The point of these personal reflections is to italicize the specific, even autobiographical, sources of rock criticism. On the "B" (theory) side, I read Lawrence Grossberg's work on popular music, a singular instance of cultural studies, as a symptom of the unexamined racial, sexual, national, and international assumptions that frequently subtend claims about the "death of rock." My focus here is the, for some, oxymoronic combination "rock 'n' theory"—in particular, what happens when rock becomes an object of theoretical speculation. Finally, in the conclusion to the chapter, a self-reflexive coda that owes a debt to Chuck Berry, I muse on the relation between contemporary youth culture and popular music as well as the generational fantasies that underwrite so many rise-and-fall histories of rock music.

Chapter 2, "Roll Over Adorno: Beethoven, Chuck Berry, and Popular Music in the Age of MP3," reflects—in the idiom of the essay, Adorno's favored form—on the classic cultural-industrial problematic in the context of popular music. In this, the title chapter, I concentrate on the medium of music rather than, say, film or TV not simply because music is arguably the most ubiquitous art form today, from radio to MP3, but because it offers a unique lens with which to focus the various questions that motivate this book: the status of popular culture and audiovisual media at the beginning of the twenty-first century; the tension in postmodernism between aesthetics and politics, art and entertainment; and the role of critical theory and popular-cultural studies in the present conjuncture. The premise is that if Berry is something like the wild dialectical other of Adorno, this binary opposition is not a simple one nor, as I demonstrate in my reading of the two, does it necessarily demand the sort of pat reversals one might imagine (where, for example, Berry's bad-boy persona is a counter to Adorno's mandarin asceticism). Rather, true to the performative logic of deconstruction, "Chuck Berry" is employed in this chapter as a vehicle (to sample the automotive rhetoric of his songbook) for staging some of the contradictions of Frankfurt School cultural critique and contemporary media culture.

The reprise to part 1, "Beethoven's Hair," reviews the issue of popular music from a slightly different angle than either chapter 1 (which uses the proclamation of the death of rock to reflect on its discursive history) or chapter 2 (which tests the Adornian critique of popular music by eliciting the black "hillbilly" sound of Chuck Berry). In this reprise I look at yet another crossroads in the history of twentieth-century American culture when high art, embodied in this case by concert-hall music, collided with its popular-cultural other (that formerly "low," "native" form of American music known as "jazz"). While one might argue that the historical occasion for this reprise, Paul Whiteman's "Experiment in Modern Music" (1924), represented a superfluous, not to say wrongheaded effort to legitimize "jass," it can also be seen as a quintessentially American instance of cultural synthesis where the disparate worlds of Tin Pan Alley and pre-bebop jazz briefly came together to produce an originary work of art: George Gershwin's *Rhapsody in Blue*.

Part 2, "Sound Film," segues, via sound, from popular music to cinema in order to examine the relation between post–Screen theory and what Michel Chion calls "audio-vision." Chapter 3, "The Suture Scenario: Audiovisuality and Post-Screen Theory," revisits the discourse of suture, perhaps the most significant conceptual legacy of Screen theory, itself a high-octane synthesis of Freud and Marx. The aim of this chapter is to ascertain whether the concept of suture has anything left to say to contemporary film studies. Referencing Slavoj Žižek's critique of both the Althusserian notion of subjectivization and the Screen account of suture as ideological closure, I propose, via a close reading of audiovisuality in Marlon Riggs's *Tongues Untied* (1989) and F. Gary Gray's *Set It Off* (1996), that the future of suture theory depends on, among other things, rearticulating it with recent film formations such as "queer cinema" and the "new black movie boom." As a critic with an unabashedly powerful transference with American popular culture, the trajectory of the text also reflects my increasing interest in discursive sites that foreground the fantasmatic intersection or crossing between different mass media (for example, the "blue" drag-queen sequence scored to Billie Holiday's "Lover Man" in *Tongues Untied*) and between different, even clashing, representational categories. So, in the second, illustrative section, I detail how Queen Latifah's performance as Cleopatra Simms in *Set It Off* draws on the hyper-masculine codes of gangsta rap—in particular, the seminal "West Coast" sound of Dr. Dre (who plays Black Sam in the film)—to generate a compelling portrayal of a gangsta butch or "butch n the hood."

Chapter 4, "Audiophilia: Audiovisual Pleasure and Narrative Cinema in *Jackie Brown*," opens with a brief account of cinephilia and then turns to the issue of scopophilia as adumbrated in one of the most influential texts of Screen theory, Laura Mulvey's "Visual Pleasure and Narrative Cinema" (1975). Though it's now clear that the category of sexuality, not to mention race, thoroughly problematizes the classic feminist account of the "male gaze," the question that propels this chapter is: How does the acoustic or auditory dimension of film complicate received notions about visual pleasure and narrative cinema? The fourth section of the chapter endeavors to answer this question by offering a close reading of Quentin Tarantino's *Jackie Brown* (1997) in the context of what the director himself calls the film's "funky '70s soul" soundtrack as well as what I call, after Chion and Kaja Silverman, the "acoustic" gaze. In the remainder of the chapter, which attempts to think the relation between race and music in Tarantino's film, I return to the feminist critique of scopophilia by way of the character of Melanie Ralston (Bridget Fonda) in order to broach a counter-reading of Tarantino's striking, if fraught, sense of cinephilia and audiophilia.

"Alex's 'Lovely Ludwig van' and Marty McFly's White Rock Minstrel Show," the reprise to part 2, exploits the musical conceit from which the title of this book takes its inspiration, "Roll Over Beethoven," to reexamine the cinematic use of the music of Beethoven and Chuck Berry. While my first example, *A Clockwork Orange* (1971), suggests the sort of radical and even, for some, dubious ends to which canonical music can be put—Kubrick's film draws on both the classical and film-musical traditions (the Ninth Symphony and "Singin' in the Rain" respectively)—my second example, Zemeckis's *Back to the Future* (1985), presents a rather different, arguably more problematic illustration of the politics of appropriation. In Zemeckis's film, the romance of race rather than, say, the attractions of sex and violence provides the impetus for the narrative's recourse to one of the most famous songs in the canon of rock music: "Johnny B. Goode." The question that this second film poses is: What does it mean for Marty McFly (Michael J. Fox) to perform Chuck Berry before, as it were, he became Chuck Berry?

Part 3, "TV: Television, Telephilia, Televisuality," engages the issues of televisuality and telephilia or, more properly perhaps, *my* telephilia, tracking from Fox Gen-X melodrama to psycho-gangster soap opera. Chapter 5, "Gen-X TV: Political-Libidinal Structures of Feeling in *Melrose Place*," discusses one of the paradigmatic programs of the first half of the 1990s, *Melrose Place* (Fox, 1992–99). In this chapter, which investigates the intersection of race, class, and sexuality in *Melrose Place* in addition to other issues central to the show such as fashion, female address, and the romance of postfeminism, I argue that the program's social politics are an index, however mediated, of larger economic forces associated with post-Fordism. While the intradiegetic accent in *Melrose Place* on advertising is one indice of this political-libidinal artic-ulation, yet another indice is the program's pace, the velocity of which reveals its considerable debt to music video or, more pointedly, MTV. Indeed, as the last format suggests, the telephilia or specifically televi-sual pleasures of *Melrose Place* cannot be understood apart from its generic and generational conditions of possibility. In this sense, just as *The Sopranos* (HBO, 1999–present) is part epic, part exposé, at once post-Gotti and post-*Godfather*, so *Melrose Place* derives not a little of its appeal from its Gen-X and melodramatic sources.

Chapter 6, "Shot/Countershot: Sexuality, Psychoanalysis, and Postmodern Style in *The Sopranos*," is composed, not unlike a diptych, of two parts. While the first part concentrates on what I take to be the dominant formal aspects of *The Sopranos*—seriality, citationality, and self-reflexivity—the second part tackles the dominant issue with re-spect to content, sexuality, and the intimate double of sexuality, ag-gressivity. In general, the dual or dialectical composition of the piece is intended to reflect not only one of the fundamental telefilmic tropes—the so-called shot/reverse shot—but the psychoanalytic scenario itself, which is structured, as in *The Sopranos*, around the shot/countershot of the "talking cure." As Tony Soprano (James Gandolfini), the irrepress-ible gangster analysand, says at one point to his psychoanalytically-trained analyst, Dr. Jennifer Melfi (Lorraine Bracco), laying bare his very real fears about engaging in the sort of emotionally inflammatory and, for him, suspiciously feminine colloquy that epitomizes psycho-analysis, "Is this a woman thing? You ask me how I'm feeling, I tell you how I'm feeling, and [then you] torch me for it?"

The third and concluding reprise, "Tony Soprano, Meet Buffy the Vampire Slayer," returns to the autobiographical mode with which chapter 1 commences. My topic here, however, is not the popular music of my youth but my experience of Mob life growing up in western New York State. More generally, the final reprise uses the postmodern generic hybridity of *The Sopranos* as a jumping off place to talk about the televisual appeal of "Once More with Feeling," the musical episode of *Buffy the Vampire Slayer* (WB, 1997–2001; UPN, 2001–03). A tour de force of cult television in the cable and satellite age, "Once More with Feel-ing" proves that it's not only possible to cross a blond, pun-happy ex-cheerleader with the action and horror genres but to marry the balletic stunts of vampire slaying with the conventions of the classical Ameri-can musical. The result is a pop-cultural confection of the first order: quality prime-time TV about big-picture issues—life and death and the undead—that you can also tap your feet to.

Introduction

Critical Theory, Popular Culture, Audiovisual Media

Why is kitsch a so much more profitable export than Rembrandt?

—Clement Greenberg, "Avant-Garde and Kitsch"

In Masscult (and in its bastard, Midcult), everything becomes a commodity, to be mined for $$$$.

—Dwight Macdonald, "Masscult and Midcult"

In "A Theory of Mass Culture," Dwight Macdonald commences his famous salvo against what for him is sometimes mistakenly called "popular culture" by insisting that its "distinctive mark is that it is solely and directly an article for mass consumption, like chewing gum."[1] Though this sort of complaint is familiar enough, it's hard to imagine a more patronizing attitude toward popular culture, as if its products were somehow beneath contempt.

Still, in retrospect, what's striking about Macdonald's essay is the decidedly stark binaries that structure its argument: "A statistically significant part of the population . . . is chronically confronted with a choice between going to the movies or a concert, between reading Tolstoy or a detective story, between looking at old masters or a TV show."[2] The argument of "A Theory of Mass Culture" is based, it is clear, on the logic of mutual exclusion. Indeed, so deeply engrained are the cultural protocols of the day (and Macdonald's are not so much exceptional as exemplary) that it never occurs to the author that it's possible to both enjoy and be instructed by both a nineteenth-century Russian novel and a contemporary detective story.

Moreover, despite the loaded rhetorical valences associated with the final opposition (Tolstoy "good," detective fiction "bad"), the differences between these cultural objects or practices are not as self-evident as

1

they may seem—even, it's important to note, at the time that Macdonald was composing his essay (an earlier version of which was published in *Politics* in 1944 as "A Theory of *Popular* Culture").[3] In this political and historical context, consider a passage from Raymond Chandler's *Farewell, My Lovely* (1940):

> They had Rembrandt on the calendar that year, a rather smeary self-portrait due to imperfectly registered color plate. It showed him holding a smeared palette with a dirty thumb and wearing a tam-o'-shanter which wasn't any too clean either. His other hand held a brush poised in the air, as if he might be going to do a little work after a while, if somebody made a down payment.[4]

Anybody who is even remotely familiar with Chandler's work will not be surprised by his invocation of one of the capital Old Masters as a way to ironically comment on his own iconic creation, the private-eye Philip Marlowe (whose surname itself recollects Conrad as well as Shakespeare's great contemporary and adversary, Christopher Marlowe).

To be fair, when in the very first paragraph of "A Theory of Mass Culture" Macdonald claims that detective fiction is one of the "new media" which the "serious artist" rarely comes into contact with, he is specifically thinking of sensational authors such as Dashiell Hammett and Mickey Spillane or, to employ his own shorthand, not "Dupin-Holmes" but Spade-Hammer. The irony is not only that Marlowe is the "vanishing mediator" in the series "Spade-Hammer," but that very few people who are conversant with detective fiction, as Macdonald appears to be, would compare Hammett to Spillane, whereas many would compare Hammett to Chandler.

If it's surprising that Macdonald never mentions Chandler in his brief survey of detective fiction, subtitled "Sherlock Holmes to Mike Hammer," it's even more surprising that the author, who was also a practicing film critic, omits any discussion of film noir. Now, one might argue that noir as a popular film genre predates Macdonald, who is writing in, roughly speaking, the mid-1940s and 1950s, though *The Maltese Falcon* (directed by the literary-minded John Huston from a novel by Hammett) appeared in 1941 and the genre coalesces, by common consensus, in 1944. The key to this particular mystery lies, I think, in the term itself: *film noir*. The passing critique of Gide (who, according to Macdonald, "was foolish enough to admire Hammett"[5]) indicates as much. In other words, film noir would have been suspect because it was invented by the French, first by Frank, Chartier, et al. in the early 1940s and later, more definitively by Raymond Borde and Étienne Chaumeton in *A Panorama of American Film Noir* (1955).[6] In fact, in one of those loopy moments that deconstruct the critically policed borders between criticism and popular culture, there's a well-known photograph of Robert Aldrich on the set of *Kiss Me Deadly* (1955)—for Borde and Chaumeton, the terminus of classic film noir—holding up a copy of their book.

The interest of *Kiss Me Deadly* in the context of Macdonald's essay is not simply that Aldrich's film trumps its lowbrow, sensationalist source, alluding to everything from Greek mythology to Christina Rossetti,[7] but that its politics are resolutely postwar ones—that is to say, post-1944. A paradigmatic midcentury, mass-cultural text (and it's a real text), *Kiss Me Deadly* offers a stunning counterpoint to Macdonald's theory of mass culture, dramatizing both its aesthetic and political conditions of possibility. These preconditions are, to tender an equation, anti-mass culture = anti-Soviet Union politics. The key term here is "Europe," meaning Western Europe,[8] where the Old World remains, French "culinary" eccentricities like Gide's admiration for Hammett aside, the bastion of elite, aristocratic culture as opposed to both Soviet and American mass culture or, more precisely, Soviet propaganda and American middlebrow culture.[9]

Of course, the problem with this formulation, a problem that has been with us since "sometime after 1960," as Louis Menand remarks in "Culture Club: The Short, Happy Life of the American Highbrow," is that most Europeans had become interested, like their transcontinental counterparts, "in Elvis Presley and Marilyn Monroe."[10] Indeed, the French (and here we return to Macdonald's issues with Gide) "were even interested in Jerry Lewis."[11] From this perspective, an essay like Macdonald's "Masscult and Midcult," which appeared in 1960, reads like an epitaph not so much on the death of high culture as of the absolute, politically efficacious distinction between "highbrow" and "lowbrow": between looking at a Rembrandt (say, a late self-portrait) and reading a detective story such as *Farewell, My Lovely* or, more expressively perhaps, between attending an opera performance at the Met and watching *The Sopranos* on HBO.[12]

Popular Music

> Beethoven's pathos of humanity can be . . . debased into a ritual celebration of the status quo. This change of function gave Beethoven his position as a classic, from which he ought to be rescued.
>
> —Theodor Adorno,
> *The Philosophy of Modern Music*

> Were it not for the dynamics of racism in our society,
> the man who would most likely have been crowned
> the "King of Rock 'n' Roll" was . . . Chuck Berry.
>
> —Reebee Garofalo, "Black Rhythm
> and Blues to White Rock 'n' Roll"

The double, highly pessimistic conclusion of "A Theory of Mass Culture"—"The Future of High Culture: Dark," "The Future of Mass Culture: Darker"—owes something to the baleful predictions of the Frankfurt School, which was not exactly upbeat about the "affirmative" aspects of the culture industry. In this light, Macdonald's citation of Adorno's essay "On Popular Music" in the final paragraph of his article is hardly accidental and suggests that his criticism of mass culture is deeply indebted to Adorno's seminal and more original critique.

Ironically enough, Adorno's writings on popular music have become the definitive statement of his—and, by extension, the Frankfurt School's—position on mass culture.[13] Although such a reading does not, of course, do justice to either, it does say something about the current critical conjuncture. The first is that unlike Adorno's writings on other media (say, on film or TV), his essays on popular music bear an intimate relationship to the art form he was most knowledgeable about and invested in: classical and, in particular, avant-garde music. The second thing to say about the extraordinary interest in Adorno's work on popular music is that it has been associated not so much with jazz (which is the main, generic focus of his work) as with rock, where rock, more so than jazz, is itself linked to a wide array of affects and practices, intensities and apparatuses. Finally, it should be noted that the singular status of a piece such as "On Popular Music" is temporally coincident with the rise of popular music studies and the precipitous decline of classical musicology.

About the last development, I think it's safe to say that when Chuck Berry recorded "Roll Over Beethoven" on April 16, 1956, at the Chess Records studio (session 5!), he could not have imagined that his revolutionary gospel would eventually come to pass. What we're talking about here is "cultural sovereignty."[14] As Robert Fink observes in "Elvis Everywhere: Musicology and Popular Music Studies at the Twilight of the Canon" (2002), classical music—"for the first time in a century"—"has lost even its symbolic or ritualistic power to define hierarchies of taste within the larger culture."[15]

The golden age in question—from roughly the late nineteenth century to 1964 (when, say, the Beatles covered Berry's "Roll Over Beethoven")—is a relatively brief period of time, but even if not everyone listened to *classical* music, "almost everyone accepted that Beethoven was Music the way the Mona Lisa was (and still is) Art."[16] Put another way, even if the words and music of "Roll Over Beethoven" were authored by Chuck Berry (and this issue of authorship is one salient difference between Elvis and him), Chuck Berry made *music*, not that culturally reified thing: "Music-with-a-capital-M."[17]

Needless to say, things have changed since 1956. Popular music critics can speculate endlessly about the "death of rock" (as I discuss in detail in chapter 1), but the temperature of classical music is not simply falling, the corpse is getting cold. Fink's post-mortem pretty much says it all: "As aging audiences quite literally die off, school music programs vanish, regional orchestras collapse, and U.S. classical record sales drop below 2 percent of the industry total, we must all admit it: Beethoven has finally rolled over."[18]

One artistic consequence of this *petit récit*—what one might call, with just a touch of irony, "the decline of Western civilization"—is that classical musicians are now aggressively appropriating rock. Hence the phenomenon of *True Love Waits: Christopher Riley Plays Radiohead* (2003), which classical-music "cover" itself comes in the wake of Brad Mehldau's jazz transpositions of Radiohead in *Art of the Trio, Volume 3* (1998). Another consequence of the above decline, one implicit in Fink's state-of-the-art meditation, is that classical-music critics are taking on popular music. Perhaps the most prominent example of this trend recently appeared in the *New Yorker*, in which their resident classical-music critic Alex Ross proffered a close reading of Justin Timberlake's "Cry Me a River" in a column titled "Pop 101." In his reading, subtitled "The Timberlake Perplex," Ross, while giving due props to the ex-'N Sync member's "plaintive" vocals (if not his soul phrasings), makes the convincing case that the "genius" behind the recording is Timbaland (the well-known rap producer Tim Mosley) and, moreover, that hip hop production today is the "site of some of the . . . wittiest thinking in pop music."[19]

However, in what is for me an even more insightful moment, Ross remarks that "Cry Me a River" (no apparent relation to the standard) "has the *inward* delight of a song that is better than it needs to be."[20] The history of popular music is writ small here since, contra Adorno, the beauty of songs like "Cry Me a River" is that its formal intricacy spectacularly exceeds its exchange value. In other words, classical music as a genre has historically been associated since Kant with the formal autonomy of the aesthetic while popular music has been linked, like mass culture in general, with the necessity of the commercial sphere. Yet it is precisely the immanent, delightful formal symmetry and complexity of "Cry Me a River" that differentiates it from other Top-40 hits.

Chuck Berry is particularly provocative in this context because, unlike Timberlake (who knows better than to claim he's doing it all for the Benjamins), Berry is on record claiming, in a wonderfully alliterative locution, that "the dollar dictates what is written."[21] The point is, just as classical music has never been wholly inseparable, as Adorno would be the first to point out (see epigraph), from the processes of fetishization and commodification, so popular music is relatively autonomous—depending on the artist, genre, and specific historical moment—from these very same processes. Beethoven, to echo Macdonald, is just as much an "idol of consumption" as Elvis.

As for the issue of production (a standpoint that ultimately drives both Adorno's and Macdonald's critiques of mass culture), it's significant that the two biggest developments in popular music over the last ten years or so have involved a technology (MP3) and a genre (rap). Since I discuss the impact of MP3 and P2P technologies in the conclusion to chapter 2, I would only note here that these file-sharing formats have the potential to revolutionize the prevailing modes of production, distribution, and consumption of popular music. In fact, to a great extent they already have, if the recent contraction of the music industry is any indication.[22]

The following passage from the introduction to Steven Daly and David Kamp's third volume of "The Rock Snob's Dictionary" captures, for all its parodic po-mo tenor, something of the current pop-musical *Zeitgeist*:

> Today the culture industry is so avidly strip-mining every last exploitable seam of black vinyl that nothing, it seems, is sacred. The snob learns, to his consternation, that one of his carefully-hoarded out of print LPs has been rendered into CD-ready zeros and ones by some hip-to-things label. The binary results are then attractively retro-packaged by some Skechers-slippered Power Mac jockey and soft-sold with expert sleeve notes. . . . By the time. . . Starbucks has excerpted one of the CD's tracks for its latest point of purchase . . . the Snob's original copy of said LP (mint condition; mono mix) has become valueless, *no longer fit for Snob discourse.*[23]

The wonderful thing about this passage, in addition to the passing allusion to Adorno, is that it exhibits the hyper-discriminatory taste that was once the province of classical-music patrons and, later, jazz enthusiasts but is now common in rock discourse (so common, in fact, that it can be parodied).

More generally, Daly and Kamp's irony-festooned complaint evinces the radical democratizing effect of digital reproduction: the cult object—fit to be framed, if not played (since actual use might degrade, ever so slightly, its pristine condition)—is rereleased into general circulation by an "indie," and then, after being touted by the glossy monthlies (which lavishly praise not the original but the remastered product as an "undiscovered gem"), is promptly synergized to sell a coffee-franchise compilation. The net result: muzak to drink mocha cappuccino to. The music in question, which was once only available on vinyl (and thus appreciated only by the select audiophilic few), is now everywhere, pervasive as the pollutants in the atmosphere.

This process of strip mining is not, of course, new; what is new is how lightning fast and omnivorous it has become since the onset of the digital era. At the same time, the by no means negligible pathos that underwrites Daly and Kamp's parody puts a fresh spin on the Adornian equation of pop culture with the culture industry, since from the Rock Snob's perspective, the problem is not popular culture per se but the way the various extra-cultural industries reappropriate mass-cultural commodities for the purposes of marketing and promotion, publicity and advertising. For example, you know that rap has finally become completely assimilated into the mainstream when you see a McDonald's commercial for the Big Mac featuring hip hop music.

My illustrative recourse to rap is not, as it were, innocent since rap itself has an overdetermined relation, via sampling and layering, to technology and commodification. In fact, in part because of these economic and technological determinations (but only in part, since race is also plainly an integral aspect of rap's appeal), it's gradually become the dominant popular-music genre in the United States. A quick glance at "The Top 25 Albums" of 2002 confirms its musical hegemony.[24] While the only remotely rock recording among the first fifteen "albums" is a reissue of Elvis Presley (*Elvis: No. 1 Hits*), three of the top five are rap-related records: *The Eminem Show*, *Nellyville*, and the soundtrack to *8 Mile*. Moreover, while there are numerous rappers not on this list who have arguably maintained both longevity and credibility (Nas, Jay-Z, Snoop Dogg, P. Diddy), it's difficult to dispute the preeminence of Eminem. (The runaway success of Em's protégé, 50 Cent, simply reinforces the point.)

The significance of Slim Shady and, more generally, gangsta rap in the culture at large is that they dramatize in explosive form the perennial problem of politics and aesthetics. For example, improbably enough, Eminem—a white guy from the wrong, black side of "8 Mile" in Detroit—has conjured up the original racial matrix out of which early rock 'n' roll, in the sublime figure of Elvis, first emerged. That he blatantly acts out the "dirty" side of this story, albeit with not a little panache (and adroit production touches courtesy of Dr. Dre), is just one of many things that makes up his controversial persona: "I am the worst thing since Elvis Presley / To do black music so selfishly / And use it to get myself wealthy."

There is doubtlessly not a little signifying at work here, given that Eminem's confession, a crazy mix of boasting and contrition, is ultimately predicated on an absurdly inflated comparison of himself to Elvis. However, these sorts of performative contradictions, snarled up as they are with Eminem's whiplash flow and mad lyrical skills, are also what make him so compelling a figure. Question: Which album better represents America in the first flush of the twenty-first century, *The Eminem Show* or Bruce Springsteen's *Rising* (2003)?

Although this particular comparison may not be a fair one (if only on base, generic grounds), it's possible to argue that Springsteen's post-9/11 record sonically invokes the past, as in the Steinbeckian dolor of *The Ghost of Tom Goad* (1995), in order to envision an ideal republic, what America can still be, whereas Eminem's angry rapping, highlighted on songs like "White America," reflects these not-so-United States in all their sound and fury. Eminem's politics, such as the in-your-face, take-no-prisoners misogyny and homophobia that the narrators of his songs chronically indulge in, are not pretty, but who ever said art was supposed to be pretty?

Sound Film

> We never see the same thing when we also hear; we don't hear the same thing when we see as well.
>
> —Michel Chion, *Audio-Vision*

> Godard did to movies what Bob Dylan did to music: they both revolutionized their forms.
>
> —Quentin Tarantino, interview in *Film Comment*

In "Reflections of a Disappointed Music Scholar," Lawrence Grossberg, whose work provides the pretext for my own reflections on the rock formation in chapter 1, argues that the reason popular music studies has not progressed as a discipline is a simple one: it has not undertaken, like Screen theory, "the necessary theoretical project in a serious and collective way."[25]

While I do not share Grossberg's estimation of the success of popular music studies (and, in any event, am not interested in handing out grades on its progress), his more general point about the productivity of certain critical formations such as Screen theory is, I think, an important one. Like the Frankfurt and Birmingham Schools as well as *Cahiers du cinéma*, the so-called Screen debates represented a dynamic, multiaccentual reconsideration of the "relation between politics and aesthetics."[26] Drawing widely on semiotics, Marxism, and psychoanalysis, Screen theory changed the way people think about film, and two of its most influential contributions—the concept of suture (theorized most productively by Stephen Heath by way of Jacques Lacan and Jacques-Alain Miller) and the "male gaze" (which Laura Mulvey ingeniously derived from Freud's work on scopophilia)—have had a significant impact on media studies.

As I recount in chapter 3, suture is the cinematic process whereby the spectator is continually stitched back into the diegetic world of the film via découpage or classical continuity editing. So in the most uncomplicated version of the theory, the second or counter shot in a shot/reverse shot sequence sutures the lack or absence opened up by the first shot (where this lack or absence threatens to disrupt the spectator's ostensibly tenuous suspension of disbelief). As in Heath's reading of suture, Mulvey's interpretation of visual pleasure, which operates as the transitional topic in my discussion of cinephilia and audiophilia in chapter 4, assigns it a central place in the history of mainstream cinema. In fact, her global account of the gaze promised a full-blown theory of *the* Hollywood movie where, in brief, the main male action of a film is dependent on the spectacle of the idealized female form in all its castratory force.

Although the concepts of suture and the male gaze have each acquired extensive critical histories since their inauguration in the mid-1970s, one of the more remarkable methodological lacunae evident in both theories—again, if only in retrospect—is their consistent neglect of the sonic or acoustic dimension of film. Thus, to take one celebrated example, Hitchcock's use of POV shots of Scottie (James Stewart) trailing Madeleine/Judy around the hilly streets of San Francisco in the first part of *Vertigo* (1958) clearly sutures the spectator into a voyeuristic position so that the body of "Kim Novak," stylishly outfitted in curve-hugging tailored suits, is a fetishistic spectacle of the first order. (Of course, in the second part of the film, after Scottie learns that he has been duped by Judy, his noirish investigation of her takes on, as Mulvey has argued, a distinctly sadistic cast.)

The question is, would *Vertigo* be the extraordinary film it is without Bernard Herrmann's haunting, vertiginous score?[27] Since this question might appear too obvious to bear repeating, it's worth recalling that the sound film has historically been the object of intense criticism. For example, in *Composing for Film* (1947), which appeared the same year as the first mass edition of Adorno and Max Horkheimer's *Dialectic of Enlightenment* (1944), Adorno and Hans Eisler issue a detailed inventory of the problems with film scoring in the age of the studio system: the stock employment of quasi-Wagnerian motifs, the dual prejudices of illustration and unobtrusiveness, and the hackneyed overreliance on euphony and melody (a habit that can be traced back to Schubert's melodic displacement of the thematicism perfected by Viennese classicists like Beethoven).[28] The difference, however, between the Adorno and Horkheimer of "The Culture Industry" and the Adorno and Eisler of *Composing for Film* is that the latter proceed to entertain the "aesthetic potentialities of mass art in the future."[29]

The same cannot be said for Macdonald, who writing "A Theory of Mass Culture" in roughly the same period as *Vertigo*, parrots the unilateral, Adornian line on the sound film laid down in "The Culture Industry": "The coming of sound, and with it Broadway, degraded the camera to a recording instrument for an alien art form, the spoken play. The silent film has at least the *theoretical* possibility, even within the limits of Mass Culture, of being artistically significant. The sound film . . . does not."[30]

A little history—even of a rudimentary, history of film sort—is instructive here. To wit, *The Jazz Singer* popularized the use of synchronous sound in 1927, some thirty years before Macdonald's essay. This single historical anecdote, combined with Macdonald's outright dismissal of the sound film, provides, in turn, a context for the following passage from Chion's *Audio-Vision*:

> Films projected in theatres have had soundtracks for sixty years now, and for sixty years this fact has influenced the cinema's internal development. But for the past sixty years as well people have continued to wonder whether the cinema did right in becoming "the talkies." One form of this unconscious prejudice is the widespread opinion that in all this time no valuable contributions . . . have been made by sound. The Sleeping Beauty of talking cinema forever awaits her prince, her new Eisenstein or Griffith.[31]

Forget about Ford, Hawks, Lang, Welles, Renoir, Hitchcock, Lubitsch, von Sternberg, and so on. Forget as well about "pit" music. For classic masscult critics like Macdonald, it's as if the art of cinema expired with the silent era.

Chion, however, not only puts the sound back in sound film, his work transvalues the terms of the long-standing debate between concert and film music. Thus, in a theoretical move that can be said to sublate the classical-musical Adorno, for whom the sonata form was the ne plus ultra of art, and the stridently anti-Hollywood Adorno, who was nonetheless able to appreciate the Strauss and Puccini Romanticism popularized by composers such as Korngold and Steiner during the studio system's classical period, Chion adverts to Beethoven in order to effect a comparison between Dolby sound and an eight-octave grand piano:

> Let us recall that Beethoven wrote his piano sonata for a smaller instrument than the piano of today: where he reached the limits of his keyboard, we have another two or three octaves. In this sense it is perhaps more correct to play Beethoven on the piano of his era. But there would be something absurd in seeing today's composers writing pieces for modern pianos with the same limitations as those that constrained the author of the Pathétique.[32]

Adorno would no doubt have categorically refused the terms of this comparison (since for him Beethoven's achievement is more about his compositional genius than the relative technological superiority of the instrument on which he composed), but both Chion and Adorno would agree that, in the language of *Composing for Film*, music should not have a "subordinate role in relation to the picture."[33]

Yet precisely because Chion does not share Adorno's habitual bias against film (that, for instance, the music of Beethoven is art while Hollywood movies are commodities pure and simple), he is able to do justice, at once technical and aesthetic, to the complex play of sound and image built into the "audiovisual contract." For example, Adorno—perhaps understandably, writing as he is in the 1940s—repeats the truism that the standard practice in Hollywood filmmaking is that the "spectator should not be conscious of the music": in other words, film music should be unobtrusive.[34] The problem with this prejudice, as I elaborate in chapter 3, is that it tends to go hand-in-hand with reflexive critiques of mainstream movies, not to mention theories of the cinematic apparatus such as suture that assume a passive, sound-benumbed spectator.

But imagine, if you will, an active *audio*-spectator (to inflect Chion's term) and some of the complexity of the sound/image configuration becomes audible. An excellent instance of what I call "audiovisual suture" occurs in Steven Spielberg's *Minority Report* (2002). It's 2054, and Det. John

Anderton, played by Tom Cruise, is trying to escape along with a precognitive named Agatha (Samantha Morton) from his ex-colleagues in the crime prevention unit. (He has inadvertently murdered, as the "precogs" forecasted, the man who purportedly killed his son six years earlier.) While Agatha waits in the car, "tired of the future," Anderton leaves to get some new clothes for her so that they can freely move about in public. He enters a Gap store and after the ID machine scans his newly implanted eyes, a hologram-salesgirl cheerily greets him: "Mr. Yakamoto, welcome back to the Gap. How did those tank tops work out for you?"

As Anderton hurriedly looks at racks of women's clothes, the ambient on-the-air sound in the store is Billie Holiday's "In My Solitude" (1947). In this scene, the extraordinary extension of Holiday's voice—ravaged, blue, and as unique as any in the history of popular music—fills the open space like some alien presence and produces what can only be called a sonic spectacle. As such, it's decidedly obtrusive. It also acts as an aural counterpoint to the film's dyspeptic vision of the nation's capital, subtly reinforced by Janusz Kaminski's monochromatic cinematography, where brand-name commodities in the form of gargantuan motion pictures dwarf the people in the street. Finally, if the force of this audiovisual passage has everything to do with its projection of a brave new phantasmagoric world of commodity simulation that is nevertheless haunted by a trace of the real, Holiday's voice is not simply a disembodied figure for the pathos that motivates the main character—bound up as it is with the loss of a child, *the* Spielbergian topos (cf. *A.I.* [2001])—but is, as well, a more general, determinate figure for the loss and alienation that pervades the artificial kingdom of the metropolis.

Now, while Spielberg is arguably the most popular director of the last quarter century,[35] it's safe to say that no director has received more attention, warranted or not, than Quentin Tarantino (whose *Jackie Brown* is the object of the fourth, "audiophilic" part of chapter 4). A well-documented cinephile and audiophile, Tarantino is unconditionally committed to scopophilia understood in the widest sense as visual pleasure. That is, the visual pleasures of Tarantino's films, which are both various and many, are always already overdetermined by his considerable cinematic and pop-musical investments, the cathexes of which are all exorbitantly on display in *Pulp Fiction* (1994). Still, "for all its investment in the mass culture visuality of post-modern experience," *Pulp Fiction*, as Dana Polan remarks in his BFI "Modern Classics" monograph, "is also a very writerly film."[36] In every sense of the word, then, Tarantino is an auteur, his films stamped with his unmistakable signature.

Fig. 1. Pulp Fatale: Uma Thurman as Mia Wallace, Vince Vega's smokin' dance partner, in *Pulp Fiction* (Tarantino, 1994).

In *Pulp Fiction*, this auteur effect is best illustrated by the now classic dance sequence performed by Vince Vega (John Travolta) and Mia Wallace (Uma Thurman) in Jack Rabbit Slim's diner. "This is Jack Rabbit Slim's," Mia says to Vince as they make their druggy entrance, "An Elvis man should love it." As her own pop-culture-studded repartee suggests (Mia has already established that there is a pronounced, generational difference between Elvis and Beatles fans), Jack Rabbit Slim's is a pop-culture diorama, recollecting the sort of "googy" clubs featured in '60s cult films like *Speedway* (1968), a film that itself featured Elvis and Nancy Sinatra. Indeed, with its Douglas Sirk steaks and Martin-and-Lewis milkshakes, not to mention its manqué Sullivan maitre d' (in real life, to quote Vince, "a wax museum with a pulse"), Jack Rabbit Slim's is a miniature version of *Pulp Fiction*, a virtual treasure trove of mass-cultural kitsch and bric-a-brac.

And yet, the model for Vince and Mia's improvised twist, an amalgam of the Swim and the Watusi, the Monkey and the Top Cat Shake, is not so much Chubby Checker as Godard, the Godard of *Band à part* (1964). The delicious irony here, one that cinephiles savor like a "bloody as hell or burnt to a crisp" Douglas Sirk steak, is that the allusion to Godard's film is also a classically postmodern gesture since *Band à part*, with its Hollywood allusions and self-reflexive style, destabilizes the tendentious opposition between Hollywood and avant-garde cinema that was one of the main presuppositions of "high" Screen theory.

Still, the real coup de grâce of the dance contest in *Pulp Fiction* is that the song accompanying Vince and Mia's twist is none other than Chuck Berry's "You Never Can Tell" (1964). In the song Pierre and his mademoiselle, teen audiophiles, own a "hi-fi phono" and "seven hundred little records": "All rock, rhythm and jazz." Berry's song, composed in prison after he was incarcerated for merely "having the intention" of committing a sex-related crime (see chapter 2), reinforces one of many blackly comic subtexts of *Pulp Fiction*: Vince and Mia may only be two wild kids out for a night on the town, but Mia's husband, Marsellus (Ving Rhames), has eyes in the back of his head, and playing with Daddy's Little Girl, as "foot massage" aficionado Antwan has haplessly discovered, is playing with fire.

Finally, Berry's song literally underscores the film's status as a sound film since the twist sequence can also be seen as a musical number. Tarantino has stated his admiration for the way Godard fractures the narrative of his films, as he does with the shuffle by Odile (Anna Karina), Arthur (Claude Brasseur), and Franz (Sami Frey) in *Band à part*, by introducing musical bits out of the blue. In this context,

"You Never Can Tell," as Tarantino has said, doesn't sound French or, even for that matter, especially twisty, but the song's use of "Pierre" and "Mademoiselle" gives it a uniquely '50s "French New Wave dance sequence feel."[37]

In fact, as I delineate in chapter 4, one of the things that separates Tarantino as a director from his multifarious wannabe peers has been the "unrivalled precedence he grants music in the creative process."[38] In this, his films, not unlike the musical, can be said to valorize music over sound, audio over vision. This attention to the sonic register also reflects Tarantino's status as a "post–baby boomer raised on a cultural diet" of, inter alia, MTV.[39] Of course, its titular identity as *music television* notwitstanding (TV minus the M), MTV's recent, much-publicized reliance as a channel on non-music-related or reality programming signals its difference from the Tarantinian aesthetic, which remains enthusiastically committed to exploring the changing field of audiovisuality even as it presupposes all the pleasures of scopo- and cinephilia.

Television

> In essence I consider the usual television dramas to be politically more dangerous than any political program ever was.
>
> —Adorno, "Fernsehen und Bildung,"
> *Erziehung zur Mündigkeit*

> Our understanding of culture has now been pluralized so as to include . . . popular music and the . . . vulgar entertainment of soap operas.
>
> —Heinz Steinert, *Culture Industry*

In "Avant-Garde and Kitsch," an essay that in the course of its schematic argument refers to Macdonald and key members of "the Institut" (Benjamin, Horkheimer, etc.), Clement Greenberg invokes a cultural phenomenon for which the "Germans gave the wonderful name of *Kitsch*": "popular, commercial art and literature with their chromotypes, magazine covers, illustrations, ads, slick and pulp fiction."[40] It probably goes without saying that Tarantino's films are, from the forward perspective of Greenberg's essay, the very definition of kitsch.

From another, more medium-specific perspective, however, they can be seen as a rich example of Tarantino's telephilia, an enthusiasm that may be more indicative of his avant/arrière sensibility than either his cinephilia or audiophilia. Talking about his generation, one that came of age in the '70s, Tarantino has commented that the "number one thing we all shared wasn't music, that was a Sixties thing. Our culture was television."[41] A random list of some of the TV programs referenced in *Pulp Fiction* confirms his observation: *Speed Racer, Clutch Cargo, The Brady Bunch, The Partridge Family, The Avengers, The Three Stooges, The Flintstones, I Spy, Green Acres, Kung Fu, Happy Days*, and last but not least, Mia's fictional pilot, *Fox Force Five*.

Although the term "television" encompasses all sorts of programming, daytime and prime-time, comedic and dramatic, fictional and nonfictional, the above list, with the possible exception of *The Avengers*,[42] suggests that *Pulp Fiction* has less of an elective affinity with the cinematic avant-gardism of Godard than with mainstream network programming. For just this reason, a film like *Pulp Fiction* is, at least for those critics trained in the Greenberg-Macdonald tradition, a prime example of the pernicious, oozelike influence of mass culture exemplified by their bête noire: TV.

So, in *Revolt of the Masscult* (2003), Chris Lehmann, waxing critical as if he was José Ortega y Gasset, maintains that by "repackaging trademark masscult reflexes," Dave Eggers has managed to consolidate his "position as a darling of the avant-garde."[43] The result is a "dialectical synthesis unimaginable to the likes of Clement Greenberg" not unlike (and here's the rub) "the endlessly allusive, casually nihilistic and character-resistant cinema of Quentin Tarantino."[44] Lehmann's most damning criticism of Eggers, though, characteristically invokes not cinema but its abject little other: "Eggers' memoir is . . . TV on the printed page."[45] The basis of Lehmann's conceit is its seemingly shocking conflation of literature and television, as if the virginal purity of the Mallarméan page were abruptly replaced by a TV screen and thereby defaced like da Vinci's *Mona Lisa*.[46]

There is another, institutional side to this revolting story. For Lehmann, the cultural revolution represented by the likes of Tarantino, "revolt of the masscult," has been aided and abetted by clerkly but treasonous intellectuals associated with American Cultural Studies. The narrative is compact as an entry in a *Reader's Digest*: "In the 1980s . . . American cultural critics began experimenting with the Birmingham School's fledgling themes of subcultural revolt as class politics by other means," and, presto!, "the American cultural studies movement was born."[47]

Although one might imagine this sort of crude caricature is confined to prickly, self-styled mavericks like Lehmann, in the postscript to his otherwise highly illuminating essay, "Adorno in Reverse," Andreas Huyssen cuffs the ears of American "cultstuds" for not being sufficiently receptive to the kinder and gentler version of the Frankfurt School featured in *New German Critique*: "The image of Adorno as high-cult theorist was so established that an attack on the German professor routinely accompanied celebrations of the radical aspirations of the new cultural studies approach. To be sure, this line was not argued by the Birmingham school of cultural studies itself, but by Birmingham disciples and progeny in the US."[48] In other words, the culprits are not Raymond Williams but John Fiske, not Stuart Hall but Henry Jenkins, not Angela McRobbie or Meaghan Morris but Lisa Lewis or Constance Penley.

Now, this is clearly not the place to propound a more nuanced history of the intricate relation between the Birmingham and American schools of cultural studies, not to mention the Frankfurt-influenced "political economy" approach and the audience-oriented one tarred and feathered with the catchphrase "cultural populism." Suffice it to say that "if cultural studies and TV studies are not the proverbial twins separated at birth," they nonetheless emerged at roughly the same time and "often get mistaken for each other by friend and foe alike."[49] This said (and given the sort of logic that typically animates the critique of mass culture—"mass culture is culture," "all culture is popular,"[50] and TV is the preferred, stigmatized figure of popular culture), I want to propose that one path out of these dark woods can be found in an essay by Adorno written around the same time that rock 'n' roll was first taking the United States by storm.

In "Television and the Patterns of Mass Culture" (1954), reprinted in the auspicious collection, *Mass Culture: The Popular Arts in America* (1957), Adorno declares that, on one hand, it would be the height of romanticization to claim that art was "once entirely pure, that the creative artist thought only in terms of the inner content of the artefact and not also of its effect upon spectators," and, on the other, that "vestiges of the aesthetic claim to be something autonomous, a world unto itself, remain even within the most trivial products of mass culture."[51] While it has become a commonplace of postmodern theory that the historical distinction between high and low culture has vanished, it would no doubt be more accurate to say that even if this hierarchy is not as tenacious as it once was, it continues to exert a certain force. One difference, as my earlier example of *Pulp Fiction* indicates, is that the high/low distinction has now migrated into the very fabric or inner content of the work of art, so that in that world unto itself which is *Pulp Fiction, Band à part* indiscriminately commingles with, say, *The Brady Bunch*.

The high/low distinction also remains, as Pierre Bourdieu's work demonstrates, as an indice of taste and class, prestige and appreciation— of, in a word, discrimination. Indeed, class-based, aesthetic politics tends to be a recurrent feature of classic mass-culture critique. So, in "A Theory of Mass Culture," Macdonald contends that the problem in the United States circa 1957, an acute one, is not that a prolific mass culture has overrun the carefully cultivated garden of Art like so many weeds; rather, the line or boundary between kitsch and the avant-garde has been irreparably "blurred": "If there were a clearly defined cultural elite, then the masses could have their kitsch and the elite could have its high culture, with everybody happy."[52] To paraphrase Marie Antoinette, Let them eat kitsch!

Macdonald's policy is, to say the least, problematic, especially if one considers that the repressed figure of mass culture typically embodies foreign elements having to do not only with class but race and sexuality. (Rap in its gangsta as opposed to political guise[53] is only the most obvious instance of the way a popular-cultural practice gets politicized with the end result that both the overt, aesthetic form and buried, social content are dismissed.) Still, to continue with the dialectical tack I have taken with Adorno, I'd be remiss if I didn't mention that the Macdonald of "Masscult and Midcult" is not without real insight into, and even foresight about, future positive developments in both mass culture and TV: "One possibility is pay TV, whose modest concept is that only those who subscribe could get the program, like a magazine; but also like a magazine, the editors would decide what goes in, not the advertisers; a small gain but a real one."[54]

Macdonald's prediction about pay TV touches on one of the most important trends in the television industry: the rise of basic cable services and the appearance of "premium" brands such as Home Box Office. HBO—which became, in 1972, the "first company to build a national distribution network for television programming using satellite communications"[55]—is perhaps the most spectacular example of the impact that the cable and satellite revolution has had on the medium. For example, in terms of textuality and political economy, the success of HBO has arguably transformed the commodity relation between audiences and the producers of TV programming from a "second" to a "first order" one.[56] In other words, stations like HBO are no longer dependent on advertisers or corporate sponsors for their livelihood; rather, subscribers, as Macdonald predicted, pay for TV.

As I relate in chapter 6 by way of The Sopranos, one aesthetic upshot of this more direct relation is that television continues to erode the once substantial mediatic divide between the big and small screens.

Accordingly, the considerable achievement of *The Sopranos* is a result not simply of its televisuality (for example, its lush, filmlike production values, including exterior location shooting in New Jersey[57]) or even its incessant, Tarantinoesque sense of citationality, but its cinematic flow (the last a direct function of the absence of commercial interruptions).

In addition, *The Sopranos*—along with *Oz* (HBO, 1997–2002), *Sex and the City* (HBO, 1998–2003), and *Six Feet Under* (HBO, 2001–2005)—reflects a new, signal mode of consumption, so-called avid fandom, that repeatedly transgresses cultural-capital lines.[58] The fact that one of the very first books on *The Sopranos* bears the imprimatur of the *New York Times* indicates its far-ranging cultural influence as well as the erosion of the longstanding division between televisuality and intellectuality (where an "intellectual" used to be someone who never watches TV or, at least, someone who never admits to doing so. *Desperate Housewives* [ABC, 2004–present]? Never). Of course, earlier, basic-cable cult programs such as *The X-Files* (Fox, 1993–2002) and *Buffy the Vampire Slayer* (WB, 1997–2001; UPN, 2001–03) have also blurred the line between viewer and intellectual—in the best, Gramscian sense—so that it is no longer possible to "insist that 'we' (the intellectual) watch television one way, while 'they' (the masses) watch it another."[59]

To adopt such a vox populi position is not, needless to say, to claim there are no differences between either TV and film (there are, to echo Sal "Big Pussy" Pompensiero [Vincent Pastore], real differences between *The Sopranos* and *The Godfather*) or even between HBO and Fox (since the former has acquired a specific cachet relative to the latter). Nor is it to dissolve the very real differences between critics and fans, as if one could somehow magically transmute, with an alchemical wave of the hand, cultural dopes into organic intellectuals. Distinctions not only remain, they remain to be described and explained, analyzed and evaluated. And here I would only reiterate that as with popular music and MP3 (or P2P) technology, HBO is not, in the last, economic instance, equally available to everyone. In other words (to reverse perspective), one might well argue that programming like *The Sopranos* represents a whole new species of class stratification inasmuch as the viability of HBO is predicated on the economic capital of those "privileged segments of the audience residing on the upside of the 'digital divide.'"[60] In short, it's not called "premium" for nothing.

While class conflict is by no means absent from *The Sopranos* (Tony himself suffers all the petty anxieties and tribulations of the nouveau upper-middle-class American citizen adrift in the suburbs), soap opera—which, in the Gen-X form of *Melrose Place*, is the topic of chapter 5—is the TV genre that has most consistently dealt with the issue. If you factor in that the genre, from its early inception on radio, has also been inextricably linked with the domestic sphere, it's clear why soaps have consistently been aligned with low culture. As Francesco Casetti puts it, summing up the two main tendencies of Screen theory, there are those who are committed to the avant-garde and those who attend to popular culture, or: "soap-opera deceptions" to be demystified and Brechtian alienation effects to be deciphered.[61]

The phenomenon of *Peyton Place* in its various literary, cinematic, and televisual incarnations presents a case in point. With its pedigree in literature and film (Grace Metalious's 1956 best-selling novel was made into a feature film in 1957), *Peyton Place* became the very first soap opera to cross over to prime time in 1964. This transition, in conjunction with the relative autonomy of television vis-à-vis literature and film, marks a crucial moment in the history of soap opera. If the television version of *Peyton Place* did not have the same immediate impact as, say, the Beatles' appearances on *The Ed Sullivan Show*, it did eventually lead the way for mega-popular prime-time serials such as *Dallas* (CBS, 1978–91). The worldwide popularity of *Dallas* eventuated, in turn, in ground-breaking, theoretically informed critical studies on the genre such as Ien Ang's *Watching Dallas* (1985), which advanced one of the first enlightened analyses of the ideology of mass culture.

Though it should be clear by now that the sort of counter, affirmative ideology that Ang proposes does not represent a sufficient response to the continuing ideological struggle or, depending on your perspective, pas de deux between elite and base culture, the advantage of a popular-cultural aesthetic is its "affirmation of the continuity of cultural forms and daily life."[62] One absolutely unique example of such an aesthetic is the *Melrose Place* art project initiated in the 1990s by the GALA Committee, the first prime-time "public art project in television history."[63] Spearheaded by Mel Chin and composed mainly of students at CalArts and the University of Georgia, the GALA Committee collaborated with the writers and producers of *Melrose Place* in order to instigate what they called "MP Art." The heart of the project revolved around so-called "PIMS" or "product insertion manifestations," site-specific, MP-inspired art objects that were strategically inserted into the mise-en-scène of particular episodes as a way to foreground the interactive potential of mass-produced culture.

So, for example, in the episode "101 Damnations" (March 4, 1997), Michael Mancini (Thomas Calabro) is looking for his ex-prostitute wife, Megan Lewis (Kelly Rutherford), "who has returned to the streets," and goes to a "seedy hotel" where the night clerk is reading François Lyotard's *Libidinal Economy* (1993), a "postmodern art-theory text" that employs the prostitute-pimp relation to illustrate the thesis that "all systems of exchange are libidinal."[64] More generally, MP art—in the form of viral invasions of the "kitschy," "surprisingly clever soap opera, *Melrose Place*"—represented a fan- and Net-linked "effort to creatively fuse the worlds of art and television."[65] As the GALA Committee website puts it, imagining a future where such projects presage a "truly interactive" relationship between culture and everyday life, "We used to watch TV. Now we live in it."[66]

⁂

In the conclusion to *Soap Opera*, Dorothy Hobson observes that "rock music may be the soundtrack of our lives," but that soap opera—the "ultimate twentieth-century mass media form"—is more intertwined with the "reality of our lives."[67]

With the recent mercurial rise of reality TV, critics are again lamenting the end or death of art, as if soap-operatic shows like *The Osbournes* (MTV, 2002–2005) weren't the height of artifice, artfully edited slices of life spiced up with the shock of the new. In fact, in its compelling use of nuclear-family dynamics, popular songs as ironic commentary, and plots recycled from the history of broadcast television, *The Osbournes* is a virtual encyclopedia of American popular culture. I mean, who could have guessed that *The Osbournes*, featuring the sight of the former bat-biting, head-banging Prince of Darkness spewing profanities as he stumbles around his pet-infested LA mansion, would be the true heir of Ozzie and Harriet?

The Osbournes may be the end of civilization as we know it, but then civilization, like rock, has been periodically dying and being reborn since its invention. The popular-cultural revolution continues apace, and, yes, it's being televised. Hail, hail, Chuck Berry, whose rockin' guitar sounded the first electrifying notes of this cultural revolution: roll over Adorno and tell Horkheimer the news.

Part 1

Popular Music
Hi-Lo Fidelity

1

Rock 'n' Theory
Cultural Studies, Autobiography, and the Death of Rock

This chapter is structured like a record—a 45, to be exact. While the A side provides an anecdotal and autobiographical take on the birth of rock (on the assumption that, as Robert Palmer writes, "the best histories are . . . personal histories, informed by the author's own experiences and passions"[1]), the B side examines the work of Lawrence Grossberg, in particular his speculations about the "death of rock," as an example or symptom of the limits of critical theory when it comes into contact with that *je ne sais quoi* that virtually defines popular music ("It's only rock 'n' roll, but I like it, I like it!"). By way of a conclusion, the coda offers some remarks on the generational implications of the discourse of the body in rock historiography as well as, not so incidentally, some critical comments on the limits of the autobiographical narrative that makes up the A side.

A Side: The Birth of Rock, or Memory Train

> Don't know much about history.
>
> —Sam Cooke, "Wonderful World"

In 1954, one year before Bill Haley and the Comets' "Rock around the Clock"—what Palmer calls the "original *white* rock 'n' roll" song—became number one on the pop charts, marking a "turning point in the history of popular music,"[2] and one year before Elvis covered Little Junior Parker's "Mystery Train" (then signed, under the self-interested tutelage of Colonel Parker, with RCA), in 1954—the same year the Supreme Court ruled racial segregation unconstitutional—the nineteen-year-old and still very much alive Elvis Presley walked into the Memphis Recording Service and cut Arthur "Big Boy" Crudup's "That's All Right."

This is Elvis recollecting Phillips's phone conversation with him: "You want to make some blues?" Legend has it that Elvis hung up the phone, ran fifteen blocks to Sun Records while Phillips was still on the line . . . and, well, the rest is history: by 1957, one year before Elvis was inducted into the army, Chuck Berry, Fats Domino, and Little Richard had crossed over to the pop charts, and the "rock 'n' roll era had begun."[3]

The irony of the above originary moment, at least for me, is that I somehow missed the Mystery Train. Over the years I've come to appreciate Elvis's music, especially the early Sun recordings (and, truth be told, later kitsch, cocktail-lounge stuff like "Viva Las Vegas"). But to invoke the storied lore of family romance, Elvis is a formative part of my sister Cathy's life in a way that he'll never be for me. Though she's only a year older than me, Elvis for her is *it*, the Alpha and Omega of rock; for me, Elvis has always been more icon than influence, and a rather tarnished one at that.

The seminal musical moments in my life are both later, post-1960, and less inaugural. For instance, I can still remember sitting with a couple of other kids in the next-door neighbor's backyard, listening to a tinny transistor radio (one of the new technologies that transformed the music industry in the 1950s), and hearing, for the very first, pristine time, "Johnny Angel" (1962). I'm not sure what it was about this song that caught my attention—the obscure, angelic object of desire does not, for instance, have my name, as in "Bobby's Girl" (and "girl group rock," as Greil Marcus calls it, was mostly about "The Boy"[4]), but I'm pretty sure sex, however sublimated and prepubescent, had something to do with it.

I can also distinctly remember watching Shelly Fabares sing "Johnny Angel" on an episode of *The Donna Reed Show* (ABC, 1958–66), a program—like *The Patty Duke Show* (ABC, 1963–66)—that was de rigueur or must-see TV at the time. Though Ricky Nelson performed regularly on *The Ozzie and Harriet Show* (and even Paul Peterson had his fifteen minutes of fame with the lugubrious "My Dad" [1962]), Fabares's small-screen version of "Johnny Angel"—sung, if I remember correctly, at a high school dance—remains a touchstone of sorts for me.

Indeed, "if you were looking for rock and roll between Elvis and the Beatles" (as I no doubt was at the time), girl groups were, as Marcus says, the "genuine article."[5] Who can forget hokey, genuinely hokey, "teen morality plays" like the Shangri Las' "Leader of the Pack" (1964), which my sisters, all four of them, would listen to over and over again on my cousin Karen's plastic portable record player? Or the sublime teen romanticism of Lesley Gore, whose songs I still listen to (on my Sony CD player), returning to some fugitive, long-lost source of pleasure, replaying it over and over again like any good arrested adolescent? "Suck—suck your teenage thumb . . ."

In the interregnum—between, that is, Elvis and the Beatles—there were of course other standbys, like the Four Seasons and the Beach Boys (East Coast and West Coast, Italian-American doo-wop and So-Cal surf music, respectively), but all this changed, forever, in 1964 with the British Invasion. In his *Rolling Stone* contribution on the topic, Lester Bangs contends that the Beatles phenomenon, set off by their first, tumultuous appearance on American television (February 9, 1964!), was a belated, libidinal response to the national mourning and melancholia that ensued in the wake of JFK's assassination.[6]

Indeed, it's hard to imagine two more dramatic and diametrically opposed moments than the depressive, wall-to-wall television coverage of the JFK assassination and the Beatles' first manic appearance on *The Ed Sullivan Show* (CBS, 1948–1971). The '60s, in all their liberatory excess ("sex, drugs, and rock 'n' roll"), are born, like some Frankensteinian thing, out of this vertiginous moment.

Although Elvis had already appeared on *Ed Sullivan*, Ed's now notorious reservations notwithstanding, with a "sneer of the lip" and a "swivel of the hip,"[7] the Beatles, with their hook-happy songs and shaggy telegenic appeal, were made, like JFK, for network television. For one thing, unlike Elvis or, later, the Stones, you didn't have to shoot them from the waist up or expurgate their lyrics. However, even as the Beatles were producing pop-romantic masterpieces like "Yesterday" (1965), the Stones were making up for lost time fast with songs like "Satisfaction," their seventh U.S. single, which not so subtly hinted that rock 'n' roll was not, in the final analysis, about romance but, as Mick's snarling voice insinuated, that down-and-dirty thing: sex. If the lyrics of "Satisfaction" mime the slow, painfully pleasurable climb of sexual arousal ("Cause I try, and I try, and I try . . .") only to climax with one of the most exhilarating anti-climactic lines in the history of rock ("I can't get no . . ."), the rhythm, set by the steady four-in-a-bar beat, totally subverts this negation, aurally delivering what the lyrics ostensibly deny.[8] Not that the lyrics were superfluous, mind you, since I spent many an hour listening to this song, trying to determine whether the third verse was, in fact, "about a girl who wouldn't put out during her period."[9]

Given that they're still alive and rockin', the Stones would be a convenient and appropriate place to conclude this, the anecdotal part of this "record." I would definitely be remiss, though, if I did not touch on the third element in the holy trinity of post-'50s youth culture: drugs. If the first wave of rock 'n' roll ends, according to received wisdom, around 1957, the second period, rock and roll (without the apostrophes fore and aft), reaches its musical and psychedelic apex in 1967 with the Beatles' *Sgt. Pepper's Lonely Hearts Club Band*.

Some thirty-five years later, I can still remember retreating to the basement of my parents' home to play *Sgt. Pepper's* for the very first time. Though I spent hours gazing at the cover, Elvis one face in a sea of famous faces, the song that kept haunting me, déjà vu all over again, was "Lucy in the Sky with Diamonds": with its surreal lyrics and trippy melody, it sounded like nothing I had ever heard before. For some reason, perhaps the color of the back cover, I always associate it with the color red, the color of revolutionaries, and *Sgt. Pepper's*, vinyl turning round and round on the turntable, turned me upside down, transporting me, like LSD later, to another, phantasmagoric world.

1967 was also the year a next-door neighbor—I can still recall his name, if not his face, Donnie—turned me on to Jimi Hendrix's *Are You Experienced?* in the basement of his parents' house, basements being the preeminent place of domestic refuge for teens in the late '60s, premall suburbs. Hendrix was subversive for me not so much because of his psychedelia (though I certainly registered this aspect of his music) but because Donnie's parents were racists, albeit the classic sub rosa upstate, New York sort. In other words, it was a black and white thing. It was also, needless to say, a sexual thing, since I can vividly remember Donnie telling me about seeing Hendrix live in concert in Buffalo and how he would look at the white girls in the front seats. I wasn't exactly sure what all this meant (I was thirteen, altar-boy Catholic, and definitely not experienced), but like *Sgt. Pepper's*, *Are You Experienced?* spoke of mysteries of race and sexuality elusive as that sky-diamonded girl, Lucy.

Since rock, especially punk, is inseparable from the culture of amateurism,[10] I would also be remiss if I did not mention that I spent many hours in the mid-'60s playing drums on an incredibly cheap drum kit (one snare, one bass drum, one non-Zildjian cymbal, no tom-tom, no hi-hat), and that one of the things that the kid behind me in high school endlessly talked about was Mitch Mitchell's drumming on "Fire," whose percussive effects we would try to duplicate on our ink-scarred desktops to the consternation of our long-suffering Franciscan instructors. Given Mitchell's rapid-fire drumming, it's not surprising that

"Fire" became our standard. The point is: part, a very big part, of the kick of rock music for me was the beat. How else can one explain the fact that years earlier, at recess, out on the asphalt playground at St. Pete's, my grammar school, I wanted to be Ringo? Think of it: not John or Paul or even George, but Ringo!

By way of a musical-historical peroration (and before I flip this "record"), I might add that by 1970, even as Elvis was beginning to make his glittery way in Las Vegas, Hendrix was dead, the Beatles had disbanded, and the Stones, post-Altamont, were all "black and blue."

B Side: Rock in Theory

> Much like rock, [cultural studies] has always been for me empowering and enabling, and like rock, it is always fun.
>
> —Lawrence Grossberg,
> *Dancing in Spite of Myself*

The Stones aside (though it remains almost impossible, when talking about rock, to set the Stones aside for very long), it would not be until that annus mirabilis, 1977, the year that Elvis finally left the building for good, that the world of popular music would begin to understand what had come to pass in the preceding decade—which is to say, in the 1970s, now cinematically immortalized in all its sleazy glory in *Boogie Nights* (1997). "Sister Christian" anyone?

1977 was the year that the Sex Pistols celebrated Queen E's silver jubilee with their outrageous version of "God Save the Queen," the lyrics of which ("God save the Queen, the fascist regime") couldn't be further from the faux pastoral sentiment of Elton John's threnody to Diana, "Candle in the Wind" ("Songs for Dead Blonds," as Keith Richards later acidly put it[11]). 1977 was also the year that Lawrence Grossberg first began teaching classes on rock music. Although the comparison is not a little bathetic, from the national punk-sublime to the pedestrian academic-pedagogical, it underscores an important theoretical moment in the discourse of cultural studies, a moment when, as in *Resistance through Rituals* (1976) and *Subculture* (1979), British cultural studies began to examine the impact of popular music on "culture and society."[12]

While there are numerous critics associated with the field of cultural studies who have written on popular music (too many in fact to name), Grossberg, unlike a lot of his American cohorts, not only studied at the Birmingham Centre, he is the "dean of academics writing on popular music," the "CEO of cultural studies."[13] Grossberg himself cannot, of course, be made to stand as some sort of synecdoche for either cultural or popular music studies (especially given that the latter has only recently achieved any semblance of disciplinary coherence), but his writings on rock are nonetheless symptomatic, I want to argue, of a certain unexamined death drive at work in popular music studies.

For example, in *Dancing in Spite of Myself*, a collection that gathers together Grossberg's work on popular music, he persuasively argues that rock is a necessary object of critical investigation because it has frequently been mobilized, often negatively (as in the neoconservatism that he critiques in *We Gotta Get Out of This Place*), as a discursive token in the ideological contest over what he calls the "national popular."[14] Thus, in "Another Boring Day in Paradise," he contends that it is only with *Born to Run* (1975) and *Darkness on the Edge of Town* (1978) that Bruce Springsteen emerges as a national-popular sign of the body and sexuality, a set of signifiers that receives its most visceral, economic expression in the figure of dancing. For Grossberg, dancing not only bespeaks the body, it embodies release from boredom and anomie—from, that is to say, the sometimes repressive, imprisoning routines of everyday life. It's not for nothing, then, that the title of his collection on rock recalls the trope of dancing—dancing in spite of, or despite, one's self—since as he says in "'I'd Rather Feel Bad Than Not Feel Anything at All'" (1984), "Someone who does not dance, or at least move with the music, is not prima facie a fan" (D 87).

Still, given Grossberg's fascination with the body in motion, or what I prefer to think of as the "body in dance,"[15] one of the retrospective ironies of his interpretation of Springsteen, virtually the only close reading to grace his voluminous work on rock, is that it somehow neglects to mention the moment when the Boss, live onstage in St. Paul performing his top-ten single, "Dancing in the Dark" (1984), pulled a pre-*Friends* Courtney Cox out of the audience and, in an Instamatic MTV moment, became a fully-fledged pop-idol-cum-sex-symbol.[16] Later, Simon Frith, writing in the aftermath of the 1984 presidential election (when "Born in the U.S.A" was opportunistically appropriated by Ronald Reagan's campaign handlers), concluded that Springsteen's *Live* (1985) was a rock monument, albeit a monument to the death of the "idea of authenticity."[17]

The Culture of Rock

I repeat the above MTV instant not to rehearse the familiar, now-dated critique of Springsteen but because Grossberg, like Frith, has frequently seized on this national-popular moment in Springsteen's career to deconstruct the idea of authenticity, replacing it with what he calls "authentic inauthenticity" (W 230). In fact, Frith's account of the end of authenticity points up, if only by inversion, the privileged place of authenticity in Grossberg's account of rock: say, the way in which early rock 'n' roll, drawing on the racially charged subtext of rhythm and blues (itself a not so latent critique of white, "I-like-Ike" America), was a highly affective cultural compromise formation, a way to both rock against and roll with the times.

If rock assumed this particular existential function in the 1950s, it consolidated this position in the 1960s, so much so that the proper, analytical object of study for Grossberg is not so much rock music as the *culture* of rock or what he calls the "rock formation": "the entire range of postwar, 'youth'-oriented, technologically and economically-mediated musical practices and styles" (D 102). Although Grossberg has typically been more concerned, true to his Deleuzian-Foucauldian cast, with charting the spatial elements of this formation, I want to focus on the temporal or historical register of this project because in his recent work, "Is Anybody Listening? Does Anybody Care?," he has been "obsessed" (his word) with the death of rock.[18]

To be fair, in the revisionary introduction to *Dancing in Spite of Myself*, Grossberg observes that the proposition that "rock is dead" is not so much an evaluative judgment about "particular musical practices or variants of rock culture" as a "discursive haunting within the rock formation" and—a crucial if somewhat contradictory afterthought—a "possible eventual reality" (D 17). In fact, as Grossberg himself seems to recognize (D 103), his speculations about the death of rock are neither new nor news. In 1971, for instance, in *The Sound of the City* Charlie Gillett had announced the death of "rock 'n' roll," if not "rock and roll" or "rock" per se.[19] And more recently, in "Everything Counts," the preface to *Music for Pleasure*, Frith himself composed the following epitaph:

> I am now quite sure that the rock era is over. People will go on playing and enjoying rock music . . . but the music business is no longer organized around the selling of records of a particular sort of musical event to young people. The rock era—born around 1956 with Elvis Presley, peaking around 1967 with *Sgt. Pepper's*, dying around 1976 with the Sex Pistols—turned out to be a by-way in the development of twentieth-century popular music, rather than, as we thought at the time, any kind of mass cultural revolution.[20]

For Frith as for Gillett, rock is effectively dead as a mass-cultural force because for all its revolutionary energy and excitement, anger and anarchism, it has finally succumbed to those twin demons: capital and technology.

Now, insofar as rock has not historically dominated the popular-music market (see, for example, Dave Harker's analysis of the 1970s, which convincingly argues that the representative sound of the era was not, say, punk but Elton John[21]), one might counter that Frith's reading of the death of rock is predicated on a substantial misreading of the music industry. Frith's claim about the death of rock also betrays a not so residual romanticism where, as in the ideology of high modernism, the artist-as-rocker steadfastly refuses the Mephistophelian commercial temptations of late capitalism.

Accordingly, it might be useful, before I broach a critique of Grossberg's claims about the death of rock, to review his account of its present state. As Grossberg sees it, rock's original historical conditions of possibility have undergone a radical transformation over the last forty or so years. On one hand, the liberal quietism of the 50s, a political consensus that underwrote the affluence and conspicuous consumption of the period, has been superseded by a neofundamentalist conservatism intent on destroying the last vestiges of the welfare state (one hypervisible target of which agit-prop militancy has been rap music).[22] On the other hand, youth culture, once the ground of the performative ethos of communtarianism, has been subjected to the microdifferentiation and super-fragmentation of the contemporary media market.

As for the structure of feeling (which in the 50s could be summed up by one word, *alienation*), postmodernism has gone from being an emergent to the dominant cultural-political formation, so much so that everything now, including and especially rock, has come under what Grossberg calls, after Walter Benjamin, the "antiaura of the inauthentic" (D 117)—in other words, not alienation but simulation, not parody but pastiche. Finally, in the industrial-technological sphere, even as the "indies" enjoy a less contentious relation with the majors (to the point in fact where leisure-and-entertainment multinationals have come to view independent labels as their "minor league"[23]), revenues derive less and less from sales and more and more from merchandising and secondary rights associated with other, synergetic sources such as film, TV, and advertising.[24] Put another way: in an age of digital reproduction (not LPs but CDs or MP3), rock has become a commodity like any other commodity, at best a depoliticized form of fun and, at worst, Muzak to divert you while you're home shopping.

A number of these transformations, including the paradigm shift from oral-print to cyber-visual culture, are reflected in the studied affectlessness of contemporary rock. To be sure, the concept of affect as it appears in Grossberg's discourse is not simply a synonym for emotion or feeling since it is a function of, among other things, cathexis and libidinal quantification. Moreover, for Grossberg as for Deleuze and Guattari, affect is a "structured plane of effects."[25] Affect, in other words, is the key to what Grossberg calls "mattering maps" or the maps people construct in order to articulate what matters most to them in their everyday lives. Rock is therefore a fundamental "affective articulatory agent" because, to repeat one of Grossberg's favorite maxims, it "helps us make it through the day" (D 20).

Rock, Rap, and Riot Grrrls

While Grossberg's theorization of everyday life, together with his neo-Gramscian elaboration of affect and the rock formation, represents an important contribution to the critical discourse on rock, the problem, as the above Deleuze-inflected synopsis suggests, is that his writing on popular music tends to be extraordinarily "abstract and speculative" (D 30) or, in a word, affectless. Grossberg has freely conceded—too freely, for my money—the limits of his project, observing in the apologetic preface to the Dylan-titled *Bringing It All Back Home* that "almost everything he has written on rock music," operating as it does on a "particularly high level of abstraction," is "too theoretical"; that his work has, in sum, become a "constant detour deferring the concrete."[26]

One, dare I say glaring, manifestation of this pervasive theoreticism is his persistent neglect of issues of race and sexuality.[27] Although John Gill's and Angela McRobbie's critiques of, respectively, gay disco and subcultural theory (to adduce only two examples[28]) indicate that rock is by no means a function of identity politics, I think it's fair to say that Grossberg's preemptive, categorical disregard of gender has blinded him to recent transformations in rock music. To wit, despite what sometimes seems like the hard-wired masculinism of rock (though as Robert Walser has shown, even heavy metal is not without its moments of gender trouble), Riot Grrrl music suggests—if, say, Patti Smith or Joan Armatrading hadn't already—that women can rock too.[29]

As for race, though Grossberg has summarily discussed the role of "Black music," in particular R&B, in everyday life (D 151–52), he has had surprisingly little to say about rap. I say "surprisingly" because rap has been viewed, as Grossberg himself attests, not only as a "site of authenticity" but as the heir apparent to rock's potential as a symbolic mode of resistance (D 104). Accordingly, if it is true, as Grossberg has claimed, that he is less interested in the death of rock than in "rock's becoming something else" (D 22), it follows that his work, "abstract and speculative" as it is, would benefit from some consideration of the specific preconditions and continuing longevity of rap as well as, more generally, hip-hop culture.

History, in fact, is instructive in this regard since the very first rap records, such as the Fatback Band's "King Tim III" and the Sugarhill Gang's "Rapper's Delight," appeared in the immediate wake of the so-called punk apocalypse and are therefore an integral part of the rebirth of postpunk popular music. (Significantly, both records were released in 1979.)[30] Although rap did not cross over to the mainstream until well into the next, disco-driven decade when Run-D.M.C.'s Aerosmith-spiked "Walk This Way" (1986) became hip-hop's first MTV hit, in the process thrusting rap "strategies of intertextuality into the commercial spotlight" (and rap records into the "hands of white teen consumers"[31]), rap music, it is clear, has irrevocably altered the rock/pop landscape.

The point is, from Afrika Bambaataa, one of the seminal old-school master of records, to Run-D.M.C. and new school, pre-"Walk This Way," rap 'n' rock tunes such as "Rock Box" (1984) and "King of Rock" (1985), rock has been part and parcel of that eclectic mix that is rap, a musical mélange forever memorialized in the lyrics of "Payoff Mix": "Punk rock, new wave and soul / Pop music, salsa, rock & roll / Calypso, reggae, rhythm & blues, / Master, mix those number-one tunes."[32] An exchange between Rolling Stone and P. Diddy (aka Puff Daddy) confirms the intimate/extimate relation between rock and rap. *Rolling Stone*: "What bands do you like now?" P. Diddy: "Radiohead."

I hasten to add that if the relation between rap and rock is not one of simple exteriority, this is not to claim, as Grossberg does, that "for practical purposes," there are "no musical limits on what can or cannot be rock" (W 131). On this particular score, one must, I think, be vulgar: rock is, first and foremost, music—with the critical proviso that, to paraphrase Roland Barthes, if a little formalism turns one away from history, a lot brings one back to it.[33]

I'm not talking about musicology here, useful as it is (especially in the proper hands),[34] nor am I suggesting that the issue of reception, or even fandom, is negligible, since one of the very real virtues of Grossberg's work has been its extensive investigation into the various extra-musical contexts of rock reception. What I am suggesting, to "bring it all back home," is that it's difficult to talk about rock or popular music in the 1990s without engaging the issue of both genre and production.

World Musics: After Rock Imperialism

On the constitutive difference between rock and the pre–rock 'n' roll tradition of popular music, Robert Palmer has written:

> Today's popular music could hardly have evolved out of "Your Hit Parade" and the pre-r&r popular mainstream. . . . Rap, metal, thrash, grunge have different attitudes towards the organization of sound and rhythm. Their distance from pre-r&r norms cannot be explained by advances in musical instruments and technology alone. Far more than musical hybrids, these sounds proceed from what amounts to a different tradition, different from the old mainstream pop and different right on down to the most basic musical values.[35]

Given Palmer's riff here on rock's traditional difference from the popular music that precedes it (for example, Frank Sinatra or, before him, Bing "The King of Croon" Crosby), it would appear that although one can speak of rock as a species of popular music, one cannot make the opposite claim (not all popular music is rock).

This distinction would appear to be commonsensical enough, but rock imperialism, as Keith Negus has demonstrated, is pervasive in English-language writing on popular music. One problem with such an approach, of which Grossberg's work is a paradigmatic example (as his assertion about musical limits indicates), is that it consistently ignores "vast numbers of generic distinctions made by musicians and audiences across the world."[36] The net result is a rockist methodology that, paradoxically enough, is at once inclusivist and exclusivist—inclusivist because generically different kinds of music such as rap are reflexively included as rock, and exclusivist because generically related kinds of music such as country are simultaneously excluded.

This problem is compounded when the universalist category of rock is applied to popular music in the global context, so-called world beat or world music. Thus, if it is true, as Negus states, that there is a lot of music "being listened to by the 'youth market' that would be described using a label other than rock," it's equally true that "for many music fans across the world, there are numerous musics that cannot be rock."[37] Not so incidentally, the global deployment of the concept of rock also tends to reproduce the classic division between rock and pop, where rock refers to the "musical and lyrical roots that are derived from the classic rock era" and pop to rock's "status as a commodity produced under pressure to conform by the record industry."[38]

The way this binary gets played out in the context of the rock/ world music opposition is, alas, all too predictable: American Western-style rock is "impure" or passé (passé because impure), while virtually all non-Western popular musics are "authentic" and, therefore, "vital." Not so surprisingly (especially if one remembers that rock was originally black slang for "having sex"), this sort of racial-ideological thinking is frequently the product of a colonialist mentality. As Timothy D. Taylor puts it in *Global Pop*, "rock music, which used to be pure sex, has lost its grinding energy; musics by others (read: people of color) still have something to do with sex."[39]

Still, the real political-economic paradox is that although world musicians are considered inauthentic if they begin to sound too much like their Western counterparts, they are doomed to a discourse of authenticity "since the structures of the music industry exclude virtually all world musicians from the venues, visibility, and profits that might make them appear to be sellouts to their fans."[40] This, then, is the bottom line of the asymmetrical relations of production that subtend the global music marketplace. Due to the concentration of capital in a handful of multinational corporations (which are located, in turn, in a handful of core countries), Western popular music is increasingly available in the traditional peripheries, but the semiperipheries do not have the same access to their own music. Hence the distinctly inequitable system of distribution that currently obtains where, say, "it is much easier to buy . . . Madonna in China than Cui Jian, the leading Chinese rock musician, in the US."[41]

Production of Culture

I will return to these issues in the context of contemporary youth culture, but this might be an appropriate place to mark the limits of the classical-Marxist account of the mode of production and propose instead what I take to be a more immanent, constructive model of the music industry. An innovative work in this regard, innovative because it draws equally on both reception and production studies without the theoretical baggage of either approach, is Negus's *Producing Pop* which in displacing the methodological emphasis from the "*production* of culture" to the "*culture* of production" retains a role for what Marxists used to call the "primacy of production" even as it demarcates a space for what Negus calls the "cultural practices of personnel" (press officer, A&R person, studio producer, and so on).[42] Noting that writing on popular music often works from unexamined predicates about art and commerce, creativity and capitalism, Negus insists that such a perspective tends to "overlook the temporal dimension which cuts through the production of commercial music"; equally importantly, it also underestimates the extent to which the various personnel involved in producing music are actively "contributing to the aesthetic meanings employed to appreciate the music," thereby substantially defining the contours of what in fact popular music means at any given time.[43]

The value of the culture-of-production approach is that by concentrating on what Pierre Bourdieu calls "cultural intermediaries," it usefully blurs the hard-and-fast distinction between labor and leisure, production and consumption. Rather more to the point, Negus's perspective emphatically reaccentuates the music in the music business, foregrounding the sorts of music that people in the business actually listen to. To tender such a claim is not, of course, to proffer a covert defense of the music business; in fact, Negus's work provides a trenchant critique of the way in which the "recording industry has come to favor certain types of music, particular working practices, and quite specific ways of acquiring, marketing, and promoting recording artists" (and here issues of race and sex-gender rematerialize in all their social-institutional force).[44] Simply put, Negus's approach, attuned as it is to both the cultural and industrial demands of the music industry, elucidates the intricate, conflictual web of relations out of which popular music is wrought.

As for Grossberg, in his anxious swerve away from anything that smacks of Marxism or economism (which sometimes appear to be the same thing for him), he has been intent to develop what he calls a "spatial materialism" (D 10). While this spatial-materialist perspective might conceivably offer a novel way to talk about the production and consumption of popular music, the aggressively theoreticist cast of Grossberg's approach is evident in his palpably thin description of his project: "to find a radically contextual . . . vocabulary that can describe the ongoing production of the real as an organization of inequality through an analysis of cultural events" (D 24). In other words, if Grossberg's analytical focus on space in rock provides a valuable complement to the general underdevelopment of spatiality in the discourse of Marxism, this very same valorization also comes at the direct expense of a proper consideration of the dialectical other of spatiality: temporality or, more precisely, historicity.

Bluntly, it will not do, on one hand, to ruminate about the death of rock and, on the other, confess that one has "given too little attention to the changing shape of the rock formation across space and over time" (D 19). Given this performative contradiction, though, what, one wonders, is driving Grossberg's obsession with the death of rock?

Forced Choice: Britney or Avril?

The above not simply rhetorical question about the death of rock returns us to the beginning of this chapter—to, that is, the birth of rock and the formative popular-musical influences in my life. My life aside (for the moment!), I want to submit that detailed, medium-specific attention to the temporality and spatiality of rock suggests that it has by no means died but has merely become, among other things, "more geographically mobile."[45]

The value of this geopolitical perspective is that it assumes one of Grossberg's signature Deleuzian themes, what one might call the "mobility of rock" (classic rock 'n' roll is frequently about, as almost any Chuck Berry song proves, automobility), and situates it in a specific national-historical context. In other words, it's not merely that rock has become part of transnational capitalism (though this proposition is undoubtedly true and has any number of implications for the present rock formation[46]); rather, it's more that a certain form of rock may well be dead, or at least embalmed, in the United States or North America but is flourishing elsewhere—say, in Cuba or China, Argentina or South Africa, Eastern Europe or the former Soviet Union.[47]

As for the United States or North America, some form of postrock music is obviously here to stay, at least for the foreseeable future, given that it has become an indispensable part—along with the iPod—of contemporary youth culture. But if MTV is youth-skewed (as opposed to, say, VH1), what exactly does it mean to invoke the category of youth today, early in the twenty-first century?

Although there is a statistically determinate audience, defined by age, for rock/pop music (say, conservatively speaking, fourteen to twenty-four), the idea of youth, as Donna Gaines has documented, is simultaneously a "biological category," a "distinctive social group," and a "cultural context."[48] Moreover, while there's little doubt that age-driven demographics drive corporate marketing and advertising, it's also no secret that in the age of Viagra, cosmetic surgery, and hyper-health and fitness, the "signifier 'youth' has been detached from the age-grade and made available to everyone"[49]—to, in other words, anyone who has the requisite desire and economic resources. With the last scenario firmly in mind, it's clear that rock is no longer, if it ever was, the "music of youth."

One consequence of this process of democratization is that the concept of youth today retains only a residual, even vestigial, connection to its biological referent. In fact, the rapidly changing cultural construct of the term since World War II—from, say, youth culture to counterculture to youth subcultures (the last with a decidedly post-Parsonian emphasis)—has thoroughly dedifferentiated its social distinctiveness. For one thing, the category of childhood, of which youth is the antithesis and adulthood the synthesis, is shrinking by the moment: "People as young as eight or nine years old are sharing in the youth life-style in terms of consumption of products such as clothing, leisure activities . . . and knowledge of the 'real world'—sexual, political, ecological, etc."[50] For another, the social idea of youth has expanded so fast that young people, as Deanna Weinstein remarks, "have become marginal to the idea of youth itself."[51]

Since the central feature of youth culture, at least in the United States since the 1950s, has been music, *rock* music, this trend—what one might call the colonization or reterritorialization of youth—has had a profound influence on contemporary music. In an epigram: "Rock, like youthful looks, is no longer the province of the young."[52] As in some grade-B werewolf movie, the rock-around-the-clock teenagers have become the classic-rock baby boomers, and the latter constituency, in turn, a prime target for the increasingly competitive music industry. More specifically yet, since the youth market cannot productively sustain long-term artistic development (and, consequently, new artists are no longer aimed at youth in the restricted biological sense), there are powerful economic imperatives to appeal to the expanding class of middle-aged consumers.[53]

To be sure, "young people" have actively, sometimes even violently, resisted the wholesale appropriation of their subcultures. If this has occasionally meant distancing themselves from adulterated discourses such as, precisely, rock (hence the pejorative epithet "rockist"), in other cases it has involved a complex process of reappropriation of the popular-cultural terrain. (Witness the revival of Rat-Pack-styled lounge music.) More generally, this ritualistic resistance has involved the formation of subcultures that entail a determinate dialectical relation not only with the dominant parent culture (itself in the process of being made over in the eternal image of youth) but with the dominant, corporate-sponsored youth culture.

The good news is that genuine youth subcultures have emerged by "marginalizing themselves from the leisure culture's free-floating definition of 'youth.'"[54] The bad news, as if the double alienation consequent on the above self-marginalization were not enough, is that young people are now free to choose from among a bewildering "array of confrontational youth subcultures"[55] where "free-floating" is not so much a term of liberatory potential, however slim, but a euphemistic signifier for the forced choice that is postmodern consumer capitalism. In a nutshell: Britney or the anti-Britney, Avril.

While one might argue that the current musical culture is merely yet another moment in the ongoing cyclical history of pop/rock (where, to revisit the late 1950s and early 60s, the choice between the Crystals and Chiffons, Ronettes and Shirelles or, to attend to the "boy groups," the Four Seasons and the Beach Boys was for some no choice at all), the difference between the immediate post–rock 'n' roll period and the present moment is the sheer volume of recorded music that is now available.[56] The almost exponential increase in the production of rock/pop music has resulted in an almost infinite array of musical subgenres, as a recent postcard survey distributed by Atlantic Records illustrates: Children's/R&B/Pop/Rock/Dance/Singer Songwriters/Traditional Jazz/ Contemporary Jazz/New Age/Ambient/Classical/Country/Metal/ Alternative/Rap/Theatre Music/World Music/etc.

About this list, I would make only two observations. First, most, if not all, of these genres can be further subdivided. For example, to take just one genre, "New Age/Ambient" can, and probably should, be divided into two separate categories, where Ambient or, more properly, Electronica can then be divided into various subgenres such as Techno, Jungle, Trip Hop, Drum and Bass, and so on. Second, the culture of rock or what Grossberg calls the "rock formation" may still exist for contemporary youth (see, in this context, the introduction to chapter 2), but rock music is arguably now only one genre or category among a host of genres and categories, subgenres and niche markets.

My Generation

> Drivin' around in my automobile . . .
>
> —Chuck Berry, "No Particular Place to Go"

Although the concept of youth is crucial, it is clear, to any future discussion of the death of rock, another, perhaps more pointed way to reframe this issue—to return to the larger, historical shifts in the meaning of youth culture—is to reconsider the generational axes of rock. Thus, to recite Frith, conventional wisdom has it that rock was born around 1956 with Elvis, peaked around 1967 with *Sgt. Pepper's*, and died around 1976 with the Sex Pistols. Or, as Negus metaphorically puts it, in the mid-1970s, "the blooms start wilting, the body decays, and rock starts dying."[57]

This late-Spenglerian vision—*Verfallsgeschichte* made flesh—offers a peculiarly seductive image for some people of the history of rock, with rock consuming itself, never mind Nirvana, in one final catastrophic conflagration with punk. Indeed, with the late Elvis and Sid Vicious squarely in mind, the one bloated from food and drugs almost beyond recognition, the other an early poster boy for heroin chic, it sometimes seems, if only in retrospect, that the banks of flowers on the cover of *Sgt. Pepper's* were funereal after all, florid intimations of rock's mortality, "flowers in the dustbin" (to echo the Sex Pistols).[58]

Still, as Negus's meta-organic metaphor insinuates ("the blooms start wilting, the body decays . . ."), it's probably inadvisable to interpret musical genres such as rock "as if they were living bodies which are born, grow, and decay."[59] When it comes to composing the history of rock, one might do better to attend, as Barthes advises, to the form of the music, a turn that inevitably returns one to history, to the form of history and the history of the form, where the former signifies the various, sometimes radically divergent histories such as rap that have generated what Palmer calls the "rock tradition" and the latter references historicity itself in all its gross materiality.

In fine, if writing on rock is going to matter today, it must remain alive to a veritable forcefield or constellation of factors: to the various histories of rock with all their zigs and zags, swerves and curves; to the "culture of production," at once macro and micro; to the complex play of identities, raced, sexed, gendered; and, of course, to the music itself. As for theory, if it's going to matter, if it's going to rock, it must not only move with the times, it must also remember that as in dancing or cruising (and this is the trickiest part), the point is, as Chuck Berry says, there's "no particular place to go."

2

Roll Over Adorno

Beethoven, Chuck Berry, and Popular Music in the Age of MP3

> If exchange value really gazes out from the capital letters of the hit song like an idol, it is redeemed once the word "penny" falls. Its magic broken, like that of the Medusa when Perseus confronts her with her own reflection. Where the possibility of happiness is no longer conceivable, where it is replaced by naked numbers, dream finds its hiding place.
>
> —Adorno, "Commodity Music Analyzed,"
> *Quasi una Fantasia*

The recent resurgence of garage rock—The Hives, The Vines, and The Strokes, to cite only three of the most highly hyped bands with monosyllabic monikers—suggests that if rock was momentarily pronounced D.O.A., its death, as I argued in the previous chapter, has been greatly exaggerated. Rock, like Bix, lives!

While there are any number of reasons why the state of rock has become an issue of perennial interest to cultural critics, not the least of which can be traced to the periodic demands of the marketplace for quasi-new commodities, in the United States at least the discourse of rock continues to function as a barometer of both popular music as well as popular culture in general. That is to say, as rock goes, so goes American pop culture. The interest of Adorno's work in this context is that his global critique of mass culture involves a regional defense of the values of classical music, epitomized by the heroic figure of Beethoven, and a corresponding depreciation of popular music, a position represented here by the early rock 'n' roll of Chuck Berry.

43

At the same time, one of the most striking ironies of Adorno's career—a career that took him to, of all places, Los Angeles, the capital of the culture industry—is that he was somehow never able to complete his projected book on Beethoven. Indeed, the conceit of this chapter is predicated on the, for me, serendipitous fact that Adorno stopped working on his Beethoven book the very same year, 1956, that "Roll Over Beethoven" appeared. This historical accident poses, in turn, any number of questions pertinent to the on-going debate about so-called mass culture: What can Chuck Berry and classic rock 'n' roll tell us about the Adornian valorization of Beethoven as one of the avatars of "serious" music? If rock music is itself, as I have observed, a privileged figure of American popular culture, what does a song like "Roll Over Beethoven" say about the Adornian conception of the aural, autonomous work of art? Finally, if the magic spell or riddle character of the work of art is true for both classical and popular music, where exactly does this leave us? In sum, what is the significance today, in the first years of the new millennium, of the historical division between the two spheres of music?

With its manifestly anticapitalist interests and concerns, Adornian culture critique would appear to be dramatically opposed on the face of it to those of popular culture. Thus, from the perspective of Anglo-American cultural studies, which has steadily progressed from the counterhegemonic elements of what Raymond Williams called "common culture" to the radical ecstatic potential of club or rave culture (Ravers of the world unite![1]), Adorno and Co., with their programmatic, for some unremitting, stress on the dire machinations of the culture industry, seem absurdly out of touch with the times, imprisoned like so many Madame Tussaud wax figures in the now outdated critical dress of the period, but without the endless trivial pursuit possibilities of retro or kitsch appropriation.

Cyber-subcultural Adorno? I don't think so.

As Jürgen Habermas once said of his mentor at the University of Frankfurt, "When you were with Adorno you were in the movement of his thought. Adorno was not trivial; it was denied him, in a clearly painful way, ever to be trivial."[2] Let's face it (to invoke the social Darwinian world of *Survivor*): Adorno would have been the first one kicked off the island.

Mass Culture, Ersatz Kantianism

I will return to the pathos as well as what I take to be the repressed element of the above characterization below, but first I want to address the conceptual and historical limits of the Adornian problematic. Take, for example, Adorno's theory of art. In *A Philosophy of Mass Art* (1998), Noël Carroll has observed:

> Adorno exemplifies a tendency of other philosophical critics of mass art . . . [who use] the Kantian theory of free beauty to presuppose a theory of art proper. . . . [O]nce this sort of theory, or parts of it, are enlisted as a framework for analyzing mass art, mass art predictably is seen to be problematic in virtue of its very nature—its tendency toward the formulaic, its commitment to entertainment, to predetermined effects, and to easy and accessible consumption.[3]

If one serious repercussion of Adorno's appropriation of the Kantian analytic of free beauty is that his theory tends to be "categorically inhospitable" to art en masse, this constitutive inhospitability to mass-manufactured art also has quite determinate side effects, since judgments of free beauty (where, famously according to Kant, we mobilize the free play of the faculties) do not represent the primary model of aesthetic appreciation. Rather, aesthetic appreciation for Kant typically involves "judging works as a certain kind of genre," in the process subsuming particular judgments, contra Adorno, under general concepts.[4]

In other words, while Carroll's characterization of Adorno's position as an "ersatz" Kantianism itself courts the charge of reducing his philosophy of art to a caricature, the fact remains that at least within the domain of popular music, Adorno failed, and rather spectacularly at that, to discriminate between different genres or styles. It's not simply that he "frequently classified *all* nonclassical music as jazz" ("based on the dubious belief that jazz was the dominant and paradigmatic form of popular music during his lifetime"[5]), but that in his later writings he was also inclined to blur his own earlier, crucial distinction between folk and popular music. Moreover, even if one were to minimize the extent of this particular problem, one would still have to insist against Adorno that the commodity aspect of popular music as a whole (assuming of course, as I've suggested in chapter 1, that one can still speak of such a thing) by no means exhausts its aesthetic appeal.[6]

Since I have already dealt with what I call the commodity-body-sign elsewhere,[7] I want to turn my attention here to a related thematic that is immanent, even hospitable, to Adorno's own theory of art. One recurring, enduring motif of this theory is the need to historicize aesthetic judgments, a critical imperative which implies that aesthetic norms and values are not static or essential—not transcendental like, for Marx, the commodity—but "culturally emergent."[8] The critical merits of this perspective is that it recognizes the specific culture or way of life out of which any art-commodity necessarily emerges even as it introduces Williams's asynchronous conception of culture as composed at any given moment of residual, dominant, and emergent elements.[9] Such a conception also suggests a possible bridge, a musical one, between Adorno and his popular-cultural critics.

From Beethoven to Fascism

Beethoven. The name is virtually synonymous with the idea of musical genius, not to mention Western classical music in general. For Adorno, however, Beethoven is very much a *locus genius* and is, as such, the product of a specific time and place—say, the era of the rising revolutionary bourgeoisie.[10] "A classicism without plaster of Paris," so Adorno describes Beethoven's famous middle period (which stretches from, roughly, the Third Symphony of 1803 to Piano Sonata no. 2 in B-Flat, op. 106 of 1819), a tumultuous period that is also arguably the musical equivalent of the French Revolution.[11] But perhaps it would be more accurate to say, since in Germany at this tempestuous moment in time, music's mirror image lay not so much in poetry as philosophy, that Beethoven is the musical analogue of Hegel: "In a similar sense in which there is only Hegelian philosophy, in the history of Western music there is only Beethoven."[12]

Although Adorno obviously reserves a privileged place in his philosophy of history for the composer of the Ninth Symphony, he nevertheless understands Beethoven's achievement from a certain catastrophic perspective: "everything—his language, his subject and tonality, that is the whole system of bourgeois music—is irrecoverably lost to us, and is perceptive only as something vanishing from sight"[13]—as, Adorno laments in a characteristically provocative afterthought, "Eurydice was seen."[14] In this dense, allusive fragment from *Beethoven* (1993), a volume of fragments, Adorno seems to be suggesting something not only about the past (for example, that it is irretrievable, a commonplace enough proposition) but about the history of music and, by way of the figure of Eurydice (and despite the earlier cavil about poetry in the bourgeois era), lyric art as a whole.

One especially illuminating context for this Orphic fragment appears in a passage from the *Philosophy of Modern Music* (1949) where, in a discussion of the decline of the hermetic work of art, Adorno reflects on the primal scene of music: "'Tears dim my eyes: earth's child I am again'—this line from Goethe's *Faust* defines the position of music. Thus earth claims Eurydice again. The gesture of return—not the sensation of expectancy—characterizes the example of all music, even if it finds itself in a world worthy of death."[15] This highly poetic passage constellates a number of, to revert to a rather elementary critical vocabulary, Adornian themes. One is that the classical as opposed to modern work of art—say, Beethoven's *Eroica* versus Stravinsky's *L'histoire du soldat*—is formally hermetic or blind to the everyday world.[16] Another, related theme is that the truth content of what Adorno after Benjamin calls "aural art" is intimately tied to the blinding recognition, like Eurydice's tearful epiphany, of the materiality of human mortality: to be human is to be a child of earth, dust of dust. Still another theme is the apparent historical-philosophical paradox, dear to Adorno, that the classical world of art may be hermetic, but if its decline happens blindly or unconsciously, "it degenerates into the mass art of technical reproduction."[17]

This last proposition—which also owes something, however antithetically formulated, to Benjamin ("technical reproduction")—speaks volumes about Adorno's philosophy of history and the tendentious way he conceives of the transition from the aural to the mechanical work of art. Indeed, in a footnote to the section of the *Philosophy of Modern Music* from which I've been drawing ("Cognitive Character"), Adorno contends, in a startling conceptual reduction, that the "hermetic work belongs to the bourgeois [period], the mechanical work belongs to fascism, and the fragmentary work, in its state of complete negativity, belongs to utopia."[18] In this strict historicist context, the word "degenerate" in the above passage inevitably takes on a pronounced derogatory aura: technically reproduced mass art is akin to fascism.

Given such a supremely Hegelian philosophy of history (which, despite the utopian negativity of the fragmentary work, is also determinedly dystopian—it's a long Luciferian fall from Beethoven to Riefenstahl), one is tempted to pose the following question: If *Beethoven* is the most utopian, because most fragmentary, work of Adorno's career, why did he abandon this work?

The short answer to this question is, I want to submit, Chuck Berry.

Amerika: Beethoven or Bikinis

Benjamin's striking aphorism from *One-Way Street*—"To great writers, finished works weigh lighter than those fragments on which they work throughout their lives"[19]—might well have been written about Adorno's long-proposed work on Beethoven. While the first scattered fragments were produced in 1934, the second year of the Nazi regime and shortly before the beginning of Adorno's exile to America, the first surviving notes for the book-length project date from 1938. Moreover, even after he had returned to Germany after the war, Adorno "continued to write notes of the kind he had been accumulating more or less continuously since 1938."[20] But in 1956—the year that, a continent and cultural worlds away, Chuck Berry recorded "Roll Over Beethoven"—the notes for his Beethoven book abruptly break off.[21]

In lieu of his projected magnum opus, which was to be titled *Beethoven: Philosophy of Music*, Adorno went on to write a similarly titled book that would prove to be instrumental to his corpus: *Philosophy of Modern Music*. As he observes in "Scientific Experiences of a European Scholar in America," a telling recollection of the expatriate years he spent in the United States, *Philosophy of Modern Music* "implicated everything I wrote about music later."[22] This seminal text—which should be read, according to Adorno, as an "extended appendix" to his and Horkheimer's great collaborative work of the period, *Dialectic of Enlightenment*[23]—was emblematic in other, more personal ways as well.

In fact, one doesn't have to press too hard against the grain of, say, "On Popular Music," which was one of four English-language studies he conducted for the Princeton Radio Research Project (1938–1940), to sense how profoundly alienating Adorno's experiences as a European scholar in America were. Barred from returning to Europe, the home of Goethe and Beethoven and the repository of the great hermetic art works of the bourgeois period, Adorno was stranded in Kafkaesque Amerika: the republic of advanced, technically reproduced mass art, of jazz and Westerns, torch songs and gangster movies.

"Like a child who once burnt shuns fire," he reminisces in "Scientific Experiences," "I had developed an exaggerated caution; I hardly dared anymore to formulate my ideas in American English as undisguisedly and vividly as was necessary to give them dimension."[24] This confession may come as something of a surprise to anyone who is familiar with the magisterial pronouncements of "On Popular Music": "Where [the masses] react at all, it no longer makes any difference whether it is to Beethoven's Seventh Symphony or to a bikini."[25] Adorno, who saw himself approaching the empiria of American popular culture "more as a musician than as a sociologist," also made the astonishing claim that he could objectively measure the inadequacy of the mass musical audience by "analyzing the *score* of a Beethoven symphony."[26]

However, the following fragment from the very beginning of Adorno's planned book on Beethoven sheds a rather different, more sympathetic light on the above claims even as it highlights what for Adorno were the very origins of musical experience and even, perhaps, of pleasure itself or *jouissance*:

From my childhood I can clearly remember the magic emanating from a score which named the instruments, showing exactly what was played by each. Flute, clarinet, oboe—they promised no less than colorful railway tickets or names of places. If I am entirely honest, it was this magic far more than the wish to know music as such that induced me to learn how to transpose and read scores while still a child, and which really made a musician of me. So strong was this magic that I can still feel it today when I read the *Pastoral*, in which, probably, it first manifested itself to me.[27]

The fascination of this fragment for me is its frank accent on the power of magic as opposed to, say, cognition or understanding. The names of the individual instruments—"flute, clarinet, oboe"—are themselves promises, like "colorful railway tickets," of unseen pleasures and distant magical places.

The irony, of course, is that whereas Beethoven's *Pastoral* awakened in Adorno a certain wanderlust, this desire was predicated, contra *Faust*'s Eurydice (and like the pastoral itself), on the impossibility of return, a paradox that is the very definition of the utopian. For Adorno, it was not simply that there would be no going back to the Arcadian pleasures of childhood or the revolutionary period of Beethoven; there would also be no going back to pre-Fascist Germany—which is to say, there would be no going back after America. In this sense, America for Adorno was positively traumatic, a reaction that is aurally registered in the following extraordinary fragment from *Beethoven*: "It is conceivable that Beethoven actually *wanted* to go deaf—because he already had a taste of the sensuous side of music as it is blared from loudspeakers today."[28]

Radio Days

Adorno, it is clear, was deaf to the magic spell of popular music. Not that this constitutional incapacity nor, for that matter, the "prohibitively difficult task" of ascertaining the "subjective content of musical experience"[29] kept him from attempting to taxonomize what in the *Introduction to the Sociology of Music* (1962) he calls "musical conduct." This taxonomy or typology extends from the expert listener (which even at the time of the book's composition was, Adorno conceded, already "more or less limited to the circle of professional musicians") to the "musically *indifferent*, the *unmusical*, and the *antimusical*."[30]

And yet, the most significant and, in some ways, most interesting type is the "entertainment listener," who is that ever elusive thing: the common-denominator object of desire of the culture industry. The mode or conduct that corresponds to this type of listener is characterized by "deconcentration" and "comfortable distraction." In fact, listening to music sheerly for entertainment purposes is, according to Adorno, as addictive as those two great accoutrements of popular (dance) music: alcohol and cigarettes. Still, an adequate description of this kind of listener is only possible (and this is retrospectively the most remarkable aspect of Adorno's characterization of popular music) from the perspective of the mass media: "There can be no more drastic demonstration of the compromise character than the conduct of a man who has the radio on while he works."[31]

I'd be lying if I didn't admit that this description cuts pretty close to the bone since not unlike, I imagine, a lot of people, I almost always work while watching TV or listening to my radio or stereo. Even now, as I sit typing at my computer, I am listening, true to the multi-media disposition of the moment, to my CD player, which is set to "concert" and is playing Beethoven's Fifth Symphony. The point is, music for me—whether classical or popular, Beethoven or Chuck Berry—is an indispensable part of my everyday life, as basic to my well-being as reading or watching movies. Bumpin' music in my car, on my CD player, may constitute "inadequate" or even "regressive" listening from a hard-core Adornian standpoint, but as anyone who listens regularly to music in a car can testify, this conduct is pretty conducive to musical reception.

More to the point perhaps, such "motorvatin'," to sample Chuck Berry's "Maybellene" (1955), is not necessarily incompatible with other kinds or modes of listening. So, in *Rhythm and Noise*, Theodore Gracyk argues that "intelligent listening occurs when one makes appropriate intertextual links and responds in terms of both musical and social contexts."[32] While intelligent listening is obviously not the only, or even best, way to respond to music (since, presumably, an adequate response to dance music would be to dance), for Gracyk rock music is heard "most adequately" when one has a "sense of the story that stretches from Elvis Presley and Chuck Berry to Madonna and Nirvana" (a narrative that I have recapitulated in chapter 1).[33] Simply put, the social context of jazz or rock 'n' roll is arguably as complex as that for classical or modern music.

Thus, to cite only one example from the history of rock, in 1949, the very same year that Adorno finally returned to Europe, the social context of popular music underwent a dramatic sea change, one that usefully complicates the fixed historical coordinates of the Adornian problematic. "October 29, 1949," for example, is the second entry in James Miller's history of the rise of rock 'n' roll (the first is Wynonie Harris's 1947 recording of "Good Rockin' Tonight") and references the day that Dewey Phillips first aired his groundbreaking radio program *Red Hot and Blue* on WHBQ in Memphis, Tennessee. As Miller chronicles, it was only a matter of weeks "before Phillips was on the air from 9:00 till midnight, hawking flour, spinning records and changing, forever, the way white people would hear black music."[34]

This last construction—"the way white people would hear black music"—is, needless to say, a long and complicated story. A chapter within a much larger, collective tale, Phillips's (Dewey's, not Sam's) story is about the sudden introduction into postwar American life of commercial television—that new, cool medium—and the attendant historic shift in the radio industry from local to national programming (and, equally significantly, from live entertainment to prerecorded music). Phillips's story is also about the fast-developing relation between a new, hipper breed of DJs and the novel musical formats they adopted in order to attract both white and black audiences.

Indeed, the rise of rock 'n' roll is inseparable from consumer culture and, especially, black consumption. Though much has been made of the "age of affluence" that blossomed like some economic atomic bomb in the aftermath of World War II, the intimate dialectic between successful DJs like Dewey Phillips and the first, emerging crossover markets elucidates the libidinal and political stakes behind the music, *race* music:

> After the war, the income of African Americans, historically depressed, grew even more quickly than that of whites. In a city like Memphis certain commodities were disproportionately bought by blacks. . . . [R]adios, once beyond the means of the average black family, had become a standard appliance. . . . Advertisers eager to reach this newly affluent audience naturally turned to radio shows that featured race music.[35]

One might imagine that African Americans responded immediately to the sort of race-skewed radio format that Phillips featured, but such an assumption would singularly fail to capture the contradictory complexion of the audience in this particular place, Memphis (the birthplace of Elvis), and at this particular moment in time, circa 1949.

For example, the kind of music that Phillips generally played—"barrelhouse boogie" and "old-fashioned country and blues," music for a midnight ramble or a Saturday-night function—was considered demeaning by many educated blacks who preferred the more "urbane and jazz-oriented fare" (Basie, Ellington, etc.) broadcast during the day on WHBQ's rival station, WDIA.[36] Moreover, during this time it was far easier for a "white deejay like Phillips to air unrefined Delta blues on a predominantly white station like WHBQ than it was for a pioneering black deejay like Nat Williams to play the same music on an all-black station like WDIA."[37] Yet another twist of the screw (one that goes some way toward articulating, if not explaining, the performative contradiction that is early rock 'n' roll) is that this music—rude, down-and-dirty Delta blues—acquired prestige for black audiences precisely because it was being played on a primarily white station.[38]

One product of this aural mixing or miscegenation was a new kind of musical community: from one perspective, invisible as air waves (since the audience members were effectively sequestered in their pre-TV homes); from another, palpable as the electricity before a summer storm. In other words, if it's fair to say that the race format, itself what one might call "separate but equal music," was a direct result of segregation, it's also fair to say, as Miller does, that the emergence of this new *sensus communis* signified, if not the end, then the "beginning of the end of segregation."[39]

For white teenagers at the time, the utter foreignness of the music Phillips played not only made it a "powerful antidote to boredom" (this much, at least, Adorno understood), its sheer distance from any world these young people had personally experienced also made it an "image of freedom" and "an invitation to fantasy."[40] Out of this matrix of image and invitation, dream wish and magic spell, this freedom to fantasize (which, perhaps, is not so different after all from Adorno's Faustian account of music), issued the inimitable music of Chuck Berry.

"Roll Over Beethoven"

Chuck Berry was the premier architect and poet laureate of rock 'n' roll. His first song, "Maybellene," recorded on May 21, 1955, was a "fast-car fantasy" with racy lyrics to match: "I saw Maybellene in a Coupe de Ville / A Cadillac arollin' on the open road / Nothin' will outrun my V8 Ford."[41]

The difference between Berry and Adorno on this particular subject, cars, couldn't be greater. Where Berry's early songs celebrate America's love affair with the automobile (a consequence of the time he spent working on the assembly line at General Motors), Adorno's view of the popular hit song was stringently anti-Fordist, likening the "calculated process of rearranging various 'frills' and 'ornaments' with the factory customizing of automobiles."[42] As Gracyk, mobilizing the appropriate vehicular trope, puts it, "Consumers make purchases based on minute differences, but everyone drives away in essentially the same vehicle."[43]

To be sure, Berry and Adorno came from very different places. Unlike Adorno, who was born into a musical family (his mother had been a professional singer and, as a teenager in Frankfurt-am-Main, he attended the local music conservatory, eventually going on to study composition with one of the principal composers of the second Viennese school, Alban Berg), Chuck Berry was a musical autodidact who taught himself how to play the guitar from *Nick Mannaloft's Guitar Book of Chords*. Born in St. Louis, a musical crossroads situated on the Mississippi, itself a "waystation for the railroad and river traffic that brought southern blues musicians to the industrial North," Berry's brand of rock 'n' roll—one part rockabilly, two parts boogie, and with a killer backbeat and guitar riffs only a fool could lose—embodies all the subtle and not so subtle contradictions of the border state he grew up in.[44]

In fact, if borders are all about the law and also tacitly, if not inevitably, transgression, Berry's outlaw persona was all about border crossing: "Restin' on charges of an unnamed crime / He was sittin' in the witness stand." Arrested in 1944 at the age of eighteen for being present in a stolen car and later convicted of auto theft, he went on to spend nearly three years in reform school, an experience that provided him with two of the dominant themes of his lyrics: the stultifying atmosphere of school life and the exhilarating freedom of being out of school, on the open road, driving. (The fact that Berry was charged in 1959—under rather dubious, even racist circumstances—with a federal violation of the Mann Act, which "prohibited transporting a minor across state lines with intent to commit prostitution,"[45] casts an even longer, more tragic shadow on his early songs.)

So when in 1956, having moved to Chicago and after his legendary meeting with Muddy Waters (who recommended him to Phil and Leonard Chess), Berry recorded "Roll Over Beethoven," he was not unfamiliar with the transgressive kicks and harsh penalties associated with breaking the law. As Berry once remarked in a gloss of "Thirty Days," "I have found no happiness in any association that has been linked with regulation and custom."[46] In this overtly rebellious context, "Roll Over Beethoven," what one critic has dubbed the "universal slogan for rock,"[47] can be seen as a direct-address assault on the musical Law of the Father and its repressive code of conduct:

> You know, my temperature's risin'
> And the jukebox blows a fuse
> My heart's beatin' rhythm
> And my soul keeps on singin' the blues
> Roll over Beethoven and tell Tchaikovsky the news.

If the bourgeois musical tradition is, for Adorno, "grounded in an essentially contemplative mode of listening" associated with the concert hall and "requiring 'understanding,'"[48] "Roll Over Beethoven" sounds as if it was made for motion, for dancing and driving.

In "Types of Musical Conduct" Adorno observes that popular music "attaches itself to technology,"[49] and early rock 'n' roll is not only inconceivable without the portable radio, it seems to be made on the go ("Go, Johnny, go!"). In fact, although Adorno claims in "On Popular Music" that the production of hit songs remains, like serious music, in a "handicraft stage," neither musical notation nor composition, which was as necessary to Tin Pan Alley composers as it was to Beethoven, was standard practice in rock 'n' roll, which was completely transformed by the use of magnetic tape recording (a new technology that had a formative impact on Berry's own career).[50] "We didn't write songs," Leiber and Stoller once quipped, "we wrote records."[51]

The records in question were not those long-playing, high-fidelity shellac ones that my father kept locked in the compartment under his console phonograph but brightly colored light-as-plastic singles, only slightly bigger than a hand, that every teen lusted after. (A hoard of 45s was something then, more valuable by far than money itself, because richer.) These 45s might have needed more RPMs than their unwieldy predecessors, 45 revolutions per minute versus 33 1/3, but their effect was no less revolutionary. For, as a teen in 1956, you might not have had enough money to buy an LP but you probably had enough to buy a 45: say, #1626 on the silver-top blue Chess label, "Roll Over Beethoven."

Magic Spell and the Two Spheres of Music

With rock 'n' roll, as Peter Wicke comments in "'Roll Over Beethoven,'" the opening chapter of *Rock Music*, "popular music appears for the first time within a cultural system of reference which allows it to become a *fundamental experience*."[52] Not unlike the historical avant-garde as opposed to Adorno's prized artistic formation, modernism, rock 'n' roll dissolved the "barriers between the formerly separate spheres of art and everyday life," so much so that everyday life, revivified by daily infusions of rock 'n' roll, itself became an art form.

This process of deaestheticization is, of course, diametrically opposed to the way in which Adorno understands both art and musical experience. For Adorno, the experience of music can only be a fundamental one when it is informed by both "interpretive experience" and "interpretive understanding." That is, whereas experience or *Erfahrung* "involves the capacity to immerse oneself within the work, to follow its dynamic unfolding 'blind' . . . while also being able to grasp it as a whole,"[53] understanding or *Verstehen* is the analytical or cognitive aspect of the previous intuitive-affective act of mimesis.

Such a cognition-heavy approach would appear to be totally alien to the experience of rock music (which Adorno would probably consign, like Benjamin, to the category of *Erlebnis* or mere "lived experience"), but he nevertheless insists, true to what I take to be the deep musical and aesthetic roots of his personality, on the irreducibility of the magic spell or riddle character of the work of art. Indeed, according to Adorno, proper listening not only necessitates falling under this magic spell but such listening, even as it aims via experience and understanding to comprehend the formal logic of the work of art, must relinquish, paradoxically enough, the possibility of fully deciphering its "constitutive enigma."[54]

Now, it may well be that Adorno's conception of the enigmatic dimension of the work of art is merely the false inverse of his sociological zeal to articulate *the* truth content of music. However, his abiding recognition of the sphinxlike character of the *Vexierbild* suggests, at least to me, that his work on popular music isn't as petrified as it sometimes seems; that there is, as it were, an Adorno after Chuck Berry. For example, in the introduction to "On Popular Music," Adorno asserts that the study of the "actual function of popular music in its present status" (which is the de facto topic of his essay) itself presupposes another, more originary problematic: the historical division between the "two main spheres of music."[55] In other words (and Adorno never forgot this), the real problem with popular music was not the music but the division itself: "The question of the truth and untruth of music is closely linked with the relation of its two spheres, the serious one and the lower one, unjustly termed the 'lighter Muse.'"[56]

From this perspective, the greatness of a song like "Roll Over Beethoven" is that it announces the historic moment when the musical spheres abruptly reverse places: Beethoven and Tchaikovsky are out, Berry and Presley, Bo Diddley, Little Richard, and Jerry Lee Lewis are in. More generally, "Roll Over Beethoven" represents the rise of mass-popular culture and the demise of high sublime culture understood—as both Kant and, later, Adorno did—as the autonomous antithesis of the lower spheres, of the merely beautiful for Kant and, for Adorno, amusement or entertainment.

If one negative effect of this postmodernist dissolution is that certain kinds of what Adorno thought of as serious, avant-garde art appear to be vanishing like Eurydice, never to be revived, one positive result is that the antagonistic relation between the two spheres which historically sustained high art—"refined matters" for the rulers, "coarse" ones for the populace[57]—no longer exists in quite the same way as it once did (say, during the reign of Beethoven). This is especially true for the United States, a development that Adorno saw with his characteristic prescience. So, in the preface to "On Popular Music," in the context of a discussion of the European provenance of the division of the spheres, Adorno declared that the "historical background of this division applies to [American music] only indirectly."[58] (Small wonder, then, that we prefer our kings, like Elvis, to be popular-music ones.)

Adorno's observation about the American indifference to the historical division of the spheres is significant in light of his comments about the United States in the chastened conclusion to "Scientific Experiences of a European Scholar in America." Writing in retrospect (and acutely conscious, it is clear, of the European presuppositions about musical culture that he had brought to bear on his work here), Adorno recalls that he only became aware of these presuppositions while he was living in the "most technologically and industrially advanced country," the United States.[59] Though one momentous result of this industrial and technological superiority was, as he pointed out, the displacement of the "center of gravity of musical life" from Europe to America, he also intuitively realized that one could avoid the "American experience" only at the price of intellectual recidivism: "every consciousness today that has not appropriated the American experience, even if with resistance, has something reactionary to it."[60]

The phrase "even with resistance" is quintessential Adorno. Still, despite or perhaps because of this resistance, Adorno, as the above passages about the United States suggest, could be quite farsighted. What he could not see was how the intricate relations that obtained among the processes of production, distribution, and consumption in the technical reproduction of popular music would be dramatically transformed in the last quarter of the twentieth century. Adorno is on record for his withering views about the commodity production of music, which for him included everything from vulgar Hollywood scores to the bastardized performance of classical "masterpieces" (vide Toscanini). Good Marxist that he was, Adorno accorded primacy to the mode of production in matters economic, what Fredric Jameson has succinctly called the "reception of production."[61] At the same time, distribution and its circulatory mechanisms were, for Adorno, the defining features of the culture industry, which refers not so much to the production process but to the "standardization of the thing itself . . . and to the rationalization of distribution techniques."[62]

MP3

I raise the issue of distribution here, in the conclusion to this chapter, because although Adorno would no doubt have been displeased by both Chuck Berry and early rock 'n' roll (whose music he would have seen as having little enough impact on the forces of production), the interest of MP3 in the context of Adorno's critique of popular music is that this technology promises to revolutionize the music industry. With the advent of Internet file-sharing applications (and notwithstanding the demise of Napster, which was finally forced to shut down in 2001[63]), people are now conceivably able to access any and every bit of music ever recorded, from Beethoven to Chuck Berry and beyond, for free.

While it goes without saying that a whole lot more American Idols will be ripped rather than Beethoven, the long-term implications of MP3 technology for artists, the music industry, and consumers are enormous. I have intentionally placed the music industry right in the middle of this triadic series (between artists and consumers) because up until now, with notable but still limited and by no means unproblematic exceptions like Fugazi,[64] artists have had to rely on the record industry to distribute their music. The question is, What would happen if artists could bypass the music industry and distribute their wares directly, via the Internet, to their fans?

Artists and proponents of intellectual property rights remain sharply divided on this issue, with Metallica on one side and, it seems, everybody else on the other. For example, if the current illegal trend were to prevail, it's not clear how artists would be remunerated, if at all, for their labor. Megapopular and absurdly overpaid acts aside (of which there are way too many to name, but let's start with Metallica!), this is by no means a peripheral issue given that some artists, notably African Americans, are just now beginning to get "paid in full."

The MP3 problematic opens up a virtual Pandora's box of other, equally daunting questions, preeminent among them, at least for the music industry: Will people stop buying music when they can get it for free over the Internet? And, equally importantly, what exactly is driving people's use of MP3 and, more recently, P2P or "peer-to-peer" networks?

The first thing to be said about all of the above issues is that they derive from a common historical event: the introduction of the compact disk in 1983. One advantage of CDs, though this remains very much open to debate for audiophiles, is that unlike vinyl records, they do not suffer fidelity degradation, all those snaps, crackles, and pops I fondly associate with vintage records. (These imperfections remain, for me, part of the aura of pre-CD and, especially, 50s and 60s popular music: for example par excellence, those orange-and-black Capitol 45s such as the very first single in the Miklitsch household, the Beach Boys' "Dance, Dance, Dance" and the even better B side, "The Warmth of the Sun.")

Of course, the economic advantage of the CD revolution for the record industry, in addition to the wholesale repackaging of back catalogues, is that it has allowed companies to virtually double the price of LPs while, crucially, holding the line on royalty rates. But by far the most enormous consequence of the compact disk has been the digitalization of music or what amounts to the same thing, its infinite reproducibility. What the latter reproductive process has meant for the music industry can be summed up in one word: piracy. As one commentator has said about Shawn Fanning, the nineteen-year-old inventor of Napster, "The record companies think Fanning has created an evil empire of copyright-pillaging pirates."[65]

Although Napster in its anticorporate guise is now dead and gone,[66] popular P2P programs such as Morpheus have almost instantaneously blossomed in its wake like so many hydra-headed monsters, raising the spectre for the culture industry, if not for music fans, of a Matrix-like "Darknet": "a vast, illegal, anarchic economy of shared music, TV programs, movies, software, games, and pornography which would come to rival the legitimate entertainment industry."[67] Record companies, predictably, have responded to the P2P problem with lawsuits and, more constructively, legal downloading services such as Apple's iTunes Music Store which, rather than giving it away for a song, charge ninety-nine cents per song.

Still, the crowning irony of the MP3 problematic is that the core values of the people who trade music files online are arguably rock and roll values: "freedom, lack of respect for authority, and a desire for instant gratification."[68] What we may be witnessing today, then, is the death not so much of rock (whose values have already been taken up and creolized by other genres such as rap) as of the music industry itself and its, for many, outmoded—because wasteful and exploitative—mode of production.

Fantasia

Whatever happens, music—some good, some bad, but hopefully more good than bad—will continue to get made. Older artists like Sonic Youth will continue to surprise us with their ability to rock with the ages, while newer ones like Eminem will emerge out of nowhere to test our aesthetic instincts and First-Amendment pieties.

In the meantime, I'll always have Beethoven and Chuck Berry to take with me to that deserted island in the mind's eye, a castaway's dream (an artificial paradise, this) complete with electricity. And since this is my magic carpet ride, in my not so exacting fantasy I'll also bring along a copy of Adorno's *Minima Moralia* to remind me that even to be able to entertain such prime-time Robinsonnades is the height of luxury. For as the Adornian dialectic continually proposes, every fantasy of escape and dream of happiness, every magic spell of every hit song, is bound up with a recognition of the merest subsistence—the "extreme poverty" and "appalling homes"—that is, unhappily, the lot of too much of the world.

Reprise

Beethoven's Hair

> Some magnificent pieces by Beethoven sound from a distance like . . . mere "boom boom."
>
> —Adorno, *Beethoven*

Beethoven's iconicity has a long illustrious history. Here, for example, is Wagner on the Maestro after hearing the Ninth Symphony (1824) in 1839 at a Paris Conservatoire Concert: "The effect on me was indescribable. To this must be added the impression produced on me by Beethoven's features, which I saw in the lithographs that were circulated everywhere at the time. . . . I soon conceived an image of him in my mind as a . . . unique supernatural being."[1]

If Beethoven's music in the popular imagination has been associated since Wagner with the Ninth Symphony (and not, say, third-period works such as the late quartets or the *Missa Solemnis* of 1823), the history of Beethoven as an icon in the image archive of the West is arguably a function of that sublime object, his hair, "that wild mane that . . . framed his dark face in the waning years" and that symbolized, like Einstein's, his "arresting personal presence."[2] Simply put, Beethoven's hair, a deathbed lock of which scientists have analyzed to speculate about the cause of his celebrated deafness (dropsy as a result of lead poisoning!), can be seen as an indelible signifier of his romantic temperament.

Now, given that the conceit of the preceding chapter is that Chuck Berry's "Roll Over Beethoven" represents a historical reversal of the cultural hierarchy personified by Beethoven and championed by Adorno, just such a conceit also runs the risk of producing a mere reversal where, for example, rock is somehow better than classical music. In other words, while the anti-classical thrust of "Roll Over Beethoven" has real force in the context of Adorno's work on popular music, it would be entirely too convenient to forget that Beethoven himself in the process of composing the *Eroica* (1804) "struck out Napoleon's name," thereby engendering a type, the "rebel artist hero,"[3] that informs both Berry's rock 'n' roll persona and his anti-Beethoven anthem.

At the same time, the problem of what Alex Ross wittily calls "marble-bust Beethoven"[4] persists: as Marianne Moore once said about poetry, "I hate it too"—classical music, that is. Ross, who in the pages of the *New Yorker* has been engaged for some time in the thankless but necessary task of writing about "classical music as if it were popular music and popular music as if it were classical,"[5] readily concedes not only that classical music is now routinely "described in terms of its . . . resistance to the mass" but that even metropolitan sophisticates proudly wear their anti-classical badges on their sleeves: "'I don't know a thing about Beethoven,' they say, which is not what they would say if the subject [were] Stanley Kubrick."[6]

In this cultural climate, a little knowledge, whether about Beethoven or the history of popular music, is a good, because dangerous, thing. For example, it's conventional wisdom, at least from the vantage point of Adorno's aesthetic theory, to see the late Beethoven as the "presagement of the alienated music of Schoenberg."[7] Yet as Edward Said, whose understanding of the history of modern music owes an enormous debt to Adorno, acknowledges, Schoenberg's music is "completely impossible (a) to perform, (b) to understand, and (c) to listen to."[8]

While the historical trajectory from Beethoven to Shoenberg makes, alas, not a little sense, Adorno has pursued other dialectical tacks, arguing, for instance, that Beethoven's symphonies (where the recapitulation mimes the dominative *Aufhebung* of the Hegelian dialectic) are less a presagement of serious music than a "prefiguration of mass culture."[9] The interest for me of this critique of classic, middle-period Beethoven, that his music sometimes violently "manipulates" or "manufactures" transcendence,[10] is that it suggests a possible consonance between the composer of the Ninth Symphony and the "dream factories" of Tin Pan Alley. Thus, according to Adorno, when an audience hears a Tin Pan Alley song—say, "Swanee" (1918)—they "become aware of the overwhelming possibility of happiness."[11]

The catch, of course (and there's always a catch with popular music for Adorno), is that the audience's felt recognition of this transcendent moment of happiness simultaneously permits them to see "what the whole order of contemporary life ordinarily forbids them to admit": namely, "that they actually have no part in happiness."[12] Escape and temporary release therefore give way not simply to ambivalence but to the rebellion and resistance consequent upon the realization that the wish fulfillment is in fact illusory.

To be sure, the difference between Beethoven and Tin Pan Alley is, for Adorno, more a matter of kind than degree; in fact, Adorno would no doubt consider the above speculation about Beethoven and

Tin Pan Alley an example of the worse sort of sublation. Which is simply to say that if it's necessary, at this post-classical moment in time, to read Adorno not so much against as with the grain,[13] it's also imperative to admit that, at best, Adorno's positions on popular and classical music cannot be reconciled.

A passage from Richard Leppert's commentary "Music and Mass Culture" in his invaluable Adorno compendium, *Essays on Music*, reflects, in miniature, the problem: "Adorno's contribution to popular music research is unimpeachable, despite the fact that he was no 'fan' of popular music, held strong prejudices, didn't know a fraction of a repertory he attacked, and didn't change his mind (very much or often) on the topic, largely ignoring . . . the popular music of the last half-century."[14] With its extended, "Senecan" qualification, the rhetoric of this passage testifies to the extreme contradictory character of Adorno's essays on popular music. Accordingly, Adorno's positions on classical and popular music can only be squared at the price of reproducing the sort of coercion or theoretical violence he detects, in the symphonic mode, in the work of Beethoven.

With this in mind (and since the case against Adorno has frequently been made on the basis of his brief against jazz), it's worth returning to one of those paradigmatic moments in the history of American popular music when, as with Berry's "Roll Over Beethoven," "hi" and "lo" elements of the culture suddenly become activated, colliding like so many atoms. One of the most striking of these moments occurred on February 12, 1924, at Aeolian Hall, at 34 West Forty-Third Street in New York City, when Paul Whiteman staged "An Experiment in Modern Music." The highlight was a performance of *Rhapsody in Blue*, the title alone hints at its unique combination of classical ("rhapsody") and popular ("jazz") music, with Gershwin on piano, Whiteman conducting the band, and orchestration by Ferde Grofé. While this concert was not the first time that classical and jazz music had crossed paths (Henry F. Gilbert and John Powell had composed *Negro Rhapsody* and *Rapsodie Nègre* in 1912 and 1918, respectively), Gershwin's *Rhapsody in Blue*—due in no small part to Whiteman's Barnum-and-Bailey promotional instincts (presented, of course, under the august auspices of "education")—transformed the landscape of modern American music.

It probably goes without saying that Adorno was not impressed, referring in "The Radio Symphony" (1941) to the "full seven-course dinner in color of Whiteman's rendition of *Rhapsody in Blue*."[15] Though in general no fan of Brecht, Adorno's negative culinary judgment here is echt Brecht. The following passage from "Little Heresy" (1965) also suggests that Adorno felt that the melodic aspects of Gershwin's music encouraged the sort of atomistic, as opposed to structural, listening that typified classical-music dilettantes (for whom Schubert was king) and hit song-starved *teenagers* (a word that, appropriately enough, given Adorno's disdain for youth cultures, appears in English in the original):

> A music history that would not be satisfied with distinguishing between high and low music, but would see through the low as a function of the high, would have to trace the path that leads from the most drastic formulations of Tchaikovsky . . . to Gershwin, and from there on down into the bad infinity of entertainment.[16]

The Hegelian note notwithstanding ("bad infinity"), Adorno's take on popular music in this passage exhibits a functionalist cast, substituting dogma for dialectics, pique for profundity.

Jazz historians, not surprisingly, have been equally critical of Whiteman's pretensions with respect to what was billed as the "First American Jazz Concert," if not of Gershwin's *Rhapsody* per se. To wit: "A critical analysis for jazz studies arises from the attempts by certain white performers [i.e., Whiteman] . . . to 'elevate' or 'rescue' jazz from what they considered party-music status to that of a 'symphonic' art form that, they felt, properly belonged in concert halls."[17] In fact, Adorno and jazz critics, once thought to be among the most unlikeliest of bedfellows, are united in their utter contempt for Whiteman, who bragged that in his "modern jazz orchestra," "every member knows exactly what he is to play every minute of the time"[18]—so much, one might say, for improvisation.

But if Whiteman, the name itself invites ethnocentric parody, has become a big, because easy, target for Adornians and jazz purists alike, he has also increasingly become the "little other" on which to displace Adorno's own free-floating fears and anxieties about the racial matrix that is a constitutive aspect of modernism. So, writing about the all-white production number that concludes *The King of Jazz* (1930), Leppert concludes his interpretation with a rhetorical knockout punch: "Whiteman's world is white and . . . European."[19]

The problem with this sort of pronouncement, as Leppert himself seems to recognize, is the consequent implication that "real" jazz is black and American. According to this same mutually exclusive logic, Louis Armstrong is the real *Roi du jazz*. And, indeed, there's not a little truth to this reading. As Gary Giddens, who composed a biography of Armstrong, has recently remarked in the first volume of his Bing Crosby biography, *A Pocketful of Dreams*, "The same year [Whiteman] overwhelmed critics at Aeolian Hall, another landmark musical event had taken place": "Armstrong had arrived in New York to play with the orchestra of Fletcher Henderson, Whiteman's relatively low profile African-American counterpart."[20] More importantly, from 1925 to 1928, Armstrong went on to make studio-only recordings with his Hot Five and Hot Seven bands that revolutionized not only jazz but American popular music.

The above musical-historical opposition between Whiteman and Armstrong (where Gershwin in this reprise is the "vanishing mediator") is a perfectly feasible one except, of course, it's just a little too black and white. Although there have been moments in the past when it has been absolutely necessary to employ such "crude" historical binaries (to invoke Brecht again), these binaries tend to thoroughly remystify what are, in fact, complex historical conjunctures. One almost immediate as opposed to mediated effect is the generation of new "mythologies" (in Roland Barthes's sense): "poor Bix having to endure Whiteman's band, Armstrong 'selling out' in the 1930s," and so on.[21] Another, equally insidious effect is that a genuinely original composition such as *Rhapsody in Blue*, if only because of its association with Whiteman, becomes tarred with the same coarse historical brush. (This is decidedly not what Benjamin had in mind when, in his "Theses on the Philosophy of History" [1940], he advocated for interpretations that brushed against the grain.)

However, a sense of history informed by the jazz diaspora might begin otherwise, with, say, the rather big heresy that "Armstrong might have *made* music of the twentieth century, but it was not he who *made it* the music of the twentieth century."[22] For that, "we have to go to cultural and geographical diasporic spaces": Whiteman and, yes, "white men" as well as "American Jews like Gershwin."[23] Along the same lines, in his biography of Crosby (who was the "first and, for a while, the only white singer to fully assimilate the shock of Armstrong's impact"), Giddens observes that the original version of *Rhapsody in Blue* may not have been a blues, but nevertheless "shivered with blues shadings."[24]

Moreover, if improvisation, combined with blues and syncopation, distinguishes jazz, then one of the great ironies of the original performance of *Rhapsody in Blue* is that it differed from the one with which most people are familiar (whether it's the acoustic version of 1924, the electrical one of 1927 or, more recently, Leonard Bernstein's or Michael Tilson-Thomas's) since Gershwin himself improvised the cadenza and Ross Gorman, the virtuoso solo clarinetist, smeared the seventeen-note opening measure, producing the bluesy wail for which *Rhapsody* has become famous.

Indeed, according to Giddens, *Rhapsody* was a "jolting, even rickety, *montage* of orchestral bumps and moans."[25] This modernist inflection also materializes in the "final note" appended to Henry Cooper's searching reading of Adorno's "*Über Jazz*" (1936) which, significantly, endorses Adorno's interpretation of Whiteman only to mark, contra Adorno, the productivity of European misreadings of "even the most commercialized jazz."[26] Cooper cites the example of Hindemith, Mondrian, and Eisenstein, the last of whom referenced Whiteman's "Home Sweet Home" in order to make the point that the solution to a compositional problem in film resembles the "stunning effect of Negro syncopated jazz."[27]

Although the performance of Gershwin's *Rhapsody in Blue* at Whiteman's "Experiment in Modern Music" is an especially rich example of the fission produced when high and low culture meet, there are other moments of revolution and counter-revolution that testify to the tangled history of American popular musics. Thus, in the world of popular music, Gershwin would go on to compose, in addition to the scores for films such as Minnelli's *American in Paris* (1951), the opera *Porgy and Bess* (1935), while Duke Ellington, some twenty years after the first performance of *Rhapsody in Blue*, would premiere his *Black, Brown, and Beige* (1943) at Carnegie Hall.

Meanwhile, around the same time that Ellington was composing his version of symphonic jazz, Armstrong's music (which Adorno, not unlike Whiteman, would have found "crude") was being summarily negated by bebop. The irony—one lost, alas, on Adorno—was that jazz, the epitome for him of popular music, was in the process of transforming itself and, in the uncompromising mode of bebop, becoming the face of the musical avant-garde. Then again, such historical and aesthetic ironies, like Miles Davis's cover of *Porgy and Bess* (1958), are the very stuff of American popular music.

Part 2

Sound Film
Screen Theory and
Audiovisuality

3

The Suture Scenario
Audiovisuality and Post-Screen Theory

Adorno's essays on popular music, for all their habitual negativity, represent a seminal conjunction of critical theory and mass culture. Screen theory, a potent combination, like Frankfurt School critique, of Marxism and psychoanalysis, Althusserian Marxism and Lacanian psychoanalysis, first came to prominence in Great Britain in the early 1970s. The difference between the two formations is that Screen theory took its cue from *Cahiers du cinéma*, engaging Hollywood cinema without the contrary disposition that occasionally mars Adorno's, if not Benjamin's or Kracauer's, work on mass art in the age of mechanical reproduction.

Yet if Screen theory was willing to explore the performative contradictions and progressive character of the classic realist text, the journal from which the movement took its name, *Screen*, indicates its singular attention to the field of visuality. Moreover, perhaps its most distinctive contribution to cinema studies, the concept of *suture*, tended to operate at a formal level as a figure of closure in almost direct contradistinction to the textual and spectatorial indeterminacy posited at the level of theory. Given these discursive orientations, the Screen concentration on the visual field and the related, univocal conception of suture, the aim of this chapter is to reexplore suture theory in light of the audio or, more precisely, audiovisual register and in the context not so much of classical and rock music (as in the previous chapter) as of jazz and rap (i.e., Billie Holiday and gangsta rap, respectively).

More specifically, this chapter is structured in the form of a diptych. In the first theoretical part, I offer a brief history of suture theory from 1966 to 1977 as well as a synoptic review of it since Stephen Heath. One of my working premises is that if the "time of suture seems to have irrevocably passed," as Žižek says in *The Fright of Real Tears*, then rather than interpret this "disappearance as a fact," it might be more instructive to see it as an indication of the "decline of cinema studies."[1] In the second, illustrative part, I appropriate Žižek's proposition and positively invert it, examining audiovisuality in Marlon Riggs's *Tongues Untied* (1989) and F. Gary Gray's *Set It Off* (1996), mobilizing Žižek's rereading of the Screen account of suture (suture-as-desuturing) as a way to conceptualize a revised notion of suturing action that better speaks to what I take to be its complex, dialectical functioning. Indeed, another of the working premises of the chapter is that "queer cinema" and the "new black movie boom" of the 1990s provide a less monolithic, more performative model than Screen theory for thinking the relations between musicality and narrativity as well as between the apparatus and textual traditions within film studies itself.

Theory: The Suture Scenario

If it's true, as Noël Carroll maintains in his introduction to *Mystifying Movies*, that contemporary film theory originated in 1966, when Christian Metz began composing the essays that would later comprise one of the founding texts of ciné-semiology, *Film Language*, 1966 has an additional significance in that it was also the year in which Jacques-Alain Miller's essay on suture appeared in *Cahiers pour l'analyse*.[2] Jean-Pierre Oudart's "Cinema and Suture" (1969) might be said to represent the first properly film-theoretical moment of the suture scenario, but the second film-theoretical moment, marking as it does the translation of Miller's and Oudart's work into English as well as the appearance in 1977–78 of Heath's "Notes on Suture" in the same issue of *Screen*, is, in retrospect, the critical one.[3]

While Daniel Dayan's "Tutor-Code of Classical Cinema" had appeared in 1974 (and eventually became the object of William Rothman's 1975 critique[4]), Heath's essay fluently recapitulated each of its predecessors and quickly became a locus classicus of contemporary film theory. A translation of sorts of Miller's essay on suture (the latter of which was also a translation of sorts of Lacan's 1964 seminar on the "causation of the subject"), part of the importance of Heath's "Notes on Suture" was that it almost immediately migrated into other disciplines, producing determinate theoretical effects outside the field of film theory. Thus, when Ernesto Laclau and Chantal Mouffe introduced their neo-Gramscian notion of "hegemonic suture" in *Hegemony and Socialist Strategy* (1985), the reference was not simply to Miller but to Heath.[5]

Indeed, the most important moment in "Notes on Suture" is when Heath, like Laclau and Mouffe, defines suture as a *post*-Althusserian problematic:

> [A] materialist theory of the constitution-construction of the subject cannot be developed in abstraction from the discursive and ideological but, equally, cannot be developed as an account of interpellation which effectively takes the subject as given and not an effect of the signifier. The mesh of the various instances, tightening together, is difficult and crucial; suture could well be defined as the terms of that crucial difficulty.[6]

Heath's formulation here signifies a pointed critique of the Althusserian notion of interpellation, a critique that prefigures, among other things, Žižek's later revision of the Althusserian account of subjectivation.

Still, if "Notes on Suture" represents a displacement of a certain Althusserian problematic (where, to reiterate Heath, the subject is conceived as "given" rather than as an "effect of the signifier"), its relation to Lacanian psychoanalysis is rather more problematic because, I want to argue, less circumspect. For even as the Oudart-Dayan "system of the suture" is sharply criticized by Heath for, respectively, its "tragic" onto-theological and global-ideological character, Miller's reading of suture—and, beyond this, Lacan's—remains firmly in place: which is to say, beyond critique. Herein, it seems to me, lies the real problem or "crucial difficulty" of the Screen conception of suture.

Now, since the terms of this articulation are, as Heath himself remarks, both crucial and difficult, I can only gesture within the limited space of this chapter to one specific critique of Heath and one potential critical rearticulation or resignification. This critique pivots on Lacan's dual account of the causation of the subject, the first term of which is *alienation*, the second *separation*. The first concept or operation, alienation, is perhaps most economically illustrated by the slogan, "Your money or your life!," which designates, for Lacan, the division between being and meaning, the subject and the Other, and so forth. The second, related operation, separation, refers not simply to procuration—as Heath queries, "How does the subject procure itself in the signifier?"[7]—but to representation and, most importantly for me, fantasy.

With these two fundamental terms in mind, one might say that if suture refers (to cite one of the few passages where Lacan actually addresses the topic) to the "junction of the imaginary and the symbolic,"[8] separation is registered with the imaginary. One might not only say this, Heath in fact does, commenting that insofar as separation (as, for instance, in fantasy) represents the "postponement of the truth of division," "suture is towards the imaginary."[9] In light of this, for me, restricted reading of suture as what Heath calls a "certain closure," I want to argue, laconically, that if separation constitutes the "time of the engendering,"[10] it also always constitutes the space of disengendering and disidentification. Bluntly, suture is the dialectical term for the dis-"junction of the imaginary and symbolic" and as such cannot refer simply, pace Lacan, to "pseudo-identification."[11]

Indeed, I want to propose that precisely because of its rigorous and sustained engagement with the causation or constitution of the subject, the suture scenario remains one of the most historically significant answers to the question that David Bordwell correctly identifies as the main project of Screen theory: "What are the social *and* psychic factors of cinema?"[12] I hasten to add that the last proposition should by no means be construed as a carte blanche defense of Screen theory since even in its best, least programmatic version (of which Heath's essay is a paradigmatic example), it not only failed to adequately account for the historical motivation and medium-specific character of suture (I am alluding here to Rothman's and Barry Salt's critiques, respectively[13]), suture theory also failed, as I noted in my earlier critical comments on Heath, to provide a sufficiently dialectical notion of suture itself. One historical result of this conceptual blockage was that despite the explicit insistence in Heath's "*Notes* on Suture" on the partial, improvisational character of his exposition, this essay retroactively functions as a "quilting point" in the historical trajectory of Screen theory.[14] In other words, suture theory circa 1977 should be read as a privileged nodal point in the discursive history of contemporary film theory.

Post-Screen Theory: Suture-as-Desuturing

As one potential theoretical point of departure, I want to submit that a qualified notion of suture-as-desuturing—rather than, say, Bordwell and Carroll's "modified model of rational-agent social theory"[15]—provides a discursive bridge between Screen theory and contemporary cinema studies. The impact of this rearticulation or resignification can be measured by considering the trajectory of the concept of suture since Heath. In "Identifying with the Cinema," Elizabeth Cowie comments that despite the stress in Lacan on the "fading" or "flickering" of the subject, suture quickly became conflated with the work of the imaginary—with, that is, the way in which a film snares or captures the spectator for its set of meanings. Given this top-down model of spectatorship, it's no surprise that suture not only came to be understood as a systemic "enactment *upon* the subject" (with all the attendant oppressive connotations) but that it also eventually became, however moralistically (as Cowie tartly puts it), "a 'bad' thing to do, or to suffer."[16]

In fact, in retrospect even Kaja Silverman's chapter on the topic in *The Subject of Semiotics* can be said to misprize its peculiar contradictory character.[17] To be sure, Silverman is not unaware of the ambivalence associated with the imaginary register; indeed, she maintains that because its excess speaks to a "regressive potential within the system," the editing procedure most closely connected with this system (i.e., shot/reverse shot) facilitates a psychic operation that is fundamentally "at odds with its larger signifying activities."[18]

However, the problem with Silverman's account of suture, its uncritical valorization of sexual difference aside, is that it also reflexively assumes an extremely coercive, omnipotent apparatus. So, in the context of a detailed discussion of Hitchcock's *Psycho* (1960), she claims that "we want suture so badly that we'll take it at any price, even with the fullest knowledge of what it entails," including "subordination to the castrating gaze of a symbolic Other."[19] Although Silverman's account represents a powerful, even magisterial, evocation of the "machinery of enunciation," it paints a pretty grim picture of the filmic spectator: "castrated," "supremely passive," wholly subordinated to what she calls cinema's "sleight of hand."[20]

A better, because more dialectical strategy is, it seems to me, to understand suture as Žižek does as a process of suture and desuturing, conjunction and disjunction. Indeed, for Žižek, the concept of suture is the "exact opposite of the illusory, self-enclosed totality that successfully erases the decentered traces of its production process" since "such self-enclosure is *a priori* impossible."[21] Consequently, if suture doesn't refer solely to a "closure in the signifying chain, but a closure and re-opening," then any and every suture is not only provisional—more or less precarious, more or less secure—but, in the final analysis, fallible: "from which the desire arises," as Cowie says, "to start again, to see another film."[22]

Audiovisuality in *Tongues Untied* and *Set It Off*

In this, the illustrative part of the chapter, I want to exhibit a less restricted conception of suture than that offered by the Oudart-Dayan model by exploring the way sound and image work together in two quite different films, one fiction, one nonfiction, one generic, one experimental, both, at least to my mind, paradigmatic.

Before I turn my attention to these texts, it's important to observe that in *Post Theory* Jeff Smith has presented a provocative critique of psychoanalytic theories of film music, focusing on their role in suture theory. In this model, according to Smith, film music, precisely "because of its tendencies toward abstraction and inaudibility," is considered "especially well-suited to the process of binding the spectator into the world of the fiction."[23] This process is simultaneously semiotic and psychological: while music in the classical sound film typically acts "like a photographic caption" to button down the "elusive visual signifier," it also acoustically glosses over the spatial and temporal lacunae of cinematic discourse, facilitating the "spectator's absorption into the diegesis."[24]

Now, if music in mainstream Hollywood cinema frequently functions for many spectators, as Adorno and Eisler claim in *Composing for Film*, in just this seamless fashion, this is clearly not the only way it functions. Indeed, I want to reappropriate Smith's critique in order to argue that (1) audibility can in fact be seen to be integral to a revised notion of suture-as-desuturing (so that, for example, part of the force and appeal of film music is predicated on our conscious recognition of it), and (2) that such an audible model of suture can also be seen to account for a certain semiotic excess in cinematic discourse (where, for example, the cultural connotations of the music do not so much anchor the signifier as release or disseminate it). With respect to the latter signifying process, I would only add that this sonorial excess also results in a certain theatricalization, where identification has less to do with the ostensibly simple, passive pleasures of absorption than with the rather more complicated effects associated with performance.

Illustration A: *Tongues Untied*

A nonfiction film that strikingly illustrates this performative process of audiovisual binding and unbinding, absorption and theatricalization, is Marlon Riggs's *Tongues Untied* (1989). Indeed, the intermittent use of popular music in Riggs's "experimental video"[25] not only underscores the issue of audibility in the widest sociocultural sense but produces an intricate subject effect, one where the "spectator is constantly slipping in and out of the very subject position that the text has constituted for him, incessantly moving between identification and cognition, pleasure and unpleasure, belief and disbelief, rapture and distance."[26]

A representative instance of this subject address in *Tongues Untied* is the sequence featuring a drag queen sitting on a park bench smoking a cigarette as Billie Holiday's "Lover Man" plays on the sound track. Shot slightly from below, in slow motion, and in a single continuous take, this audiovisual "passage," to reaccentuate Heath's sense of the term, contrasts sharply with the various sequences that precede it. Consider, for instance, its position in the narrative syntax of the video up to this point, an autobiographical story that can be said to begin with the presentation of a black and white photograph of Riggs as a small boy accompanied by a voice-over, itself punctuated by shock cuts, detailing his growing awareness of his difference from other black and white boys.

Other relatively discrete passages follow—a zoom-out/zoom-in shot, framed by the pop-musical lyricism of Roberta Flack's "The First Time Ever I Saw Your Face" (1969), of what appears to be a high school photograph of a "whiteboy with gray/green eyes" who seduced Riggs out of his "adolescent silence"; still photos of "vanilla" pretty boys set to the disco beat of Sylvester's "Do You Wanna Funk" (1982); stock footage of buff gay white men in blue jeans and black leather gear at the Castro Street Fair in San Francisco circa 1989; and a rapid montage of "popular" images of black people: still color photos of obese mammies, complete with kerchiefs and polka-dotted bikinis, grotesquely posing for the camera ("Don't want no messy lovin'"); a S/M advertisement featuring a cropped photo of a manacled black male, white hand on pierced black breast, topped by the bold-lettered caption "Slaves for Sale"; and so on.

Over this series of racist jokes and fetishes, cartoons and caricatures (which, like the images of beautiful muscled white bodies before it, is not without its exorbitant erotic charge), Riggs, his talking head superimposed on a shot of him walking alone on a city street, acknowledges his growing recognition that despite "decades of determined assimilation," something was amiss in the land of plenty:

> In this great gay mecca,
> I was an invisible man . . .
>
> I quit the Castro
> no longer my home, my mecca
> and went in search of some place better.[27]

Cinematically speaking, the immediate response to this voice-over call is the arresting audiovisual passage with which I began: a black queen dragging on a cigarette to the sound of Billie Holiday's "Lover Man."

In terms of *Tongues Untied*'s autobiographical narrative, the most obvious thing about this passage is that it not only represents our first glimpse of that better place Riggs speaks about, it's also opposed to the gay white mecca associated in the video with the Castro. The difference between these two places—between, say, San Francisco and New York City or, more properly perhaps, between the Castro and Harlem—is not simply a matter of race, however, since the drag queen passage also implies a gendered opposition between the macho hardbodies on display at the street fair and the feminized physique and face of the drag queen.

While Riggs's decision to quit the Castro is arguably the most significant moment in *Tongues Untied*, his new home is by no means a refuge of "peace, harmony and sunshine." Rather, as he himself says in the voice-over, it is a place of truth: "simple, shameless, brazen truth." Accordingly, the tone of the first drag passage is distinctly low-key, even "blue," a point of view emphasized in *Tongues Untied* by the fact that the object of the videographic gaze is not a group (as, for instance, in the Castro passage) but a single, if quite singular, person. There is also, crucially, the issue of sound to consider, since the music for the bridge sequence is not by Sylvester or even Nina Simone (as in the Castro and second drag-queen passages, respectively) but Billie Holiday.

"Lover Man": Lady Day/Blue Boy

Billie Holiday is of course a mythical, even legendary, figure in both mass popular and gay culture. While the latter subcultural fandom is perhaps most famously memorialized in Frank O'Hara's "The Day Lady Died," the former mass-cultural iconicity or mythology, Lady Day as the epitome of the romantic, tortured artist, is notoriously on display in her ghosted autobiography, *Lady Sings the Blues* (1956), and in the Hollywood biopic of the same name.[28] Indeed, in *Lady Sings the Blues* (1972), Holiday (Diana Ross) sings "Lover Man" after her husband (Billy Dee Williams) has thrown her out of his apartment for using heroin,[29] a climactic moment in the film that, however fanciful or melodramatic, acknowledges the song's centrality to the Holiday canon.

Recorded in New York City during the peak years of Holiday's career from 1943 to 1944 with Salvador "Toots" Camarata and his Orchestra, "Lover Man" was her first recording for Decca and, unlike her previous jazz recordings on Columbia and Commodore, featured violins. Although strings are frequently frowned upon by jazz purists (and were a rarity for jazz vocalists at the time), their use on "Lover Man" arguably provides Holiday with just the sort of pop instrumentation she needed at this point in her career. In fact, the change in musical context from small instrumental combos (which had placed Holiday for some time in the "invidious position of having to compete with her past triumphs") to orchestral backing (complete with horns and a rhythm section) emphasizes the extraordinary grain of her voice with the net result that the "jazz ele-

ments of her singing" are "less important than the almost perfect symmetry between words, rhythm and personality."[30] "Lover Man," as John
Nicholson, one of Holiday's biographers, writes, is "a 'lyric moment' that
defines the singer in the character she had created for herself."[31]

The lyrics of "Lover Man," written by Jimmy Davis, Jimmy Sher-
man and Roger "Ram" Ramirez, are as simple and eloquent as Billie's
voice, full of pain and loneliness, loss and despair:

> I don't know why, but I'm feeling so sad
> I long to try something I've never had
> Never had no kisses
> Oh, what I've been missing
>
> Lover man, oh, where can you be?
>
> I'd give my soul to call you my own
> The night is cold and I'm so all alone
> Got a moon above me
> But no one to love me
>
> Lover man, oh, where can you be?

These lyrics would appear to be the consummate expression of a certain
romantic yearning and, in fact, this is one of the ways that the drag-
queen passage and, more generally, *Tongues Untied* has been read: as a
not so veiled displacement of Riggs's own desire for a new white lover
to replace the one with the gray/green eyes.

Still, if this particular moment, via the suturing action of the popular-musical format coupled with the slow-motion photography, can be
said to offer a site of affective identification for spectators, there are
other aspects to both the drag-queen passage and Billie Holiday's performance that exceed this pop-ballad romanticism. What, after all, does
it mean to cross "Lover Man," a song that itself can be said to cross form
and content (at least as it is performed by Billie Holiday[32]), with the
image of a cross-dresser?

One autobiographical answer to this question is that the first drag
sequence expresses Riggs's own personal pain, pain that is a consequence, it is clear, not merely of the racism and homophobia of the
straight white world (as seen in the jewelry store sequence) but of the
intolerance of the straight black world as well (as recorded in the gay-
bashing scene that immediately precedes the drag-queen sequences).

Indeed, reflecting on this last issue in "Black Macho Revisited," Riggs remarks that the abject other of normative black conduct, a model epitomized for him by the macho appropriation of the militant Malcolm X before Mecca, is the image of the "sissy," which is seen as cute, comic, effeminate or, at worst, as a debased, deviant, emasculated form of black masculinity.[33]

Still, indispensable as Riggs's own story is to the generic hybridity of *Tongues Untied*, this autobiographical element must also be viewed in conjunction with—and perhaps, even, disjunction from—the video's other audio and visual voices. Riggs himself stressed this social, communitarian aspect of *Tongues Untied* in an interview, observing that he made the video so *"people* won't have to go through the pain that *we* went through discovering who *we* are."[34] Here Riggs's recourse to the pronoun "we" hints that if the first drag-queen passage can be read as a trope or figure for his own life (the autobiographical suture), it's also a not so oblique signifier for a whole culture or people (the social-historical suture). Thus, responding in an interview to the charge that the "revolutionary" conclusion to *Tongues Untied* is false (because Riggs himself was involved in an interracial relationship at the time), he asserted that although the phrase "Black men loving Black men" had been interpreted in the strict sexual or romantic sense, he himself was thinking more of the social sense of the term: love in the sense of "family," "friendship," and "fraternity."[35]

En Vogue

"Lover Man" has, I want to submit, a very real resonance in this larger familial-fraternal, sociohistorical context. Part of this resonance is, of course, a function of genre. That is to say, Billie Holiday's repertoire, deeply rooted as it was in the blues, drew on "this cultural product of former slaves" to "contest and transform prevailing popular song culture."[36] Simply put, Holiday used a popular-musical form—in this case, the "torch song"—for her own intimately expressive ends. Indeed, it might not be too much to say that it is only from just such a formal, aesthetic point of view that one can begin to appreciate the utopian subtext of "Lover Man," which is simultaneously about a "fantasized future love" and another, more fundamental sociohistorical fantasy: "love and sexuality as . . . concrete daily experience and as a coded yearning for social liberation."[37]

This dialogicity or double voicedness, which is central to the performative thematics of *Tongues Untied*, is manifest in the video's verité representation of the vogue subculture later redocumented in Jennie

Livingston's *Paris Is Burning*. Just as Holiday's "Lover Man" draws on white mainstream popular music, so the gay male Afro-Latino culture of vogueing appropriates the mass-cultural style of haute couture for a "street-based culture of resistance,"[38] a subcultural act of poaching that is reappropriated in turn by popular-music divas like Madonna. In other words, if realness is all about what Nicholson in his gloss on Holiday's "Lover Man" calls the "public construction of emotion,"[39] this concept also provides a particularly apt description of the first drag sequence which, combining music and gesture, constitutes a quite sublime example of everyday vogueing.

I mean, isn't there something exquisite, exquisitely theatrical, about the way this diva acts, coolly surveying the life passing before her, coquettishly playing with her bright blue top, taking drag after drag from the cigarette burning in her right hand? This girl isn't waiting to exhale.

Although it has been argued that the drag-queen sequences in *Tongues Untied* are "nostalgic, romanticized moments" that are "quickly undermined by the voices of black homophobia" (the second sequence, for example, is followed by a shot of a black preacher shouting, "Abomination!"[40]), the first drag passage can also be interpreted as a "temporary utopia," a vision of an imagined black community where, say, the pleasures of smoking become a prized signifier for gay black pleasure (a notion intimated in *Tongues Untied* by the entrance late in the first drag-queen passage of the tall black male with the elongated cigarette dangling from his lips). In just this audiovisual sense, Riggs's music video may be said to express or signify the real material conditions of gay black men in America circa 1989, in the process making both visible and audible what Kobena Mercer calls "performative body politics."[41]

Illustration B: *Set It Off*

It may appear somewhat contradictory to turn from an experimental video or personal documentary like *Tongues Untied* to a decidedly commercial, some might say "exploitative," feature film like F. Gary Gray's *Set It Off* (1996). However, the ostensible subjects of these two works— drag divas and female gangstas, respectively—are not as far apart as they may at first glance seem. Andrew Ross, for example, has observed that there is an "unspoken dialogue" between the gangsta and the diva, where the "hardcore rapper's steady loyalty to ghetto realism (the appearance of being totally determined by one's social environment) finds its counterpart in the vogue queen's 'realness' (the ability to impersonate anything but that which you are)."[42]

Accordingly, if it's true that listening to the incomplete dialogue between the above two figures can tell us something about the sexual politics at work in contemporary black popular culture, Queen Latifah's performance as Cleopatra Simms in *Set It Off* is, I think, especially memorable. One of the most remarkable aspects of this break-out, scene-stealing performance is the way that Latifah exploits her own off-screen persona, a regal rap identity reflected in her stage name, Queen Latifah. As she recounts in *Ladies First* (named after one of her best-known songs), "Queen became synonymous with *woman* for me—the way every woman should feel or should want to feel": "proud," "dominant," "strong."[43]

Although this persona is critical to Queen Latifah's characterization of Cleo in *Set It Off*, her performance—like Ice Cube's in *Boyz N the Hood* (1991) or, say, Sean Combs's in *Monster's Ball* (2001)—draws on an important subgeneric musical distinction as well. That is to say, Queen Latifah is not only a female but an East Coast rapper, with all that this much-abused term diacritically insinuates—where, for example, "West Coast" means "gangsta rap" or, more specifically (since West Coast rap itself derives from earlier, hard-core East Coast traditions), a "style of rap that narrates experiences and fantasies specific to life as a poor young, black, male subject in Los Angeles."[44]

Cleopatra Jones Redux: Queen Latifah as Gangsta Butch Diva

I will return to the whole issue of gangsta rap in more detail below, but for the moment it's worth noting that Queen Latifah on occasion has used her own music to comment on the negative stereotypical representation of black women in hard-core rap. Consider, for example, the following lyrics from "U.N.I.T.Y" (1993):

> Instincts lead me to another flow
> Every time I hear a brother call a girl
>   a bitch or ho
> Trying to make a sister feel low
> You know all of that's got to go.[45]

It may well be, as Nelson George has argued, that hip hop has not yet produced its Billie Holiday, but the above lyrics, the last line of which recollects Latifah's first single, "Wrath of My Madness" (1988), nevertheless suggest that she has more than "filled Aretha's shoes" as a "symbol of female empowerment."[46]

Still, if Queen Latifah's persona as a strong, empowered black woman (who's definitely not into, as she's said, the "misogynistic bull" of gangsta rap[47]) makes her in many ways a logical choice for the bulldagger dyke Cleo in *Set It Off*, the real performative twist of this character is that she not only plays a butch to Ursuala's platinum-haired high femme (Samantha MacLachlan) but a gangsta butch. This rap inflection is critical, as Judith Halberstam points out in *Female Masculinity* (1998), to the multiaccentuality of Queen Latifah's performance in the film:

> [I]f blackness in general is associated with excessive and indeed violent masculinity, then Latifah as Cleo exploits this association. . . . To create a credible butch style, Queen Latifah trades off a rap version of black masculinity.[48]

In this racial-sexual context, it's instructive to compare Halberstam's reading of Queen Latifah's performance as Cleo, which is attentive to both the commercial and subcultural demands of the role, with the high-minded rhetoric that pervades the anonymous review of *Set It Off* that appears in the 1997 edition of *The Motion Picture Guide*: "The film leaves a foul taste and is simply an exploitation film dressed up with an expedient social conscience. It trades on the issue of black women's rage and then only exploits it to make another violent melodrama."[49]

While there's no doubt something to this reviewer's complaint about *Set It Off*'s "uneven mix" of social drama and exploitation film, one might argue that almost all gangster films are, by definition, "violent melodramas" and that an "exploitation film dressed up with an expedient social conscience" is also a damn good definition of one of the seminal genres of black cinema: blaxploitation. Indeed, it's important not to dismiss the blaxploitative elements which are part of the postmodern generic mix that is *Set It Off* since blaxploitation is not only central to the visual "iconography of hip hop" but blaxploitation soundtracks such as Isaac Hayes's *Shaft* (1971) and Curtis Mayfield's *Superfly* (1972) remain one of the principal links "between '70s pulp movies and late '90s youth culture" (as I suggest, by way of Tarantino's films, in the conclusion to chapter 4).[50]

G-Funk: Girlz N the Hood

Need one observe that the audiovisual suturing action of *Set It Off* is predicated on the spectator's appreciation of just these sorts of pop-cultural linkage?

Take, for instance, the first posttitle sequence of the film, which begins with a high establishing shot that drops down from a view of the factories across the way, crosses over the tops of some parked cars, then glides through the open gate of a chain-link fence, stopping in a medium shot on three of the four women—Stony (Jada Pinkett), Frankie (Vivica A. Fox), and Tisean (Kimberly Elise)—who are outfitted in retro '70s clothes for Stony's brother's (Chaz Lamar Shepard) high school graduation party.

The sound track to this sequence—the first nonscore, diegetic music in the film—is Parliament's "Flash Light" (1977), a good-time booty-shakin' party song that immediately sets up a complex musical dialogue between the '70s and '90s.[51] The key figure here is George Clinton, the parti-colored dreadlocked lead vocalist of Parliament/ Funkadelic. In other words, just as the visual look of gangsta rap derives from both blaxploitation and the gangster film (for example, Brian De Palma's *Scarface* [1983]), so the sound of classic West Coast rap comes, in large part (at least in the case of Dr. Dre), from the "funk-inspired beats" of Parliament.[52] In a nutshell, without Clinton's P-funk, there would be no Dre-style G-funk.

Given Dr. Dre's enormous influence on West Coast gangsta rap, his off-screen persona is also pivotal, like Queen Latifah's, to the complicated sorts of audiovisual suturing that characterize *Set It Off*. Who is Dr. Dre (Andre Young)? Suffice it to say that as a founding member of NWA and, later, as the creative force behind Death Row Records (in tandem with the notorious Marion "Suge" Knight), Dre was the "dominant hip hop producer of the early 90s."[53] Who better then to play Black Sam, the resident arms dealer of *Set It Off*, than Dre himself?

Cut on action: As the Geto Boys' "Point of No Return" booms in the background[54] and Black Sam sits skull-capped in the foreground, the camera gradually tracks from left to right in the cramped space of a shooting range, pausing on each woman in turn as she noisily discharges her weapon, bullets ripping into the paper targets. *Cut again*: While the camera pans up Black Sam's inner arm tattooed with shotgun shells like little headstones, Cleo, who has stolen cars for him in the past (and who has been firing away in her trademark style—with both hands), approaches him for a favor. However, when Black Sam nods at a small pistol ("Y'all can roll with that right there"), Cleo, her mind still fixed on an Uzi, nixes the idea, saying, "No way. We ain't robbin' stage coaches. I need something I can set it off with."

This scene, even as it utilizes shot/reverse shot to effect an explicit criminal connection between the two, highlights Cleo's ability to go mano a mano with Black Sam since she manages to get the guns she needs while flatly refusing his request for Frankie as sexual interest.[55] Moreover, Cleo's meeting with Black Sam looks both forward and backward. Retrospectively, it looks back to a scene near the beginning

Fig. 2. Girlz N the Hood (clockwise from upper right): Cleo (Queen Latifah), Frankie (Vivica Fox), Stony (Jada Pinkett), and Tisean (Kimberly Elise) enjoy the lush, post-heist life in *Set It Off* (Gray, 1996).

of *Set It Off* when Stevie, Stony's brother, goes to the projects to visit Lorenz (WC) and the latter answers the door with a gun. Although Lorenz's criminal identity has already been established (he's a suspect in the violent heist that initiates the film and that has cost Frankie her job at the bank), the music playing in his apartment, Busta Rhymes's "Live to Regret," poignantly comments on the fatalism of the gangsta ethos later reflected in Lorenz's ensuing death at the hands of the police. Prospectively, Cleo's meeting with Black Sam anticipates her own violent demise at the end of *Set It Off* when, like Bonnie and Clyde, she drives her car straight into a police barricade while, in a cutaway, we see Black Sam and his posse ruefully watching the event live on TV.

True to the manifold codes and conventions of the genre, Cleo's elective affinity for the gangsta life is signalled in other, more material ways as well: her masculine ghettocentric attire and hair style (plaid flannel shirts and tightly braided cornrows in the down-home style of Snoop Dogg); her drinking (unlike Stony, who shares fine wine and champagne with Keith, her banker boyfriend [Blair Underwood], Cleo drinks hard liquor and forty-ouncers straight from the bottle); her chronic use of "crank" (marijuana being the drug du jour for rappers, a usage celebrated in Dr. Dre's first solo CD, *The Chronic* [1992]); and, most importantly perhaps, her choice of music.

The last character trait receives something like its definitive audiovisual suture in the first, post-Black Sam sequence when Cleo, a lit cigarette between her lips, sunglassed face framed like a mask in the rearview mirror, breaks into a car and neutralizes the alarm. There's a brief moment of silence, then the rat-a-tat-tat sound of Cleo's voice: "Bullshit. . . . Bullshit. . . . Fuckin' bullshit." Tossing CD after CD out of the window like so much trash, a reckless gesture that Detective Strode (John C. McGinley) will later seize on to ID her, Cleo finally finds the right kind of music, early James Brown-flavored East-Coast gangsta rap: Eric B. & Rakim's "I Ain't No Joke" (1987). "Now that's what I ride to," Cleo exclaims, setting off for her first big heist, the stereo's bass seriously rocking the car's speakers.

Complex as these sorts of sutures are in *Set It Off* (and, as I hope I have established, they are quite intricate), it would nevertheless be simplistic to reduce Cleo's character to this particular audiovisual register (gangsta rap) since, as I noted earlier, she is also a "particular *type* of lesbian": "loud-mouthed, bullying, tough."[56] In other words, Cleo is not a "bitch" or "ho" but a gangsta butch. This gender-specific aspect of her character, which hardly conforms to the politically correct imperatives of the "positive image" campaign, is flamboyantly on display in *Set It Off* in a sequence that takes place in Cleo's garage apartment in the aftermath of the group's first successful caper.

Fig. 3. Scarface: Cleo, in her car, with cornrows.

The sequence opens with a low slow-motion shot of the gold wheel rims on Cleo's new Chevy lo-rider. Cut to a medium shot of Cleo sitting in the driver's seat of the car, jacking it up and down ("Fuck them niggas!") while Ursuala, cloth in one hand, forty-ouncer in the other, plays at polishing the gleaming exterior. The significance of the music playing in this scene—again, gangsta rap (Da Five Footaz's "The Heist")—is the way it literally overscores the whole relation between rap and cars, rap as the epitome of California car culture. As Dr. Dre has said, "I make the shit for people to bump in their cars."[57]

Automobility is also a determinate figure here of female masculinity—of, in other words, autonomy as well as a certain economic, if not necessarily social or even geographical, mobility.[58] As such, the above gangsta-rap suture speaks volumes about what drives Cleo, echoing as it does a scene earlier in *Set It Off* when two men in a fully loaded Chevy lo-rider, Yo-Yo's "Bonnie and Clyde II" blaring from the stereo, pull up and tease her about the beat-up car she has been chilling in.[59]

In this narratively overdetermined context, the import of the shot of Cleo whooping it up in her vintage Impala under the admiring gaze of her girlfriend is obvious enough: she's not only made it (and has the dope car to prove it), she's one of the boyz. The erotic dynamics of this moment of female-masculine ebullience are dramatized in the very next scene when, the music on the sound track suddenly downshifting from the hard brassy beats of "The Heist" to the R&B-drenched sound of Sin's "Diva's Den," the camera cuts from a close-up of a smoke-wreathed stereo to a swirling shot of Ursuala dressed in a sheer black negligee doing a languorous dance for Cleo who, seated on the hood below her, is stroking her thigh.

Crossroads

According to the tried and true conventions of mainstream Hollywood film (transgression/containment), the above lesbian scenario is abruptly interrupted by the appearance of the other three women in the group, who are not only taken aback by what they see but visibly dismayed that Cleo has already blown her share of the loot on, among other things, Ursuala's new wardrobe. This scene also sets off a violent dispute between Cleo and Stony, one that powerfully illustrates the opposing audiovisual codes and, in particular, musical cues assigned to each character.

In the first scene, Cleo and Stony, dressed in matching prison-green janitorial uniforms, sit side by side on the carpeted steps of an apartment in the luxurious high-rise where they have been working.

Although they have been best friends since childhood (and will momentarily band together again for one final bank heist), this reconciliation scene, filmed without sound, eloquently articulates their very real differences:

> *Cleo:* You know you need to come back in with us. You ain't got enough money to get out of town.
>
> *Stony:* You're right about that. But I want more than that. I mean, is this the only way? You see, I wanna be somebody.
>
> *Cleo:* Stony, you can go to suburbia and start a new life. . . . The hood is where I belong.

If Cleo, as Queen Latifah puts it, is "hard-core, from-the-hood, down and down,"[60] Stony is soft-core, from-the-hood, up and up: that is to say, upwardly mobile.

This class ambition is reflected, not unlike Stony's ventriloquism of Keith's philosophy of *embourgeoisement*, in the diverse kinds of music the film uses to characterize her relationship with him. Whereas Cleo's outlaw relation with Ursuala is generally mediated by rap music and, occasionally, R&B, Stony's association with the Harvard-educated Keith is marked by an eclectic range of musical genres from soul to jazz (e.g., Miles Davis's "All Blues") that not only bespeaks her romantic aspirations but his superior cultural and socioeconomic status. Indeed, the sociocultural differences between Stony and Keith (which, as the musical cues indicate, are anything but minor) also reflect those between Stony and Cleo.

Thus, while it's not surprising to see Stony, in one of the most lyrical moments of *Set It Off*, hanging with the other girls on a rooftop getting stoned on Cleo's stash, a beautifully modulated scene of sisterly solidarity mirrored in the softly repeating refrains of Bone Thugs-n-Harmony's "Days of Our Livez," it's virtually impossible to imagine Cleo strolling around at a corporate cocktail party at the Biltmore, as Stony does with Keith, to the exotic strains of Mendelssohn's "Italian" Symphony and Handel's "Arrival of the Queen of Sheba." If there's not a little irony to the film's recourse to classical music (if only because Stony remains decidedly nonplussed by Keith's "buppie" affluence), the spectacular dénouement to *Set It Off* nonetheless makes clear that despite a lifetime of shared experiences, Cleo and Stony face radically divergent futures.

Fig. 4. Up on the Roof: Cleo, Tisean, Frankie, and Stony, post smoke, in *Set It Off.*

As for Cleo, it is as if she's doomed, between her gangsterism and butch lesbianism, to enact a certain musical deus ex machina. Accordingly, when she later drives to her death, the music on the sound track is Lori Petty's "Up Against the Wind," a haunting dirge that functions as a mournful coda to the gangsta rap genre that has been her signature sound throughout the film. By contrast, Stony's fate, like the pop R&B used to suture her character, is rather more upbeat, if also rather more ambiguous. This ambiguity is underlined in the final sequence of *Set It Off* when, having escaped to Mexico under the benevolent eye of the law (no such luck for Cleo or, for that matter, TT or Frankie), Stony, who has everything and nothing, stands in the middle of a hotel room gazing at the stacks of cash spread out on the bed before her like so much blood money. As the happy-sad harmonies of Brandy's "Missing You" wash over a montage of recollection images, we the audience are no doubt supposed to reflect—laughter in tears, like Stony—on the heavy price that the gangsta life exacts.

Still, in the end, what one takes away from *Set It Off*, what one can't so easily forget, is not this classical moment of suture, sentimentally pleasing as it may be, nor even the final breathtaking traveling shot of Stony driving in an open red jeep along the coast of Mexico, but Queen Latifah's performance, at once hard and heartbreaking, shot through with *jouissance*: Cleo taking time out from her cleaning gig to comically diss the photo of a white family ("White people be havin' some old waterhead cryin'-ass ugly baby!"); Cleo waving her guns at the customers in a bank during the gang's first heist ("Whaddaya lookin' at? I'm a bitch with a gun!"); Cleo stubbornly refusing to drive the getaway car until one of the women in the other car passes her "mood music"; Cleo giddily raining dollar bills through the hole in the ceiling of her crib to the other women waiting below, Keith Murray's "The Most Beautifullest Thing in the World" playing in the background; or Cleo, cigarette stuck defiantly in her mouth, lo-rider jacked all the way up, racing toward the red lights whirling in the distance.

As Marlon Riggs might have said, forget about Brandy et al. (Snap!): Queen Latifah, the pre-*Chicago* MC playing the gangsta butch, is the real diva.

4

Audiophilia
Audiovisual Pleasure and Narrative Cinema in *Jackie Brown*

In "Cinema and Psychoanalysis: Parallel Histories," a retrospective essay on the historical conjuncture of cinema and psychoanalysis, Stephen Heath comments on the fluctuating fortunes of various concepts in the long wake of Screen theory. While Heath in his audit mentions, in addition to suture, fantasy, fetishism, the real, the phallus, and the symptom, ironically enough, given his express interest in sexual difference, there is no mention of the "male gaze."

This is a rather striking omission, since if it is true that suture as a concept is "not doing too well,"[1] the same cannot be said of Laura Mulvey's conception of the gaze. Although it's been over twenty-five years since "Visual Pleasure and Narrative Cinema" first appeared in *Screen* in 1975, Laura Mulvey's monumental essay still exerts an enormous influence, like some buried radioactive deposit, on discussions of cinematic pleasure. The subtitle to the second section of Mulvey's essay neatly captures her clarion call to the vanguard: "Destruction of pleasure as a radical weapon."[2]

While Meaghan Morris, in the context of a moving discussion of Claire Johnston, has commented on the esprit de corps that informed so much '70s British feminist film theory,[3] the limits of Mulvey's essay on visual pleasure also need to be reiterated. For example, would most women today confidently claim, as Mulvey does at the end of "Visual Pleasure and Narrative Cinema," that they would "view the decline of the traditional film form" with little more than "sentimental regret"?[4]

Some of the cumulative force of Mulvey's peroration as well as its anti-hedonistic agenda can be seen in "Pleasure: A Political Issue," a summary essay by Fredric Jameson that appeared in the influential 1983 collection, *Formations of Pleasure*. The conclusion to this essay, which is a response of sorts to Mulvey's, is simple as it is symptomatic and represents what one might call a critique of pure pleasure: "The right to a specific pleasure . . . if it is to become genuinely political, if it is to evade the complacencies of hedonism, must always in one way or another also be able to stand as a figure for the transformation of social relations as a whole."[5]

One can, I think, appreciate the political sentiment of this utopian, classically Adornian formulation and still wonder whether pleasure should be made to bear such a revolutionary burden. Put another, more emphatic way: If pleasure is an indispensable aspect of cinephilia in the best, most general sense, isn't it time to reconsider the critical axiom that pleasure is always already a political issue? Why it is that most forms of visual pleasure today, especially that most basic of cinematic pleasures, scopophilia, somehow seem like guilty pleasures? Finally, if it is true that the audio register, at least since the advent of the sound film, is a crucial aspect of cinematic pleasure or what Michel Chion calls "audio-vision,"[6] what can audiophilia add to our understanding of cinephilia and scopophilia?

After an overview that addresses these questions in the context of what one might call "cine-scopo-audiophilia," I will turn by way of illustration to Quentin Tarantino's *Jackie Brown* (1997) in order to demonstrate how this constellation is a manifest, constitutive aspect of the film's popular-musical imaginary.[7] My close reading of Tarantino's film will also endeavor to show how what I call the "acoustic signifier," in the form of nondiegetic as opposed to diegetic music, not only provides a unique perspective on the agency or perceived mastery of the various main characters but reflects the dynamic relation that obtains between the look and the gaze—between, in the sonic register, listening and being audited.[8]

Cinephilia

Cinephilia: love of or, perhaps, desire for the cinema.

Love. Desire. There is a difference between these two definitions of cinephilia, and depending on one's perspective, it can be said to mark a differential moment in the history of film studies. For instance, in "The Imaginary Signifier" (first published in English in 1975 in *Screen*, the same year as "Visual Pleasure and Narrative Cinema"), Christian Metz comments that the filmic institution "works to fill cinemas."[9] In other words, while it is certainly possible to talk about the

pleasure of "bad objects," not to mention the pleasures of dis- or unpleasure (say, *jouissance* or what Freud calls *Unlust*), Metz's basic point
is that "one goes to the cinema . . . in the hope that the film will please
and not that it will displease."[10] In short, the institution as a whole "has
filmic pleasure alone as its aim."[11]

Here, at the very beginning of *The Imaginary Signifier* in the subsection titled "Going to the Cinema," Metz is very close to the language
and concerns of Mulvey's essay on visual pleasure. However, where
Mulvey attacks what she takes to be the political-libidinal conditions of
possibility of the "male gaze," Metz is reacting to, among other things,
the cinephilia of certain French critics associated with *Cahiers du cinéma*
who were themselves suffering a severe allergic reaction to the so-
called Old-Guard, Tradition-of-Quality film (Carné, Claire, Clément, et
al.). *Cahiers du cinéma* was, in turn, part of a larger constellation of journals including *Positif* and *Présence du cinéma* out of which cinephilia
itself, as a determinate historical practice, emerged.

As Paul Willemen observes in "Cinephilia Reconsidered," an
essay/interview with Noel King, the only thing that united the above
factions was cinephilia, "anecdotally represented by the fact that they all
saw one another in the front rows of the cinema, grooving on their relationship to cinema."[12] Thus, although these 1950s French critics might
disagree, violently, about which films were good or bad, they were all
essentially in agreement about the social good of "going to the cinema."
Still, the real interest of Willemen's reconsideration of cinephilia is that
he configures it not so much as the "love of" but as the "desire that sustained cinema."[13] Indeed, Willemen's recourse to the word "desire," not
to mention the past tense (as if cinema, like some exotic ecosystem, were
no longer able to sustain itself), suggests that his formulation is a historical one, reflecting as it does the ascendence of other audiovisual media
such as television.

Although Willemen's periodization of cinephilia persuasively
captures the influence of French film culture and the emergence of
new media technologies, it may be more useful, at least in the Anglo-
American context, to understand cinephilia as a belated response to the
recent history of cinema studies. From this institutional perspective, the
death of cinephilia rather than, say, cinema per se can be read as a symptom of the rapid rise of structuralist and poststructuralist theory within
film criticism, an epistemological break signalled by the appearance of the
author-function "Metz."[14] Rather more specifically, cinephilia is a dis-
placed figure for all those guilty and not so guilty pleasures such as
scopophilia that have been ritualistically exorcized since the appearance
of Mulvey's timely meditation on "visual pleasure and narrative cinema."

Scopophilia

Schaulust. Jouissance du voir. Although scopophilia has a philosophical, even clinical air in both Freud and Lacan, I think it's fair to say that the term has become something of a dirty word in film studies. To say today in these tendentious, not so indulgent times that one is a scopophile, that one regularly indulges in scopophilic activities, is immediately to pronounce oneself a pervert—say, Mr. Maplewood (Dylan Baker) gazing with unrequited lust at pretty little leaguer Johnny Grasso (Evan Silverberg) standing expectedly at the plate, baseball bat in hand, in Todd Solondz's *Happiness* (1998).

To be sure, scopophilia for Mulvey is a very particular kind of perversion, gendered perversion, one endemic to the mainstream classic-realist cinema, where woman—not a prepubescent, albeit girlish boy like Johnny Grasso—is the "bearer of the look." So, presumably (to continue with the example of *Happiness*), we do not identify so much with Mr. Maplewood as with his peerless son Billy (Rufus Read) when, at the very end of the film, he finally climaxes for the first time while voyeuristically looking at a woman's wedged bikini behind. Hence Mulvey's emphasis on fetishistic scopophilia, which suggests that the holiest Hollywood film form is inextricably bound up with the castration complex and the primacy of the phallus. In fact, as Stephen Heath was among the first to point out—in an essay titled, appropriately enough, "Difference"—fetishistic scopophilia and its bad scopic twin, sadistic voyeurism, presuppose a restricted libidinal economy predicated on the masculine/feminine either/or of sexual difference.[15]

At the same time, scopophilia in "Visual Pleasure and Narrative Cinema" is something like the antagonistic pretext for Mulvey's astringent aesthetic politics: no scopophilia, no countercinema. In this regard, scopophilia functions for Mulvey not unlike cinephilia for Metz: the difference is sexual difference. So, where for Metz the theoretician—the anti-cinephile, the "one who desires to know"—"is necessarily sadistic," turning the medium like a glove inside out in order to subject all the attractions of the cinema to the "same scopic drive which made one love it" (thereby economically converting cinephilia into epistemophilia[16]), for Mulvey scopophilia and its attendant perversions (sadism, fetishism, voyeurism, and so forth) must be systematically destroyed in order to "break with normal pleasurable expectations" and, a fortiori, "make way for a total negation of the ease and plenitude of the narrative fiction film."[17]

As Mulvey, invoking the populist, lowest-common-denominator reaction to philosophical critique, famously and plainly puts it in "Visual

Pleasure," "It is said that analyzing pleasure, or beauty, destroys it. That is the intention."[18] In brief, the aim of Mulvey's radically refashioned brand of criticism is not to engender a "reconstructed new pleasure" or an "intellectualized unpleasure" but a "new language": not pleasure but desire, not "satisfaction" but "dialectics."[19] Given the last Brechtian inflection (which somehow seems to have forgotten Brecht's own intuitive aesthetic violation of his precepts about the epic theatre), it's no surprise that Mulvey's account of visual pleasure has met with so much resistance over the years.

The history of critical reception to Mulvey's essay bears out this displeasure: Mary Anne Doane on the distance afforded the female spectator via masquerade (exquisitely illustrated by Jennifer Tilly's performance as the hyperfemme femme fatale, Violet, in the Wachowski brothers' *Bound* [1996]); Steve Neale on the simultaneous disavowal and ostentatious display of male homosexuality in agonistic spectacle (of which David Fincher's *Fight Club* [1999], emblazoned as it is with Brad Pitt's bronzed torso, is a spectacular example); Jackie Stacey on the homosocial specular relations between women (where Madonna as Susan in Susan Seidelman's *Desperately Seeking Susan* [1985] is the erotic object of Roberta's [Rosanna Arquette] screwball but by no means sadistic investigation); and so on.[20]

However, the most bracing critique of Mulvey's legacy, one first broached by Richard Dyer in an essay on the complex scopic economy of the male pin-up,[21] has arguably been conducted within the deconstructivist milieu of queer film studies. Consider, in this context, Ellis Hanson's collection, *Out Takes: Essays on Queer Theory and Film*. In "Visual Pleasure in 1959," D. A. Miller, in a wondrously perverse rereading of Mulvey's argument, contends that behind the rear view of Elizabeth Taylor's famously plunging swimsuit in Mankiewicz's *Suddenly Last Summer* (1959), there is another, more originary "behind": the gay sodomitical spectacle associated with the "Homosexual Anus."[22]

The post-Mulveyan turn of the screw here is that while Miller's reading of scopophilia is not only the ripe fruit of a certain autohistorical cinephilia (in 1959, Miller confesses, "*Suddenly Last Summer* furnished me an object of considerable pubescent obsession"[23]), but precisely because of this magnificent obsession he is able to reinflect the negative, totalizing logic of Mulvey's essay and, not so incidentally, evade what Hanson calls the "ubiquitous, pre-fabricated, gullible, voyeuristic gaze of homophobia."[24] Bluntly, Miller's critique of Mulvey and, more generally, cine-psychoanalytic feminist film theory constitutes a not so veiled critique of gay criticism itself, which has historically been marked, though one imagines not indelibly, by a certain cinephobia.

Thus, teasing out the delicious implications of Corky's (Gina Gershon) posttryst line in *Bound* ("I can see again!"), Hanson claims that gay and lesbian film criticism has sought for "purely ideological reasons" to "alienate" spectators from Hollywood's classical lures: fetishism and voyeurism.[25] The net effect of this political-aesthetic strategy has been not so much "passionate detachment," *Entfremdung* or distanciation, as plain old alienation and the gross reduction of the erotic and the aesthetic to the politics of representation. The latter version of identity politics has, in turn, been reduced to the quixotic quest to find out "which movies are good for gays or bad for gays" or, in lieu of this politically correct imperative, which "movies are good for the gaze or bad for the gaze."[26]

From Scopophilia to Audiophilia: The Gaze *qua* Race

Before I turn my attention to audiophilia, the third and final term of this overview, I would be remiss if I did not note that the preceding review of the Mulveyan account of scopophilia is not without its own lacuna, a blind spot that has retained a striking persistence in this highly popular critical discourse.

I am referring of course to the racial gaze, a problematic that first appears within the purview of post-Freudian psychoanalysis in Homi Bhabha's 1983 Fanonesque essay, "The Other Question," and slightly later, within the domain of cinema studies proper, in the influential 1988 *Screen* issue titled, not without a little irony, "The Last Special Issue on Race."[27] More recently, in Robert Stam and Toby Miller's Blackwell anthology, *Film and Theory* (2000), the section devoted to "The Nature of the Gaze" comprises, in addition to Mulvey's "Visual Pleasure," bell hooks's "Oppositional Gaze" and Slavoj Žižek's "Looking Awry," which represent diametrically opposed takes on the still vexed issue of the gaze.

To wit, where hooks's piece castigates black female spectators who accede to the "pleasure of mainstream cinema" and, in the process, are summarily "gaslighted," Žižek's essay skips from pornography to montage to the death drive in order to elucidate the "logic of the gaze *qua* object."[28] More simply, where hooks argues that black female spectators "enchanted" by Hollywood (including her own sister before she was disabused of her regressive behavior by hooks herself) are thoroughly complicit with a "masochistic look of victimization," Žižek maintains that there is an "irreducible discord" between the gaze *qua* object and the spectatorial look.[29]

The difference between hooks's and Žižek's views of visual pleasure can be gauged, with a slight authorial displacement, by comparing two representative takes on one of the most influential and controversial films of the 1990s, Tarantino's *Pulp Fiction* (1994). First bell hooks, then Sharon Willis:

> [Tarantino] represents the ultimate in "white cool": a hard-core cynical vision that would have everyone see racism, sexism and homophobia but behave as though none of that shit really matters, or if it does it means nothing 'cause none of it's gonna change, 'cause the real deal is that "domination is here to stay."[30]

> We may not like [Tarantino's films]; these may not be the films we want. But, then, films are rarely about what we want. . . . [T]he symptoms that [Tarantino's films] display signal certain shifts in the terrain of racialized representation. And this bears watching, since it is watching us.[31]

For hooks, Tarantino's pornographic, politically regressive representation of "white cool" and its ugly predicates (racism, sexism, etc.) is part and parcel of a nihilistic vision that produces a blinding disjunction between looking and doing: "everyone" can see as clear as day what's up on the screen, but no one will behave any differently because everyone knows what the "real" raw deal is (that is, "domination is here to stay"). For Willis, by contrast, Tarantino's films are not about the politics of representation, about what we think we like or want, but they nonetheless bear watching, even reviewing (and this is, I think, a rather different project than hooks envisions), because "such films continually catch us out," exposing us to the performative contradiction between the look and the gaze, between what we claim we want to see and "what we do not want to own."[32]

In addition to articulating what is at stake in the "noncoincidence of the look and the gaze" (the gaze, as Kaja Silverman reminds us, is not "coterminous with an individual viewer or group of viewers"[33]), Willis's observation about the "stunning asymmetry" between Tarantino's equations of popular music and "icons of black masculinity" provides a useful point of departure for thinking about audiophilia, if not filmic sound in general.[34] Indeed, I want to suggest that there is an equally stunning asymmetry in *Jackie Brown* (1997) between the eponymous character, an icon of black femininity (Pam Grier), and the music used to articulate her point of view ("funky seventies soul"[35]). In other words, not unlike Žižek's analysis of the discord between eye and gaze, there is a subtle discontinuity in Tarantino's film between diegetic and nondiegetic music where diegetic music is a form of hearing or listening aligned with the look while nondiegetic music—in this case, popular songs as opposed to instrumental music—is aligned with the gaze and being heard or, in a word, audition.[36]

Audiophilia: Auditing *Jackie Brown*

> The thing I'm coming from is listening to music to be the guide to a movie.
>
> —Quentin Tarantino, press conference
> on *Jackie Brown*

Tarantino, of course, is as famous for his audio- as his cinephilia. Even as his cinephilia bespeaks an adolescence "spent in black movie theatres watching . . . blaxploitation flicks,"[37] his well-recorded crush on Pam Grier (whom he talks about as someone else might talk about Garbo or Dietrich) connotes a serious scopophilic investment in her figure. As Clarence (Christian Slater) says about Alabama (Patricia Arquette) in *True Romance* (1993), "She's a sixteen-calibre kitten! . . . Alabama Whitman is Pam Grier!" Or, as the authors of *The Tarantinian Ethics* (2001) describe the opening of *Jackie Brown*, "This is true romance, the love affair of lens and image. . . . The director's enamouration with this rediscovered icon of the seventies is translated into the unflinching absorption of cinematic homage, a fantasy as full as the figure who fills the screen."[38]

Tarantino's audiophilia is also abundantly on display early on in *Jackie Brown* when the nondiegetic music that accompanies Jackie's brief imprisonment is "Long Time Woman" ("I'm a long time woman / And I'm serving my time"), recorded by none other than Pam Grier for the Roger Corman-produced women-in-prison classic, *The Big Doll House* (1971). In addition, in a striking scene near the beginning of *Jackie Brown*, Jackie, while entertaining Max Cherry (Robert Forster) the morning after she has been released from the county jail, mirrors Tarantino's own self-professed status as an audiophile:

Max: You never got into the CD revolution?

Jackie: I got a few. But I can't afford to start all over. I just got too much time and money invested in my records. (86)

Needless to say, neither Jackie's audiophilia nor her choice of music (the Delfonics' "Didn't I Blow Your Mind This Time") is incidental,[39] since if her audiophilia offers a subtle commentary on her stubborn attachment to the past, the Delfonics' song marks the exact moment in *Jackie Brown* when Max goes from initial attraction to full-blown romantic infatuation. (In fact, if only to anticipate what I will take up in more detail in the coda to this chapter, Tarantino accents Max's romanticism by cutting from Louis Gara [Robert De Niro] having sex with Melanie Ralston [Bridget Fonda] to Max shopping in a music store for *The Best of the Delfonics.*[40])

While a certain classic star-driven scopic pleasure is clearly at play in Tarantino's infatuation with Pam Grier ("I've just been a big fan for a long time. She is a truly great icon"[41]), his ardent audiophilia equally clearly fuels both his cinephilia and his postmodern style of filmmaking. Thus, in a press conference for *Jackie Brown*, Tarantino remarked that he originally conceived of the film less as an "opera" in the manner of *Pulp Fiction* than as a "chamber piece," where, to mix musical genres, if not metaphors, the beat or rhythm of *Jackie Brown* is "old romantic soul-music from the seventies" (86).[42] This sonic determination is crucial because unlike a lot of directors (or, at least, pre-MTV directors), Tarantino's musical sense or taste tends to dictate his cinematic choices rather than vice versa. As he essayed in a discussion about the Dick Dale overture to *Pulp Fiction*, "I'm always trying to find the right opening credit or closing credit sequence music early on, when I'm thinking about the story. Once I find it, that really triggers me into the personality . . . of what the piece should be."[43]

"Across 110th Street": Overture

> [Jackie's] just walking down the airport and she just looks like the baddest creature.
>
> —Quentin Tarantino, interview in the Manchester *Guardian*

Now, if we can take Tarantino at his word here (and I think we can and should), the music-induced mood of the opening credit sequence of *Jackie Brown*, provided by Bobby Womack's "Across 110th Street," is wonderfully expressive, recollecting as it does *Across 110th Street* (1972), a film that is contemporaneous with *Shaft* (1971) and for which Womack wrote the title song and score. "110th Street" also summons up that larger cinematic "structure of feeling," blaxploitation, which remains the audiovisual source for the character of Jackie Brown and her inimitable predecessor, Foxy Brown.[44]

A close look at the very beginning of *Jackie Brown* confirms the significance of Womack's song, the opening notes of which precede the pre-title sequence, as if true to Tarantino's audiophilic mode of working, the film itself was generated out of this aural space. "Across 110th

Street" commences, followed by the titles "Miramax Films" and "A Band Apart" (the latter a cheeky reference to Godard), then—simultaneous with the director's signature, "A Film by Quentin Tarantino"—Jackie Brown steps into the frame. This part of the sequence, a continuous medium shot that follows Jackie on a people mover as she moves through the lobby to the gate at Cabo Air Lines, limns her current station in life. Her long hair pulled back, smartly dressed in a Cabo Air Lines uniform, a flight bag slung over one shoulder, a scarf tied loosely around her neck, Jackie Brown may be running, literally, a little late, but she is calm, cool, and collected—in a word, professional. Fred Botting and Scott Wilson restage Tarantino's scopophilic gaze: "Jackie Brown *looks* fantastic: her walk, between strut and swagger, her *look*, exudes an absolute self-assurance and self-possession, a fullness correlated with the way in which SHE fills the screen."[45]

The million or, in this case, half-million dollar question is: Where, literally and figuratively, is she going?

We later learn from LAPD officer Mark Dargus (Michael Bowen) that Jackie has previously run afoul of the law. In 1985 she was "busted for carrying drugs" for her pilot husband ("He did time and she did probation"), an incident that explains why, at age forty-four, she is still working for what Dargus calls the "shittiest little shuttle fucking piece of shit Mexican airline that there is." If this weren't bad enough ("the worse job in the industry," as Jackie tells Max over coffee), she has been slaving away in the airline business for nineteen years and her salary is "only sixteen thousand [dollars] plus benefits." Dargus sarcastically to Jackie: "Didn't exactly set the world on fire, did ya?"

Dispiriting as this narrative is, the opening lyrics of "Across 110th Street" tell a slightly different story, evoking not only where Jacqueline Brown comes from but what she wants:

> I was the third brother of five
> Doing whatever I had to do to survive
> I'm not saying what I did was alright
> Trying to break out of the ghetto was a day
>   to day fight
>
> Been down so long, getting up didn't cross my mind
> I knew there was a better way of life that I was
>   just trying to find
> You don't know what you'll do until you're put under
>   pressure
> Across 110th Street is a hell of a tester

The counterpoint at work in these lyrics suggests that although Jackie is not a "brother," she'll do whatever she has to do, whether it's "alright" or not, to survive, to "break out" of the ghettolike circumstances she's found herself in. What Chion calls "empathetic" music[46] has, therefore, an extra resonance in this sequence given Jackie's complex subject position, which is a function of age, race, and gender.

At the same time, the nondiegetic character of the music as opposed to the lyrics also intimates that for all her strut and swagger, Jackie's agency is subject to real limits, so much so that sound can be said to trump image (since it is arguably the music, not Jackie's look, which over-fills the screen). More precisely, Jackie may be a figure of fantasy, the very stuff of cinephilia and scopophilia, but this fantasy, like the screen right before she pulls a gun on Ordell Robbie (Samuel Jackson), is split.[47]

Thus, if the tracking shot of Jackie immobile on the people mover, just like Benjamin Braddock (Dustin Hoffman) at the beginning of *The Graduate* (1967), accents her imprisonment (in her current job as well as in her relation with both the law and Ordell), "Across 110th Street," true to the dialectical modality of the acoustic signifier, renders both Jackie's desperation and her desire for freedom: in sum, she moves not simply to but with the music.

"Street Life": Jackie as Femme Noire

> Pam Grier wasn't the black version of anybody.
>
> —Quentin Tarantino, press conference
> on *Jackie Brown*

Cut to the heart of the film where Jackie is on her way to the Del Amo Mall for the big "half-a-million dollar switcharoo" [*sic*] (162). The sequence begins with a front-window shot, a close-up in three-quarter profile, of Jackie driving in her Honda Civic as Randy Crawford and the Crusaders' "Street Life" (1972) plays on the sound track:

> I play the street life
> Because there's no place I can go
> Street life
> It's the only life I know
> Street life
> And there's a thousand cards to play
> Street life
> Until you play your life away

You never [let] people see
Just who you wanna be
And every night you shine
Just like a superstar

Although Crawford's song eloquently captures Jackie's mindset at this particular moment in time (she's about to gamble everything she has on her ability to pull the wool over the law's and Ordell's eyes), this sequence also includes a brief cutaway shot of Max, seen in medium shot through the front window of his Cadillac Seville, cruising down Hawthorne Boulevard on his way to the mall. The fact that "Street Life"—rather than, as in the screenplay, the Delfonics—plays under this shot indicates that even though the music is not enunciated by Jackie, her musical point of view is dominant.[48]

After a brief cut back to Jackie driving in her car ("The type of life that's played / A tempting masquerade"), the camera cuts to Louis and Melanie en route to the same mall in a Volkswagen bus. The acoustic difference between these three scenes is telling: while Max is obviously lost in a romantic reverie about Jackie (one, the sound track hints, Jackie does not fully share), Louis and Melanie are squabbling about the car stereo's volume, Melanie blithely drumming her thigh to the Grass Roots' "Midnight Confessions." More to the point, if the cutaway to Max illustrates the contrast between his romanticism and Jackie's street smarts as well as the close but occluded relation between the two (since Max cannot see that Jackie's attraction to him is a masquerade of sorts), the cutaway to Louis and Melanie emphasizes the difference between the two couples: Jackie, who has fully registered Max's look of love, knows she has him right where she wants him whereas Louis, unlike Ordell, cannot control Melanie, an issue that will have disastrous consequences for both of them.

After arriving at the Del Amo Mall parking lot, Jackie gets out of her car, opens the hatchback, and, using some pulp romance novels (*Short Blade*), arranges the fifty thousand dollars which Ray Nicolette (Michael Keaton) has marked—minus ten grand, a "little cherry on top," for Melanie. (As Jackie later says to her in the fitting room where the money exchange takes place, "What the hell did [Ordell] ever do for us?") On the sound track "Street Life" scores Jackie's actions:

Street life
But you better not get old
Street life
Or you gonna feel the cold

There's always love for sale
A grown-up fairy tale
Prince Charming always smiles
Behind the silver spoon
And if you keep it young
Your song is always sung
Your love will pay your way beneath the silver moon

Just as the aforementioned hatchback shot with its tight framing would appear to contain or restrict Jackie, so the nondiegetic music drives home the meanness of a life lived on the streets.

And yet, if the accompanying lyrics record that time is beginning to run out on her ("But you better not get old . . . / Or you gonna feel the cold"), the visual echo of the one other trunk shot in the film (where the point of view is the dead Beaumont's) suggests that Jackie—unlike Beaumont or, for that matter, Louis whom, significantly, Ordell shoots while his Volkswagen is parked—is no victim. Indeed, the opposite is the case, since at this very moment Jackie is in the process of usurping Ordell's position of power. (This reversal is confirmed by the fact that the instrumental nondiegetic music in the "Music Exchange" sequence as a whole—"Aragon," "Escape," and "Vittroni's Theme/King is Dead"—is lifted straight from Roy Ayers's score for the Pam Grier vehicle, *Coffy* [1973]: "The 'Godmother' of them all . . . the baddest One-Chick Hit-Squad that ever hit town!"[49]).

The ensuing traveling shot of Jackie walking against a bright blue tile background recalls the opening sequence of the film, but with a critical difference: as Jackie strides toward the mall with "all the confidence of a world champion" (175), she is not en route to her job at Cabo Air Lines but to another kind of "job" that will liberate her from her dead-end life. The location is crucial here: not LAX—which, with its pejorative liberatory associations ("flight"), signifies her checkered past, in particular her past subservience to her husband as well as her continuing indenture to Ordell—but the mall ("DEL AMO MALL—LARGEST INDOOR MALL IN THE WORLD") where, literally acting out her own ingenious script, she will effectively turn the tables on those who would manipulate her for their own ends: the ATF and LAPD, who are using her to get to Ordell, and Ordell himself, for whom Jackie is merely a trusted courier.

In this specific context, it's important to remember that precisely because Ordell thinks he knows Jackie like he knows Melanie ("You can't trust Melanie. But you can always trust Melanie to be Melanie"), he believes he has her under his thumb. Thus, Ordell's character's apparent

Fig. 5. Automobility: Jackie (Pam Grier), attired in Cabo Air Lines uniform, not flying but driving, in *Jackie Brown* (Tarantino, 1997).

Fig. 6. Kangol Cat: Ordell Robbie (Samuel L. Jackson) with ponytail, braided goatee, and pre–"Diddy" summer whites.

sense of mastery is acoustically established in *Jackie Brown* via, among other things, what one might call "idiosyncratic" diegetic sound[50]: the casually authoritative way he beeps his car to set the alarm and locks, his keen attention to audiophilic detail (Ordell to Louis: "You can play the volume loud as you want to. But don't touch my levels now. I got them set just like I like them"[51]), and, most importantly, the kinds of music this "brother" chooses to play in his "ride."

In fact, just as subjective diegetic music—such as, par excellence, the Delfonics—is used to delineate Jackie (which is not to say that her identity is commensurate with this kind of music since this romantic guise is only one of her various personae), so idiosyncratic diegetic music is used to characterize the real antagonist of *Jackie Brown*, Ordell. Consider, for example, the death by execution of Beaumont near the beginning of the film. Once Ordell has persuaded Beaumont to get into the trunk of his car with a pump-action shotgun (Ordell ostensibly needs backup to complete a deal for M-60 machine guns with some Koreans), the Brothers Johnson's "Strawberry Letter 23," penned by Shuggie Otis, booms on the sound track. After Ordell has taken his own sweet time putting on black gloves and getting a .38 from the glove compartment of his car, he drives around the block while, in the most audacious stylistic moment in *Jackie Brown*, the camera cranes to view the action. As Ordell drives, the music fades out, then back in. We watch and listen from a discrete distance while Ordell parks, shuts the car door, then opens the trunk, Beaumont's voice yammering away like a broken record. There is the sound of a gun blast, then another, then dead silence. We hear the trunk door close, the door of Ordell's Oldsmobile, and, finally, on his car stereo, on low, the deep soul funk of "Strawberry Letter." Life, the music suggests, goes on, business is business, potentially wayward employees have to be terminated.

Diegetic music is also employed to contrast and match Ordell and Max. While the Delfonics' "Didn't I Blow Your Mind This Time" suffuses Max's car like some exotic perfume, the music that plays under Ordell's surveillance of Jackie after he has posted bond for her, and she has shared a drink with Max at the Cockatoo Inn, is Johnny Cash's "Tennessee Stud."[52] Indeed, as the music swells, Ordell begins his preexecution routine. (What he does not know, or can't envision, is that Jackie is already one step ahead of him and, in a proleptic visual rhyme, has surreptitiously purloined Max's gun from the glove compartment of his car. To loop Johnny Cash: Ordell is no "Tennessee Stud" because Jackie is no "Tennessee Mare.")

Ultimately, however, Ordell is not nearly as different from Max as he supposes. Thus, when near the end of the film Ordell drives Max's car to the latter's office (where, unbeknownst to them, Jackie, backed up by Ray and Mark, awaits with Max's .38), the music that enlivens their deadly serious drive is, once again, the Delfonics' "Didn't I Blow Your Mind This Time," the lyrics of which song are all about a man who can't leave a woman ("Ten times or more . . . I've walked out that door"). That Ordell is subjected at this particular moment in the narrative to another person's musical point of audition (which is arguably not so much Max's as Jackie's, since she first turned him on to it) attests that, as we are about to find out, both men have, in fact, been played.

"Across 110th Street": Dénouement

> I don't subconsciously think [*Jackie Brown*] is a black film; it *is* a black film.
>
> [*Jackie Brown*] is not a black exploitation film.
>
> —Quentin Tarantino, interview in the Manchester *Guardian*

The final sequence of *Jackie Brown* provides a rich commentary on Jackie's new status. Melanie, Louis, and Ordell are all dead. Louis, in a fit of castratory rage, has shot and killed Melanie in the parking lot of the Del Amo Mall; Ordell, in turn, has shot Louis for shooting his "fine little surfer girl"; and, finally, Ordell, whom Jackie has lured to Cherry Bail Bonds by feigning being "spooked" by him ("All the time I never heard her sound scared like that"), has been shot and killed by Ray. Jackie, however, has one more bit of business to attend to before she departs the country: Max Cherry.

Crucially, Jackie arrives at Max's office, the front window of which sports a "fat red cherry" (13), in Ordell's car, a fact that does not escape Max's attention: "That's Ordell's." While Jackie's defense—"What's the matter? Haven't you ever borrowed someone's car?"—indicates a certain cold-bloodedness on her part, one that momentarily conjures up associations with the femme fatale of *film noir*,[53] Max's own response to Jackie's blasé attitude ("Not after they're dead") testifies to his own uneasy recognition of his position vis-à-vis her: after all, it could very easily have been him, and not Ordell, who ended up dead.

Jackie, sensing Max's ambivalence, cuts to the chase:

Fig. 7. Target Practice: Jackie, seated in Max's (Robert Forster) office, taking aim at an imaginary Ordell.

Jackie: I didn't use you, Max.

Max: I didn't say you did.

Jackie: I never lied to you.

Max: I know.

Jackie: We're partners.

Max: I'm fifty-five years old and I can't blame anybody for anything *I* do.

Undeterred, Jackie invites Max to go with her to Madrid, but he's more than just a little bit scared. Although he's a pretty cool customer in his own right, especially at the end when Ordell threatens to blow his brains out, he's ultimately no match for Jackie, who's "cool as the breeze" (200)—an inspired throwaway allusion to Pam Grier's *Cool Breeze* (1972)—or, as Ordell himself says at one point, "too cool for school." In fact, Max's vulnerability is graphically underlined by Tarantino when, in the film's final close-up of him as he mournfully watches Jackie walk away, we see that his lips are smeared with Jackie's cherry red lipstick—if being cherry implies a certain naiveté, Max, it is clear, is not nearly as experienced or streetwise as Jackie.

Cut to Jackie driving again, "Across 110th Street" on the sound track. This, the final sequence of *Jackie Brown*, even as it musically references the "Street Life" sequence, visually reiterates the opening of the film, with Jackie on a people mover gliding past bay windows with planes in the distance. However, the difference between the earlier driving sequence and this one—in addition to the fact that Jackie is en route to the airport, not the mall, and is shot from the front rather than in profile (so that we can read the emotions that pass like clouds across her face)—is the precise status of the sound track. Although the final sequence begins with a close-up on Jackie's face as she drives and, perhaps, reflects on her recent farewell to Max, she suddenly starts lip-synching or, depending on one's interpretation, singing "Across 110th Street":

> Pimps trying to catch a woman that's weak
> Across 110th Street
> Pushers won't let the junkie go free
> Across 110th Street
> A woman trying to catch a trick on the street
> Across 110th Street
> You can find it all in the street

There appears to be a certain irony here inasmuch as Jackie is hardly weak, nor has she had to resort to prostitution to survive or to exact revenge, as Foxy Brown does. Moreover, if the song is not playing in her head but on the car stereo—if, that is to say, the sound is source, the moment when Jackie starts singing the above bridge from "Across 110th Street" involves what Chion calls deacousmatization since the sound changes from nondiegetic to diegetic or on-the-air sound.[54]

Now, what exactly is the import of this particular—in this case, heavily accented—point of synchonization?

About this signal audiovisual phenomenon Chion comments in "Phantom Audio-Vision" that "deacousmatization goes hand in hand with [the] descent into a human, ordinary, and vulnerable fate."[55] Chion's focus here is on various *acousmêtres* (for example, the unmasking of the Wizard of Oz), but his interpretation of this process can also be applied, with some minor revision, to the final sequence of *Jackie Brown*: "Why is the sight of a face necessary to deacousmatization? For one thing, because the face represents the individual in her singularity. For another, the sight of the [singing] face attests through the synchrony of audition/vision that the [song] really belongs to that character, and thus is able to capture, domesticate, and 'embody' her (and humanize as well)."[56] Jackie is no doubt humanized in the last sequence of the film, a byproduct of the conjunction of close-up and enunciated sound, but her character is not, it seems to me, captured or domesticated by the sound track. Rather, the moment when Jackie begins to sing "Across 110th Street" (and, in the process, unconceal the source of the music) is a profoundly paradoxical one since at this point in the diegesis, she is arguably both audited and auditor, enunciator and enunciated.

Indeed, this pronounced point of audition insinuates that even as Jackie is finally making "Across 110th Street" her own, effectively internalizing it, she is still subject to another or the Other's voice, not a woman's—say, Randy Crawford's—but a man's (Bobby Womack's). In other words, Jackie may have escaped Melanie's brutal fate (a topic I will return to below) and, certainly, Spain is worlds away from the mean streets chronicled in "Across 110th Street"; however, no one, not even someone as cunning as Jackie, who has successfully come away from her encounters with both the law and Ordell intact—with, that is, both the money and her life, can completely evade the acoustic gaze. In the final analysis, as the sonic reiteration of Womack's "Across 110th Street" makes clear, Jackie Brown remains a black woman in, to dub James Brown, a (white) man's world.

Audiophilia Reconsidered: "Asking for It"

> I may come back in another form, and you know,
> I'll come back as a white man.
>
> —Pam Grier, interview in the *Onion*

In "Cinephilia Reconsidered" Willemen remarks that "there is a multiple array of pleasures" depending on the various fantasy scenarios a film puts into play, none of which is, in itself, "either good or bad, positive or negative."[57] Instead, "cinema or any other representational practice binds a variety of pleasures into narrative structures in such a way that the pleasures come to function as positive or negative indicators."[58]

The question I want to raise here is: If, as audio-spectators, we are positively invested in Jackie's victory over her male adversaries, what is the relation between her character and Melanie's? More importantly, what is one to make of Melanie's sudden death at the hands of Louis, a character who is an obvious figure of castration not unlike Melanie and the other women that form Ordell's posse (Raynelle, Sheronda, etc.). The answers to these questions are reflected not only in the sorts of highly personal musical choices Tarantino makes in *Jackie Brown*, choices that define the film's musical imaginary, this audiophilia is also inextricably intertwined with Tarantino's equally acute sense of cinephilia and scopophilia, cathexes that are driven by idiosyncratic notions of race and gender.

In the *Sight and Sound* interview that appeared contemporaneous with *Jackie Brown*, Erik Bauer observes that whereas Louis's violent act in Elmore Leonard's novel *Rum Punch* (1992) "seems like an extension of his character," in Tarantino's film "it comes as a shock."[59] Although Tarantino contends that it "gives the movie a dose of reality," Bauer not only presses the director on this point ("Isn't it important for all action to be set up, so people understand why it's taking place?") but wonders out loud about the "audience's attachment to Melanie's character when she dies."[60] Tarantino's answer, which I quote in full, is revealing for the light it sheds on his conception of Melanie's character: "I think the audience has a complete love/hate relationship with Melanie. Audiences applaud when Louis shoots her. It's impossible that someone could be asking for it, but she's asking for it. She's a fucking smartass, treacherous and all these things. But we also like her at the same time; she's a totally fun character."[61] Melanie's death in *Jackie Brown* references, of course, similar shocking moments in Tarantino's body of work such as Vince Vega's (John Travolta) accidental shooting of Marvin

(Phil La Marr) in *Pulp Fiction*. Indeed, the unexpected but oddly compelling juxtaposition of comedy and brutality that marks the above two scenes is a signature Tarantino effect, one that was first indelibly impressed on most viewers in *Reservoir Dogs* (1992) when Vic Vega/Mr. Blonde (Michael Madsen) slices off Marvin Nash's (Kirk Baltz) ear to the "sugary, bubblegum" sound of Stealer's Wheel's "Stuck in the Middle with You."[62] This is the Tarantinian universe writ small: comic-acoustic sadomasochism.

Bauer's question about setup notwithstanding, Melanie's death in *Jackie Brown* is in fact set up from the very beginning of the film and goes some way toward explaining the movie's libidinal—in this case, racially and sexually inflected—economy. For example, unlike Jackie, who first appears in motion and, crucially, fully clothed (very much in contrast, one might add, to those characters that constitute Pam Grier's iconic persona), Melanie is a classic object of the scopophilic gaze. Not only is she shot in a horizontal position, "curled up in a reclining chair" (5) in the apartment that Ordell has leased for her, silver toe rings adorning her pedicured feet, her tanned chest and legs foregrounded and fetishized as in a *Playboy* pinup, her initial appearance in the film is linked to the video which Ordell and Louis are wholly absorbed in watching. While Melanie is decidedly uninterested in "Chicks Who Love Guns," it's compulsive viewing for Ordell and Louis, Busby Berkeley for the gangsta set: "A chorus line of six beautiful bikini-clad women, all holding different automatic weapons" (37).

Still, even as the camera trains on the changing parade of phallic women on screen (the action of which, true to some B noir, Ordell narrates), Melanie exists as another, alternative focus. Instead of holding an AK 47 (as Gloria, "a tall Amazonian bikini-clad black woman" [5], does), Melanie is "smoking weed from a pipe" and perusing an issue of *Movieline* magazine (5), a detail that imbues the opening shots of her with a distinct cinephilic charge: she may not be Jackie Brown, but she's a star in her own right, a beach-bum odalisque.

Of course, even Jackie Brown is not, as it were, Jackie Brown. In *Rum Punch*, she's Jackie Burke, and in Leonard's novel, her race is unmarked—which is to say, she's white, not black.[63] The scopic, acoustic, and cinephilic implications of this racial substitution are most apparent in a scene early in the film when Max first makes Jackie's acquaintance. Here Jackie, like Melanie, is the object of the gaze (Max's as well as the audience's), but as the song "Natural High" proclaims ("Why do I feel this way? / Thinking about you every day / And I don't even know your name"), this gaze or, more properly, look is more romantic than sexual. Indeed, Max falls hard for Jackie the very first moment he sees

Fig. 8. The Look of Love: Max Cherry watches Jackie do that thing she does in *Jackie Brown*.

her emerging in long shot out of the shadows of the county jail, the dulcet tones of Bloodstone backing her entrance like some heavenly choir. Despite Jackie's ragged appearance, could this be the annunciation or, better yet (think Raphael), transfiguration of Foxy Brown?

The scopic-cinephilic punch of this moment of pure, unadulterated romanticization is retroactively confirmed in a scene in the screenplay (cut from the movie) where Max and Jackie chat in the food court at the Del Amo Mall after he has exited a matinee movie:

> *Max:* I think falling in love with movie stars is something that happens to a man as he gets older.
>
> *Jackie:* Does it happen to all men?
>
> *Max:* Well, I'd never be so bold as to speak for all men, but as for myself and a few of my friends, that's definitely the case. There's a lot of actresses out there you like, and there's some you have crushes on. But there's always one who you love. (122)

In this matinee idol context, it's interesting that Max and Jackie never consummate their relationship (as they do in Leonard's novel). In comparison, Melanie not only has casual sex with Louis but is literally fucked from behind, a sexual position that carries a potent, if ambiguous, charge in Tarantino's films. (See, for example, the scene in *Pulp Fiction* where Marsellus Wallace [Ving Rhames] is the object of white male anal rape.) In fine, whereas Jackie is an object of ciné-Platonic idealization, Melanie is an abject, sexually contaminated object that has to be eliminated (like, one might say, so much waste).

That the difference between these two figurations of femininity is a racial one can be gleaned from the music used to articulate each character. While Jackie's musical point of audition is realized via black R&B artists such as Bobby Womack and Randy Crawford, Melanie's is associated with white pop-rock bands like the Guess Who and the Grass Roots.[64] In fact, it's not insignificant that the latter musical *points de capiton* are introduced in the scenes that immediately precede Melanie's death. I have already discussed the automotive montage where Melanie, to Louis's obvious displeasure, is loudly singing along to "Midnight Confessions." This scene is itself set up by another, earlier one situated in Melanie's apartment where Louis is talking on the phone to Ordell ("What the fuck are you still doing there?!") and the Guess Who's "Undun" is playing in the background—in, to be precise, Melanie's bedroom and behind closed doors (not unlike the rape scene in *Pulp Fiction*).

Although Louis, who's "pissed" at being lectured to by Ordell ("Well, you're the one in motherfuckin' charge. . . . Go in there, snatch her by the hair, and drag her big ass out"), is arguably the one "undone" here, Melanie's choice of music, the Grassroots, contrasts unfavorably with Jackie's musical taste, which is funky, old-school cool. More generally, just as the film's sound track privileges black over white music (so that Melanie's obvious enjoyment of "Midnight Confessions" emphasizes her lack of soul), so *Jackie Brown*, subtly mobilizing white guilt, valorizes a particular, idealized version of black femininity—*Foxy Brown* (1974) without the T&A—at the direct expense of white femininity.

How else can we explain the ostensibly "totally fun" scene where Melanie is whacked by Louis? No doubt we are meant to understand this sudden brutal act of violence, per Tarantino's intentions, as payment for Melanie's treachery as well as, perhaps, for Louis's inability to deal, as Ordell regularly and good-naturedly does, with a "natural-born smartass" (181) like her. Still, such diegetic motivation hardly seems to do justice to the film's final image of Melanie, whose legs, once the object of the camera's steady fetishized gaze, now stick out from under a row of cars like the Wicked Witch of the West's. This excessive image in turn returns us, not unlike that of the repressed, to the issue of binding: If, as Willemen proposes, the valence of any given pleasure is a function of the meaning viewers attach to a particular character taking a particular action in a particular circumstance, whose pleasure are we talking about here?

Whether and to what degree Louis is a surrogate for the director must, inevitably, remain moot, but about one thing we can be sure—Louis takes enormous pleasure in killing Melanie:

Louis whips out the beretta Ordell gave him, shoots [Melanie] . . . BAM . . . in the belly. . . . BAM . . . Louis shoots her again on the ground. One; to make sure. Two; cause it felt good. (187)

Louis's recourse to force here—via, crucially, *Ordell*'s beretta—exposes him as a pale, pathetic imitation of the real thing—of, that is to say, his partner's easy sexual and physical mastery of the world around him. Meanwhile, even as Melanie lies dead in the parking lot of the Del Amo Mall, Ordell, in a bit of dramatic irony that suggests that Tarantino is not unaware of the scopic economy he's set in motion, is happily ensconced at a "titty bar" in downtown Los Angeles. In other words, when Louis shoots Melanie it's not only the beginning of the end for him, it's only a matter of time before Ordell himself has to face the music (since he's now wanted for Beaumont's and Louis's deaths).

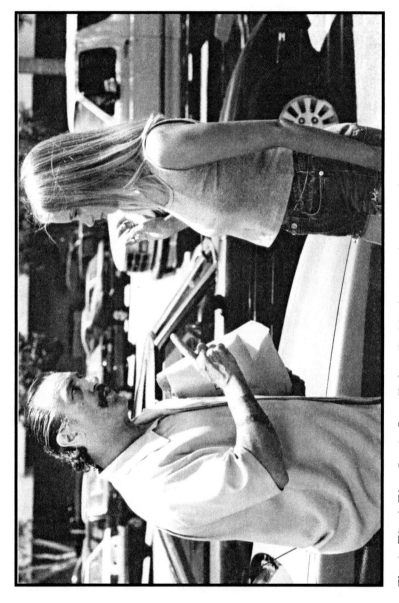

Fig. 9. Tête-à-Tête: Louis Gara (Robert De Niro) tries to lecture Melanie Ralston (Bridget Fonda) about the fine art of larceny in the parking lot of the Del Amo Mall.

Given Tarantino's own retro-blaxploitative revision of Leonard's novel, it's no accident that although Jackie practices shooting Max's revolver in his office while waiting for Ordell to arrive (having earlier, in an echo of a famously ultraviolent scene in *Foxy Brown*, pointed the same gun at Ordell's crotch[65]), she does not kill him. If Melanie is a chick without a gun, a wannabe playa who should never have left her bedroom and the sanctuary of her Playa del Rey apartment (true to the Beach Boys' fantasmatic music, she's the ultimate post-'60s California Girl), Jackie herself, even when outfitted in her "total power suit," is no Foxy Brown.

The smile that finally lights up her face at the end of *Jackie Brown* as Bobby Womack's "Across 110th Street" plays in the background enacts a double measure: Jackie's deliverance from the gangsta life that the other Foxy Brown raps about in the record store where Max, in a moony romantic haze as profound as Tarantino's, is buying *The Best of the Delfonics* and Pam Grier's own transcendence, however mixed or muted, of the caged persona with which she first made her name.

Counterpoint: Post-Soul Music or Pre-Gangsta Rap?

> I organize family style
> Lady Godiva, forever Firm Fox Boogie never lonely
> We were wed in Holy Matrimony
>
> —Foxy Brown, "Letter to the Firm
> (Holy Matrimony)"

Tarantino, like Lynch, has a thing for ears. Just as the noirish plot of *Blue Velvet* (1986) is precipitated by the severed ear that Jeffrey Beaumont (Kyle MacLachlan) finds in an abandoned field, so *Reservoir Dogs* pivots, at least in terms of imagined graphic violence, on the scene where Mr. Orange cuts off officer Nash's ear, then talks to it as if it were an anatomical microphone: "Hey, what's goin' on? Did ya hear that?" Ultimately, what both Lynch and Tarantino have in common is an uncommon interest in aurality: their art, not unlike van Gogh's (Frank Booth [Dennis Hopper] to the "ear's widow"[66]: "Stay alive, baby . . . do it for van Gogh"), is all about the colors, the prismatic tones and timbres, of cinematic sound.

There are, of course, very real differences between the two directors, one of which is that Lynch's audiovisual aesthetic derives from the 1950s (hence the use of Bobby Vinton's "Blue Velvet" [1963] as the title song for the above film), while Tarantino's musical imaginary, true to his generation, has its origins in the 1970s (see, for example, his use of K-Billy's Super Sounds of the Seventies in *Pulp Fiction*). In fact, Tarantino's explicit investment in this pop-musical structure of feeling can be gleaned from the following remark he made in defense of his adoption of Kool and the Gang's "Jungle Boogie" (1974) in *Pulp Fiction*: "Growing up in the Seventies gives you an appreciation for music that came out in the Seventies that no-one else on the planet has an appreciation for unless you grew up listening to it."[67]

Now, Tarantino's hyper-possessive take on '70s popular music is patently false (nobody "owns" the music, popular or otherwise, of any period); however, it does suggest that the audiovisual complexion of a film such as *Jackie Brown* cannot be fully appreciated without some sense of its popular-musical conditions of possibility. Consider, in addition to the sound clip from *Detroit 9000* (1973), the scene set in Melanie's apartment where Ordell is explaining to Jackie that there has been a slight change in plans because Simone (Hattie Winston) has suddenly split and absconded with ten grand of his hard-earned money. If Ordell's conversation with Jackie (and, therefore, his audio track) might be said to be foregrounded in this scene, it's also audiovisually counterpointed by what is happening in the foreground, where Louis and Melanie are lying on the couch, no doubt wasted from smoking weed, watching *Dirty Mary, Crazy Larry* on TV.

John Hough's 1974 low-budget, heist-and-car-chase flick stars Peter Fonda and Susan George as two outlaws on the lam who, as the screenplay puts it, "make jokes as they're pursued by police cars" (165). But the joke, as it were, is on Louis and Melanie, whose relationship is deteriorating by the minute and who, in the imminent future, will be at each other's throats. In other words, in this scene Tarantino not only engages the visual axis in the form of television to comment on the filmic action, he expertly plays the 1970s (the historical moment of Hough's movie) off the 1990s (the time period in which *Jackie Brown* is set).

More generally, while I have been concerned to show how Tarantino's audiophilia impacts on the narrative dynamics of *Jackie Brown* as well as its racial and sexual economy, the film's musical imaginary (which is mainly '70s soul) should also be seen and heard in conjunction with the 1990s understood as a constitutive, if mostly absent, popular-musical structure of feeling. Accordingly, it might not be too much to say that the audio format of *Jackie Brown* is not monaural but stereophonic where, say, '70s old-school soul acts as a screen of sorts for another, rather more contemporary genre of music: '90s gangsta rap. As for the film's popular-musical conditions of possibility (*Jackie Brown* appeared in 1997), 1996 not only marked the release from Death Row/

Interscope of Snoop Dogg's *Tha Doggfather* and 2Pac's *All Eyez on Me* (the first two-CD rap record), it marked the demise of Suge Knight's thuggish empire and West Coast gangsta rap in general in the charismatic body of Pac himself, who was shot and killed in September of that year.

Although *Jackie Brown* samples East Coast gangsta rap by way of Foxy Brown, it's noteworthy, especially given she was associated at the time with the Firm,[68] that Tarantino did not reference one of the bonafide heirs to Biggie and 2Pac, Nas, whose 1996 *It Was Written* was the follow-up to his 1994 smash *Illmatic*, or his soon to be lyrical adversary, Jay-Z, whose *Reasonable Doubt* (1996) was the auspicious beginning of the Roc-A-Fella dynasty. This omission, if one can call Tarantino's decision not to use West Coast rap in a mid-'90s film set in Los Angeles' South Bay an omission, may well be related to the frequently lodged charge that his films are driven by a postmodern historicism, all pastiche and retrograde aesthetics, that reduces the past to a succession of cinematic tableaux.

However, the stereophonic character of *Jackie Brown*'s soundscape suggests to me that the answer is rather more complex. First, one can certainly understand why Tarantino would want to reference the female rapper Foxy Brown (rather than, say, Lil' Kim) since the former owes her moniker and even some of her "fatal" sexual appeal to Pam Grier's blaxploitation persona. Second, whereas the extensive use of '90s gangsta rap in *Jackie Brown* might have resulted in a reduced mimetic relation between sound and image, effectively collapsing the acoustic space of the film, the steady employment of '70s R&B arguably deepens or doubles it, introducing a tension between '70s sound and '90s scenography and, in the process, producing a certain audiovisual volume. Finally and most importantly, the quite audible presence of classic soul music in *Jackie Brown* obviously reflects Tarantino's desire to showcase Pam Grier, albeit not the mythical, "super-bad-momma" that audiences associate with her younger, badder self.

Rather, as the director himself has said, it's "*Coffy* 20 years later, *Foxy Brown* 20 years later."[69] In other words, it's Pam Grier not as Foxy but Jackie Brown: not some scopic fantasy, a gangsta Lady Godiva "walking down the street to burn Harlem" to the ground, but a "woman working in this world,"[70] a woman with her feet planted firmly on the ground.

Reprise

Alex's "Lovely Ludwig van" and Marty McFly's White Rock Minstrel Show

> We're not the high brows, we're not the low brows
> Anyone can see
> You don't have to use a chart
> To see we're He-brows from the start.
>
> —George and Ira Gershwin,
> "Mischa, Jascha, Toscha, Sascha"

In a passage in his seminal essay, "On Suture" (1977/78), Stephen Heath observed in a typically thought-provoking aside that among the modes of narrativization that characterize the fiction feature film, those "working between image and sound tracks . . . still need to be examined."[1] Over the intervening years since Heath's essay first appeared in *Screen*, the notion of suture has become a cliché, yet another ornament of that monolithic entity known as Screen theory which somehow once exercised the analytical imaginations of film critics but now, with the hard right turn to the archives, can be safely consigned to history.

Heath's passing remark about "suturing" (the gerund with its sense of process and activity is indicative) suggests, however, that the resources of Screen theory have by no means been exhausted. Another hearing of Kubrick's *Clockwork Orange* (1971) not only confirms this point of view but allows that another one of the key concepts of Screen theory, the apparatus, also retains more than residual explanatory power.[2] In this unabashedly theoretical context, the sequence where Alex (Malcom McDowell) is being voluntarily reconditioned at the Ludovico facility, after having been incarcerated for the murder of the Cat Lady (Miriam Karlin), raises all manner of questions about the relation between art and fantasy.

The day before the initial treatment, Dr. Branom (Madge Ryan), prepares a hypodermic needle and, in response to Alex's query about what exactly is in store for him, tells him that they're "just going to show . . . some films." Alex's response—"I like to viddy the old films now and again"—is the diegetic cue for the acoustic transition to the next sequence: "And viddy films I would." The film's recourse to voice-over narration is a classic instance of suturing since the shift on the sound track from dialogue to voice over invites the audio-spectator to share Alex's point of audition. At the same time, it also complicates, via distanciation, spectatorial identification. In other words, voice-over narration, precisely because of its nondiegetic status (on-screen Alex = off-screen Alex), insinuates another, spectral presence which circumscribes his immediate audio-vision.

This other, acoustic gaze materializes with brutal, terrifying force in the treatment sequence proper and is associated with the film's rendition of the cinematic or ideological state apparatus as a *dispositif* of torture. Cut to an audiovisual theatre with, in the foreground, a straitjacketed Alex being administered to by a white-coated doctor, and in the background, in the last few rows of the theatre, various doctors and medical personnel. Behind them, standing in for Alex's face (which we cannot see), is the star-spoked light of the projector.

Cut again to a choker shot of Alex's face, topped by a crown of electrode thorns, as the doctor surgically clamps open his eyes so he can't shut them. The first movie (of a gang throwing a man downstairs, then beating him to a bloody pulp) is a pastiche of sorts of the first real violence perpetrated in *A Clockwork Orange*: Alex and his gang's assault on the tramp (Paul Farrell). It is also, according to Alex himself, a "professional piece of sinny": "like it was done in Hollywood." The exaggerated sounds that accompany the action on screen, captured by Kubrick himself with a hand-held camera, are, at least for Alex (if not, importantly, the audience), "very realistic" and indicate that while what we are viewing is, discursively speaking, filmic, for Alex there is little difference, if any, between art and fantasy or, for that matter, fantasy and reality.[3]

Despite the serum injection and what might be, in the context, a rather unpleasant reminder of his criminal past, Alex, as his appreciative comments intimate ("real horrorshow"), takes enormous pleasure from the spectacle unreeling before him, including and especially the "red red vino" which, he surmises like the habitual horror fan he is, must be "put out by the same big firm." Accordingly, his exclamation—"It was beautiful!"—can be seen as an aesthetic as opposed to anaesthetic judgment and highlights the film's emphasis on artifice and fantasy, spectacle and performance: "It's funny how the colours of the real world only seem really real when you viddy them on the screen."

The next film—shot, like the previous one, in the same color stock and set to Wendy (formerly Walter) Carlos's synthesized "Timesteps"—depicts a purple-haired "devotchka" (girl) being raped by one "malchick" (man) after another. This state-sponsored home movie, which is also a pastiche (in this case of Alex's earlier rape, to the tune of "Singin' in the Rain," of Mr. Alexander's [Patrick Magee] wife), arguably repositions both Alex and the audio-spectator as unwilling masochists.[4] That is to say, this time Alex, who is literally captive, cannot get out of the film's line of fire and becomes sick unto death. The juxtaposition of his anguished cries that he's going "to be sick," his first diegetic remarks in the sequence, with Doctor Brodsky's (Carl Duering) dispassionate commentary on his progress, sets up a stark acoustic contrast between the state and the criminal individual.

The second reconditioning scene, which follows a brief passage where Alex discusses his behavior modification treatment with Dr. Branom, begins straightaway with a montage in black and white, not color, of Hitler reviewing his troops, standard-bearing German soldiers goose stepping, fighter planes dropping bombs and strafing the countryside, and, among other things, a ruined cityscape where the only thing that seems to have survived intact is a sculpture of children dancing in a ring around a crocodile. When the camera finally cuts to Alex's horror-stricken face, he intones in voice over that "they flashed nasty bits of ultra-violence on the screen" but "not on the soundtrack." Instead, the background score—as the image of a Nazi herald, an eagle with talons above a wreath-encircled swastika, flashes on the screen—is, to Alex's utter horror and disgust, a "kitsch," "music-box" rendition of "Beethoven's Ninth Symphony, Fourth Movement" (arranged and performed by Carlos).[5] Alex's ear-piercing scream, "It's a sin!," punctuates a tight shot on his left eyeball, a shot that redoubles the outré, Daliesque image of bleeding eyeballs we earlier saw applied on his shirt sleeves: "Using Ludwig van like that! He did no harm to anyone. Beethoven just wrote music!"

In addition to film stock, the difference between the first two movies that Alex is forced to watch and the final one is the way the latter sutures sound (Beethoven) and image (Nazi war footage) in order to produce a certain ideological effect or subject position. Put another way, the Nazi/Beethoven movie plays like a parody of apparatus theory: Alex, after being drugged and subjected to the "sinny" discourse of the state, becomes a docile citizen, an exemplary embodiment of law and order. This said, the fine Kubrickian irony of the sequence can only be appreciated in dialectical tandem with the anterior, equally famous sequence where Alex masturbates to the "glorious music" of Beethoven.

Unlike the Ludovico sequence where the visuals can be said to drive sound (Nazi footage → Beethoven), in the first fantasy sequence of *A Clockwork Orange*, which is set in Alex's bedroom in his parents' Thamesmead apartment ("municipal flat block 18A, Linear North"), sound motivates image. Returning home from another mayhem-filled night on the town with his fellow "droogs," Alex takes a pee, then removes his false eyelashes and pastes them to a wall-sized mirror. The last prop, even as it introduces a philosophical note (the age-old question of art as a mirror of reality), reflects back the iconic black and white portrait of Beethoven that decorates Alex's window shade.

After an overhead shot of Alex taking his pet python snake, Basil, out of a bottom drawer, the camera cuts back to the mirror (and a doubled shot of Alex) retrieving a mini-cassette of Beethoven: "It had been a wonderful evening, and what I needed now to give it the perfect ending was a bit of the old Ludwig van." The close-up of the cassette in Alex's hand, a Herbert von Karajan-conducted Deutsche Grammophon recording of Symphony No. 9 in D minor, op. 125, is succeeded by a shot of Alex looking in the mirror at himself and the reflected image of Beethoven: Alex, it is clear, has a heroically romantic identification with the composer.

As the celebrated opening notes of the Ninth Symphony blare on the sound track,[6] the camera stutter-zooms in to a close-up of the eyes of "Ludwig van," then tracks down to a Katz-like drawing of a naked woman, stopping on the python, entwined on a branch, poised between her open legs. The next shot—another slow track, this time down to a statue of naked, anatomically correct Jesuses—precipitates a rapid-fire montage, cut to the exact tempo of the music, of thorn-crowned head, nail-pierced hand, and outstretched foot. This bravura set piece, which recollects Alex's earlier biblical fantasy in the prison library (with Alex as a Roman soldier scourging Christ[7]), marries the sacred to the profane, the immortal music of Beethoven to a blasphemous, Waholian image: a series of bloodied, post-crucifixion Jesuses dancing in a chorus line, their right arms raised in a Nazi salute.[8]

Alex, eyes ecstatic, is in heaven: "Oh, bliss. . . . Oh, it was gorgeousness and gorgeosity made flesh." A brief reprise shot of the larger-than-life bust of Beethoven sets off another Technicolor montage of "lovely pictures"[9]: a woman, skirts flying, being dropped through a trapdoor, hung (by pirates?); dynamite explosions; an avalanche of rocks raining down on some cavemen (a cheesy shot from the B prehistoric film, *One Million Years B.C.* [1968]); and, finally, a smoke-ringed cyclone of fire. Interspersed between these disparate shots, culled from what appears to be exploitation movies, are freeze frames of Alex leering like a vampire, fake blood dripping from his bared fangs. If Alex is clearly a blood-thirsty sadist, his fantasies are also equally clearly a product of stock Hollywood movies: he is, in a word, a ciné-sadist.

Still, for all the similarities between the Ludovico and fantasy sequences, there is a world of difference between the two. While the use of the "Turkish March" from Beethoven's Ninth Symphony in conjunction with, among other things, Leni Riefenstahl's *Triumph of the Will* (1934) is intended—according to the "eye for an eye," "fight violence with violence" principles of Dr. Brodsky's version of aversion therapy—to pacify Alex's savage sexual and violent instincts, it also evinces the state's ready recourse to propaganda. This, of course, is a not so subtle form of fascism, a fascism of the imagination, one where the totalitarian state insists on having a complete monopoly on violence, symbolic and otherwise.

By contrast, in the fantasy sequence, Alex, spurred on by the second movement from the Ninth, is freely able to exercise his fantasies, however depraved. This creative free association, which is not unrelated to the freedom to associate, is allied with the aesthetic sphere and its relative autonomy from the diktats of both the state and moral reason. Accordingly, the fantasy sequence can be said to perform a critique of ideological apparatus theory hyperbolically realized in the Ludovico sequence: that is to say, most audiences are neither captive, literally speaking, nor coerced via drugs to experience a particular movie in a particular—in this case, aversive—fashion: "Beethoven makes me sick to my stomach!"

Alex's free-form masturbatory fantasy to Beethoven also arguably desutures classic suture theory, sonically throwing into relief its unacknowledged preference for the visual economy and its devices (for example, editing) as well as disclosing the frequently arbitrary rather than strict, interpellative relation between sound and image. In the fantasmatic world of Alex, there is no incongruity, for good or ill, between Beethoven and B movies: to listen to Beethoven is to be "Hollywood."

In response to the accusation that *A Clockwork Orange* supports Alex's point of view, Kubrick once replied, "I don't think any work of art has a responsibility to be anything but a work of art."[10] For Kubrick, who has always insisted that there is a "very wide gulf between reality and fiction," that the work of art is closer to that of dream or fantasy,[11] art is not only beyond good and evil, its power derives, at least in part, from this fundamental predication. The reprise of Schiller's "Ode to Joy" from Beethoven's Ninth in the final sequence, as Alex is recuperating in a hospital after a Beethoven-prompted suicide attempt,[12] reflects the director's off-screen position: an unreformed Alex, whose incorrigible fantasy life is inseparable from his love for the composer, is to be preferred to an Alex whose basic instincts have been sublimated by the state.

Whatever one makes of Kubrick's appropriation of Beethoven (and there are critics who feel he has either besmirched the master's reputation or betrayed the spirit of Burgess's novel[13]), it is certainly radical compared to the way that, say, Chuck Berry is utilized in *Back to the Future* (1985). Zemeckis's film is, of course, one of the paradigmatic American movies of the 1980s and begins on an instrumental note. Marty McFly (Michael J. Fox) has come to Doc Brown's (Christopher Lloyd) laboratory to practice playing guitar for an after-school, best-of-the-bands audition. When he plays the first chord, though, his overloaded amplifier completely short-circuits Doc's intricately rigged electrical setup, sending Marty flying across the room. Later, one of the members of the dance committee (played by none other than Huey Lewis[14]) tells Marty and his bandmates, The Pinheads, that they won't be playing at the dance because they're "too loud" (a plot point that establishes Marty's hard-rock credentials). As he walks away dejected from the audition, his girlfriend, Jennifer (Claudia Wells), tells him that he should submit his demo tape to a record company, but Marty wonders out loud whether the record executives will simply inform him that he has "no future." (And we're not talking about the Sex Pistols here.)

The point is, Marty's rock 'n' roll aspirations are central to the main narrative arc of *Back to the Future*: Marty's desire to regenerate his parents, George (Crispin Glover) and Lorraine (Lea Thompson), so that his father will not grow up to be the loser, the abject figure of shame and humiliation, he so patently is.[15] Marty's and George's fates are also connected, albeit obliquely, with that of a black man, Goldie Wilson (Donald Fullilove), who is running for reelection as mayor but who, judging from the shape of the downtown district, which is marred by a drunk, an adult book store ("Cupid's") and run-down movie theatre (*Orgy American Style*), is more concerned with his own image than with the well-being of Hill Valley, circa 1985.

Cut to Hill Valley circa 1955 where Marty, via one of those time-travel conventions dear to science fiction, has been transported by Doc's plutonium-fueled DeLorean. (In yet another seemingly incidental but, in fact, integral plot twist, Doc has stolen atomic fuel from some Libyan terrorists.) The crucial action of the film occurs at the "Enchantment under the Sea" dance which Marty, in the alien form of a Vulcan Darth Vader bearing ear-splitting hard rock music from a tape labeled "Edward van Halen," has terrorized George into asking Lorraine to. Cut to a medium shot of a powder-blue-tuxedoed black man playing the saxophone at the dance, a member of Marvin Berry and the Starlighters, while outside, in a Chevy, to the ironic strains of Johnny

Ace's "Pledging My Love" (1955), Marty is steeling himself to make a move on Lorraine so that George can rescue her.

Instead, Biff (Thomas F. Wilson), the school bully and George's arch enemy, appears and Marty is hauled away and thrown into the trunk of the band's car. Marvin gets out to see what's going on, at which point one of Biff's gang says, "Beat it, spook." Although the gang quickly scatters when the other bandmembers get out ("Don't wanna be messin' with no reefer addicts"), the film clearly aligns Biff and his cohorts with the racist mentality of '50s small-town America. Meanwhile, as Marvin is in the process of injuring his hand trying to get Marty out of the trunk, George finds himself interrupting not Marty, as planned, but Biff.

The epitome of cowed, sissified masculinity, George is paralyzed until Biff violently pushes Lorraine face first back into the car, then—in one of the most dramatic shots in the film—the camera shows a close-up of George's hand making a fist.[16] Accessing the physical aggressivity that, the film suggests, is dormant within every red-blooded American male, George TKOs Biff with one punch. The low-angle shot of George towering over him, followed in long shot by Marty's amazed point-of-view gaze, sutures the scene: George, like Jim Stark's (James Dean) father at the end of Ray's *Rebel with a Cause* (1955), assumes his paternal legacy, the patrimony that is his gender, by finally standing up to another man.

Still, the exacting trial of masculinity that *Back to the Future* screens cannot be resolved until George also exercises his sexuality by kissing Lorraine. Hence Marty's plea to Marvin and his band to "finish the dance" so that he doesn't become "history." Marvin's reply that they can't go on unless Marty knows "someone who can play the guitar" is the inevitable, not so coincidental narrative pretext for the protagonist to assume Marvin's role as lead guitarist in the Starlighters. As Marty nonchalantly strums the first chords of the 1954 Penguins' hit, "Earth Angel," a happy ending seems imminent.

The subtle transition on the sound track from the diegetic "Earth Angel" to a tense passage from the nondiegetic score (composed by Alan Silvestri) marks, however, a new moment of crisis: suddenly, Marty can't play anymore and the people in the picture he has brought back from the future, his brother and sister circa 1985, begin to dematerialize one by one. The score rises to a crescendo when Lorraine's new Biff-like dance partner begins to maul her. Can Marty's father-to-be summon the nerve to save his once-and-future mother? As George responds to Lorraine's call for help, the orchestral music climaxes and the romantic measures of "Earth Angel" resume: "The vision of your happiness, whoa, whoa, whoa . . ." While Marvin Berry passionately sings, his bandaged hand at his side, his other hand outstretched to "all the lovers out there," Marty, flexing his magically regenerated fingers, begins playing guitar again.

The anticlimactic musical number that follows, like the feedback and audition scenes at the beginning of the film, does not appear to be essential to the main story of *Back to the Future*, since George and Lorraine have already been reconjoined and Marty can now rendezvous with Doc so that they can go back to the future. But Marvin's ad hoc suggestion, "Let's do another one," spurs Marty to come up with "something that really cooks." Assuming Marvin's place at the mic, Marty tells the audience "it's an oldie . . . where I come from," then turns to the band and says: "It's a blues riff from *B*. Watch me for the changes and try to keep up."

Now, there are no doubt innumerable audio-spectators who revel in the drama of a white kid showing some African Americans a thing or two about music—in particular, rock 'n' roll—but Marty's extempore remarks could not be more patronizing, as if rhythm and blues did not originate with black culture. The script's alibi for this startling act of appropriation is, of course, the utterance of the word "spook" earlier in the sequence. With this speech act, which separates the good ("our hero") from the bad (Biff and his gang), Marty is free to put Marvin and the Starlighters in their place, in the process shamelessly stealing not only from the history of rock 'n' roll (Jimi Hendrix's guitar acrobatics, Pete Townshend's equipment-smashing theatrics) but from Chuck Berry's signature style (duckwalking, knee-sliding, etc.).

When at the end of the song (an obviously postsynchronized version of "Johnny B. Goode" sung by Mark Campbell) Marvin calls Chuck to tell him the news—"You know that new sound you're looking for? Listen to this!"—the film has managed an extraordinary act of ideological sleight of hand: Marty (not, for example, Chuck Berry) is the true father of rock 'n' roll. Marty's post-performance remark to the audience who, standing slack-jawed, do not get his "inspired" playing, betrays the paternalistic subtext: "Guess you guys aren't ready for that, but your kids are gonna love it."

In their symptomatic reading of *Back to the Future*, Warren Buckland and Thomas Elsaesser offer a rich, concise summary of this racial inversion: "Marty . . . 'teaching' rock 'n' roll to one of the black fathers of rock [is] sweet revenge on both his white fathers" (George and the audition judge played by Huey Lewis).[17] Certainly, the film is cognizant of the fact that Marty's performance, especially the obligatory but superfluous gesture of wiping his brow, is borrowed almost entirely from African American culture. Indeed, the white minstrel show

Fig. 10. The Great White Hope: Marty McFly (Michael J. Fox) duck-walks at the "Enchantment Under the Sea" dance in *Back to the Future* (Zemeckis, 1985).

that *Back to the Future* stages (for, it is imperative to add, the nondiegetic audience) presupposes a quite specific cognitive position: for the scene to work, the audio-spectator must already know that Chuck Berry is the real father or inventor of rock 'n' roll.

Audiences also no doubt recognize "Johnny B. Goode" as a Chuck Berry number since it's not only his "greatest aesthetic triumph" but "one of the most widely known rock songs in the history of the genre."[18] "Johnny B. Goode" is, in fact, a three-minute rags-to-riches version of the American dream.[19] If it is partly about Johnnie Johnson who, after gigs, used to go to the clubs and sit in with the local bands and drink until dawn (hence Chuck's lament when he would later turn up just in time to make the next show, "Why can't you just be good, Johnnie?"[20]), the surname in the song ("Goode") refers not to Berry's pianist but to Berry's birthplace in San Jose, California: 2520 Goode Avenue.

The song itself is about a man from "way down close to New Orleans" who, "unable to read or write so well," makes the journey from a Lincolnesque "log cabin made of earth and wood" "way back up in the woods among the evergreens" to seeing his name up "in lights" and "people coming from miles around" to hear him play his guitar "like ringing a bell." Yet like most works of art, "Johnny B. Goode" is neither mere autobiography nor absolutely sui generis. Berry in Taylor Hackford's *Hail! Hail! Rock 'n' Roll* (1987) readily concedes that the song, like "Roll Over Beethoven," was composed of a "little Charlie Christian" (Benny Goodman's guitarist), a "little Carl Hogan" (a featured lead guitarist for Louis Jordan), and a "little T-Bone Walker" (the legendary electric bluesman).

Still, the most striking thing about "Johnny B. Goode," at least in terms of composition, is that the author himself changed the wording in the first verse from "colored" to "country boy." Berry claimed in his autobiography that it would have been "biased to white fans" to use the word "colored,"[21] though most critics have understood Berry's emendation as part and parcel of his lifelong desire to play to both white and black audiences. This mixed address, at once creative and commercial, echoes the philosophy of Booker T. Washington, who, in his "Atlanta Compromise Speech," wrote, "In all things that are purely social we can be as separate as the fingers, yet one as the hand in all things essential to mutual progress."[22]

While Bruce Pegg in his biography of Berry cites this famous passage from *Up in Slavery* (1901) in the context of "Johnny B. Goode," it gains additional resonance in the meta-context of *Back to the Future*, which depicts a segregated world where blacks need the inspiration of whites rather than other, more familial, black folk ("His mother told him someday you will be a man / And you will be the leader of a big old band") or soulful educators such as Washington and W. E. B. Du Bois.

So Goldie Wilson needs the moral uplift of Marty McFly ("You're gonna be mayor") to realize that one day he, too, can be mayor of Hill Valley ("I'm gonna clean up this town"). But in a "movie in which hands, one might say, *really* count,"[23] Goldie's hands are only good, really, for holding a mop with which to clean the floor of Lou's cafe (the clenched fist of the Black Power movement is, needless to say, beyond the retro-future purview of the film), while Marty's and George's are invested with life-changing dramatic significance: George punches out Biff in order to win the hand of Lorraine, and Marty performs "Johnny B. Goode," thereby showing Chuck Berry and his other R&B, pre-rock 'n' roll brethren the way.

The difference, then, between *Back to the Future* and "Johnny B. Goode" is that Berry's song is an homage to and builds on an earlier tradition of rhythm and blues, whether it's Christian's "stopped string bends," T-Bone's "chicken-pecking," or Hogan's intro to "Ain't That Just Like a Woman" (which Berry in "Johnny B. Goode" plays note for note).[24] *Back to the Future*, on the other hand, references this very same tradition in order to shade, to authorize and authenticate, its teen protagonist's comic travails, wittingly or unwittingly repeating the early tragic history of rock 'n' roll when white artists such as Pat Boone got paid in full at the expense of their more original, and usually tenfold more talented, black counterparts.

The artistry of "Johnny B. Goode"—its complicated racial address, its lyrical allusion to the history of slavery (where New Orleans, as Berry remarks in his autobiography, was the "gateway" to freedom[25]), and its cinematic synopsis of the life and hard times of a "brown-eyed handsome man" by the name of Chuck Berry—is performatively evoked in *Back to the Future* only to be erased in the end by Marty McFly's white rock minstrel showboating.

Part 3

TV
Television, Telephilia,
Televisuality

5

Gen-X TV

Political-Libidinal Structures of Feeling in *Melrose Place*

Cinephilia and scopophilia, if not audio-philia, have played a substantial role in the critical and journalistic discourse on film. Telephilia, on the other hand, has had a rather less illustrious history, as if the sort of intense affect and pleasure associated with, say, cinephilia were somehow impossible or inappropriate when discussing television. Part of this discrepancy no doubt has to do with various differences between the two media, such as the relatively small screen and square aspect ratio of TV, while another part surely has to do with the historically debased or degraded status of the medium vis-à-vis film.

Even today, TV, at least for many intellectuals (in the widest sense of the word), remains something of a guilty pleasure, even shameful. (You watch *The OC* [Fox, 2003–present]?) This is especially the case when the telephilia involves allegedly women's genres such as melodrama or, worse yet, soap opera. That is, it's one thing to say you regularly watch *Friends* (NBC, 1994–2004) or *CSI* (CBS, 2000–present)—a sitcom and forensic crime drama, respectively—but it's quite another to admit you're a fan of *Melrose Place*. It's doubly shameful if you admit to owning, as I do, the soundtrack to the show, *Melrose Place: The Music*. It doesn't matter that some pretty good artists appear on the CD—Aimee Mann, Sam Phillips, Annie Lennox, and Paul Westerberg, among others. Admitting to enjoying a pop music soundtrack to a prime-time soap like *Melrose Place* is tantamount to admitting that one's taste in cultural matters is completely bankrupt. Enjoy your symptom indeed!

This said, the following chapter, which examines the play of racial and sexual, generic and socioeconomic markers in *Melrose Place*, is predicated on a determinate telephilia, one marked by all the usual

135

symptoms: desire and identification, fantasy and fascination. At the same time, telephilia is understood here not simply as a modality of pleasure or leisure but as a mode of critique or, more dialectically, what I call, pace Adorno, "affirmative" critique. From this dual perspective, *Melrose Place* appears as a complex, even indeterminate text, a metatext that is simultaneously about melos and drama, opera and advert, sexuality and political economy.

Preview

> Soap operas are the fairy tales of capitalism.
>
> —Elayne Rapping, "Daytime Soaps"

Melrose Place, a program that emerged out of the economic and ideological ruins of the 1980s, is arguably one of the paradigmatic television programs of the early 1990s.[1] Although the received wisdom has it that Fox's success as a major network in the 1990s was a direct function of its youth-skewed programming (exemplified by its breakthrough program, *Beverly Hills 90201*), what has received rather less attention is the way its equally popular spin-off, *Melrose Place*, initially embodied many of the media assumptions about the "slacker" generation only to abandon this focus its second year in order to raise plummeting ratings. The result of this midcourse change of direction is history, with *Melrose Place* becoming, true to its Spelling provenance, the *Dynasty* (ABC, 1981–89) of the early 1990s or, as one scribe put it, "the *Dynasty* of Generation X."[2]

The working hypothesis of this chapter is that in order to understand the material conditions of possibility of *Melrose Place*, one must attend to the X in "Generation X," an X that is not merely political and economic but, precisely, libidinal-economic.[3] Moreover, these preconditions are dramatic, not to say melodramatic in character, and have everything to do with the cultural logic or structure of feeling of late capitalism, in which the free generation depicted, however politically correct or aesthetically pleasing, in *Melrose Place* collides with the determinate realities of post-Reagan America.[4] The net effect is part farce, part melodrama: postmodern capitalism, *Melrose*-style.

While the début of *Melrose Place* in the summer of 1992 was auspicious enough, beating out ABC's and CBS's offerings in its time slot, it did not fare nearly so well the following fall, despite the fact that it was in the extremely enviable position of piggybacking the 1991–92 showcase teen-angst drama, *Beverly Hills 90210*. In fact, it looked for a very long moment that *Melrose Place* would end up like the other *Bev-*

erly Hills 90210 clones of that year—*The Heights* (Fox, 1992), *Freshmen Dorm* (CBS, 1992), *The Round Table* (NBC, 1992), and *2000 Malibu Road* (CBS, 1992)—on the steadily growing Himalayan rubbish heap of failed prime-time programming.

The problem with the first full season of *Melrose Place*, according to retrospective media consensus, was that the show was too serious, that is, earnest. Not surprisingly, the producers of *Melrose Place* promptly jettisoned its emphasis on what Spelling himself called "moral lessons" for, in a word, sex.[5] As one critic put it, "Initially the show [was] about young-adult concerns like . . . sexual harassment in the workplace. Eventually the producers wised up and made the show almost exclusively about the characters sexually harassing each other."[6] In sum, the soapier *Melrose Place* became, a transformation generally attributed to the casting of Heather Locklear (the Aaron Spelling ingénue and downsized 1990s version of Joan Collins, the 1980s melodrama queen[7]), the faster its ratings rose, so much so that by the spring of 1994, *Melrose Place* had suddenly become something of a national sensation like *Dallas* (CBS, 1978–91) in its own quite heady heyday.

It's instructive, then, to return for a moment to the original 1992–93 season. In an interview with the *New York Times*, Darren Star, creator and producer of *Beverly Hills 90210* and writer-creator-producer of *Melrose Place* (under, of course, the executive tutelage of Spelling himself), commented on the show's genesis. Speaking in the drawn-out wake of the 1980s as well as the apocalyptic *Day of the Locust* scenario of the "LA riots," Star said of the "glitz and greed ideal" that had fueled the decade, "The riots woke people up to the fact that they're living in a very real city. . . . People started being a lot more politically aware, concerned."[8]

Translation: sure, there were a lot of Nautilus-sculpted bodies arranged around the pool in the apartment complex from which *Melrose Place* takes its SoCal name, but the show was really about issues, social issues. Put another way (from, that is, a more sociological perspective), if *Melrose Place* was originally conceived as a "discount *Dynasty*" or "middle-class *Dallas*,"[9] it was also partially a response to the stubborn economic recession of the late 1980s, and the social-issues accent was a moralistic reaction to the very real excesses of the same decade.

Hence Star's own inside take on the late 1980s and its impact on his generation: "We've gone from a time when money seemed fast and easy for a lot of young people coming out of college and now money's not fast and easy, and you're forced to think about things socially. And, in fact, it's become very unhip not to."[10] The irony of this pronouncement is that if the initial socially concerned *Melrose Place* was ostensibly hip but unsuccessful, the new and improved *Melrose Place* was unhip but spectacularly successful—at least with its target audience.[11] Call it "anti-PC chic."

After the Reagan Dynasty: "Help Me, Rhonda"

> I had *nothing* to do. . . . I'd just go, "*Yes*, Rhonda," or
> "Go *get* 'em, Rhonda." So when Rhonda left the
> show . . . I was like "Help me, Rhonda."
>
> —Doug Savant, cited in *Rolling Stone*

If any reading of *Melrose Place* must inevitably come to terms with that most vexing of issues, televisual pleasure, the larger issue of mass-popular culture also raises a number of related questions that have had a significant impact on the recent history of Anglo-American cultural studies. One question is the complicated issue of reception.[12] For instance, assuming individual viewers or audiences are watching *Melrose Place* and not just "watching television," what, precisely, are these viewers consuming? This, the local problem of reception, opens not only onto the more global problem of production (i.e., political economy), it opens as well onto more medium-specific issues such as genre, in particular soap opera or melodrama.[13]

Before I tackle the open-ended question of why audiences watch *Melrose Place*, I want to make a number of preliminary observations, the first being that the medium in question is, precisely, television. Although this point might seem obvious enough, what I want to emphasize here, in addition to the more intimate relation between content and advertising that obtains in television as opposed to film, is that television, as a number of critics have remarked, involves the performance of a certain practice.[14] This habitual or ritualistic aspect of watching television, so-called "regularization" or what Pierre Bourdieu calls *habitus*,[15] makes it a notoriously difficult thing to define, even if one aims merely to delimit this activity from other audiovisual practices such as film viewing. One way, however, to determine the televisual specificity of *Melrose Place* (I leave aside the more general differences between the various media) is to broach the issue of genre. From this perspective, I think it's safe to say that most viewers watched *Melrose Place* because it was a nighttime soap or, more properly, "prime-time continuing melodramatic serial."[16]

The seriality of *Melrose Place* is not, in fact, without historical resonance. It's not simply that the ratings for *Melrose Place* dramatically improved in the spring 1993 season because Spelling—an acknowledged master of both continuing weekly series and multiplot dramatic series such as, respectively, *Johnny Ringo* (CBS, 1959–60) and *The Love Boat* (ABC, 1977–86)—"decided to leave its plot lines unresolved over several episodes."[17] This decision to abandon the notion of what Star calls "self-contained episodes" must itself be contextualized, since in the late 1980s there was a growing consensus among network executives that soap operas were not "in tune with the times," the assumption being that "channel-surfing viewers would not sit still for multi-week story lines."[18] Rather more to the point, the dénouement in May 1992 of the "last of the great 80s soaps,"[19] CBS's *Knots Landing* (1979–92), suggested to not a few media pundits that prime-time serials such as *Dallas* and its Spelling derivations, *Dynasty* and *The Colbys* (ABC, 1985–87), had abruptly lost their populist currency with the fall of Reagan-style neoconservatism and the sudden ascendancy of Clintonian neoliberalism.[20]

Still, as an article in *Time* titled, appropriately enough, "1600 Melrose Place" conveyed,[21] 1980s-style soaps did not suddenly vanish with the close of the decade. The crucial piece of programming here was *Beverly Hills 90210* which, as one of the most important transitional shows of the early 1990s,[22] reconfigured the classic adult-skewed demography of the major networks even as it draped itself in the glamorous visual trappings of the 1980s. Yet if *Beverly Hills 90210* distinguished itself from glam soaps such as *Dallas* and *Dynasty* by hailing those mainstays of suburbia, "mallrats," *Melrose Place* made its name by demographically targeting twenty- rather than teen-somethings, thereby dramatically undercutting the aristocratic allure of its predecessors. Speaking in the early, "relatively unglitzy" 1990s, Spelling invoked one of the staples of Marx's famous "trinity formula" (rent) in order to capture the dreary economics of the moment: "I think the time was right for a show that [was] not all glamour, a show that says 'Jeepers, how are we going to pay the rent?'"[23]

Other less economic, more libidinal, explanations were adduced. For instance, Richard Zoglin, responding in *Time* to the media hullabaloo over *Melrose Place* in early 1994, attributed its success relative to other contemporaneous and long since forgotten prime-time serials such as *Tattingers* (NBC, 1988–89), *Homefront* (ABC, 1992–93), and *Angel Falls* (CBS, 1993) to what he called its "modest goals" and the "bland, modern universality of its characters."[24] While the notion of "modest goals" reinforces the idea, advanced by both Spelling and Star, that *Melrose Place* was a "discount *Dynasty*," this notion also suggests that *Melrose Place*—or, at least, its original social-dramatic incarnation before it became a "cheesy soap" and, later, an "over-the-top, self-conscious farce"[25]—was closer in spirit to the mundane middle-class ethos of *Knots Landing* (CBS, 1979–93) than to the ritzy upper-class ambience of *Dallas* or *Dynasty*.

Fig. 11. Original Habitués of *Melrose Place* (from first row, left to right): Jo (Daphne Zuniga), Alison (Courtney Thorne-Smith), Jake (Grant Show), Jane (Josie Bisset), Billy (Andrew Shue), Matt (Doug Savant), Michael (Thomas Calabro), and Rhonda (Vanessa Williams).

Zoglin's explanation for the surprising success of the program ("the bland, modern universality of its characters") is equally telling: "One is struck by how the personnel have blended together. There was once a black neighbor. . . . [Now] she has moved away. Michael and Jane were initially struggling young marrieds; in short order they became free-lancing singles like everyone else. With the exception of one gay character (whose plot significance is minimal), the pieces for mixing and matching are interchangeable."[26] What's striking about this passage is that Zoglin's seemingly throwaway line about the cast—"One is struck by how the personnel have blended together"—both raises and effaces substantial racial and sexual issues.

Thus, one of the not so ironic ironies of *Melrose Place* is that its second-season resurrection can be explained by the predictable, if abrupt, departure of Rhonda Blair (Vanessa Williams), the black neighbor who conveniently moved away at the end of the first season.[27] There were, naturally, good generic reasons for the substitution of Amanda (Locklear) for Rhonda, not the least of which was that this trade-off virtually resolved the problem of interracial romance. Williams's character was also expendable because, like Savant's gay character, Matt Fielding, she was almost wholly anodyne. Which is simply to say that if, on one hand, the initial appearance of Williams on *Melrose Place* promised some token attention to the fate of single black females in the new post-Reagan world order (something along the lines that not all of them were draining the last reserves of the welfare state), on the other, it's hard to imagine how Rhonda—shoehorned into a leisure-service stereotype (aerobics trainer) and eventually situated safely outside the sacrosanct precincts of Melrose Place—could ever have shouldered such a heavy representational burden.

Williams's character in fact confirms Christine Geraghty's study of prime-time soap operas where, as she puts it, "the black character as an individual disappears under the responsibility of carrying the 'race' issue and is used largely to demonstrate the notional tolerance of the largely white community."[28] The paradox here, at once aesthetic and socioeconomic, is that while soaps "aim to present black characters as if being black was of little importance" (a position that is of course hysterically affirmed in *Melrose Place*), "the structural position of the single black figure means that his/her function too readily becomes that of representing and explaining difference to the audience of whites both inside and outside the soap."[29] In this sense, Rhonda remains a perfect figure for the LA riots and the so-called rage of the black urban underclass. In a phrase: out of sight, out of mind.

Zoglin, then, is correct at least about this: for all the talk about multiculturalism and the politics of difference in 1990s America, *Melrose Place* is universal with a vengeance and with all the attendant, retrogressive post-'60s racial implications. In other words, the blend is not so much bland as blond, where the Madonna-like platinum blondness of Amanda is a not so subliminal racial code. Simply put, it's just assumed (as in "common sense") that no black character, no matter how attractive or successful, would be a part—or, perhaps, would *want* to be a part—of the sort of urban, upwardly mobile lifestyle that is featured in *Melrose Place*.

This much, at least, gangsta rap has taught us.

From Race to Sex-Gender: Kiss Kiss, Bang Bang

> Television dramatists have presented the plight of (white, middle-class) gay men with AIDS, but their particular concern is the agony of the families/ friends who have to face the awful truth: their son (brother, boyfriend, etc.) is, gasp, gay!
>
> —Larry Gross, "Out of the Mainstream"

In an early review of *Melrose Place*, John O'Connor had this to say about the "minority contingents" on *Melrose Place*: "Rhonda and Matt, relative outsiders, are best friends, of course."[30] O'Connor's sarcastic afterthought ("of course") perfectly encapsulates the liberal-pluralist logic of *Melrose Place* and its restricted libidinal economy. Thus, despite Zoglin's claim that the show's "chief appeal" resides in its "infinite possibilities" ("The combinations are," he says, "unlimited"[31]), it's pretty clear that the sexual and romantic *combinatoire* that constitutes the political-libidinal deep structure of *Melrose Place* is in fact quite finite, just as, to reverse tack, the status of Matt's and Rhonda's characters relative to the Melrose Place community is not so much relative as absolute. In other words, these sorts of things are, precisely, structural.

The question nevertheless remains why Matt, whose character in the first two seasons was just as marginal as Rhonda's, did not suffer the same untimely fate. One explanation for this asymmetry of narrative emphasis, Williams's reported unhappiness as an actress aside, is that the gay angle was somehow more popular with viewers than the black one. The very real downside of this popularity, "of course," is that gays can be gays so long as they don't actually act on their sexual preferences. The assumption here is that queer sex cannot be the object of the direct heterosexual gaze. O'Connor sums up the heteronormative logic that subtends this view: "Matt doesn't figure . . . in the earlier episodes. Evidently the producers have decided he's someone you wouldn't want to sleep with."[32]

While it's difficult to disagree with O'Connor's industry-inflected take, it's also important to account for the extant textual evidence, such as the now notorious nonkiss which transpired during the final episode of the second season. In this episode, which revolved around Billy's impending never-to-be-consummated marriage to Alison (Courtney Thorne-Smith), Matt "babysat" Billy's best man, Rob (Ty Miller). Later, upon returning to the Melrose Place courtyard, Billy watched in bewilderment from the windowed privacy of his fiancée's apartment as Matt and Rob kissed—or so one had to infer, since the camera cut away at the very last moment to Billy surreptitiously watching from the cloistered heterosexual space of Alison's apartment. The relay of the televisual gaze from Billy to Rob and Matt illustrates the way that prime-time writers and producers, in this case, at the heavy-handed behest of the network (who in turn were slavishly responding to the threats of advertisers), endeavor to manage viewers' anxiety about gay male sex.[33]

True to the accelerated pace of prime-time commercial television (and particularly *Melrose Place*, whose narrative tempo is almost as fast as an MTV video), Billy comes to terms the very next day with the forbidden truth of homosexuality. His overnight reconciliation with his friend's sexual preference is negligible, however, since Rob is only a visitor, like Matt's ex-sailor lover, Jeffrey (Jason Beghe), to the world of Melrose Place. Consequently, the baring of the secret of homosexuality in this episode is ultimately less about Matt and what it might mean to be gay than about what Billy and we, the audience, are supposed to do or feel about this problem.[34] In brief, the program's sexual politics are, like its racial politics, emphatically liberal-pluralist. That is to say, it's all about tolerance.

If Billy's epiphanic recognition scene sutures the "perverse" homosexual space briefly opened up by Rob's dramatic coming-out, my second example—Matt's on-again, off-again relationship with Jeffrey—exhibits just how constricted *Melrose Place*'s libidinal economy is.[35] So, in apparent contradistinction to the program's compulsive-heterosexual law of desire, Matt is finally permitted, "just like everyone else," to have a real sexual-romantic relationship. Yet even as we watch Matt attempt to rekindle his relationship with Jeffrey (who has, at his father's insistence, resigned his navy commission), we learn in the very same episode—on the beach, no less—that Jeffrey is HIV-positive, as if gay sex equals HIV seropositivity and HIV seropositivity equals AIDS.[36]

Now, I would not want to rule out the progressive potential of this sort of melodramatic encoding, but you don't have to be an especially skeptical spectator to realize that the relative sexualization of

Matt's character is almost immediately linked to the social problem of AIDS. Although AIDS activists have tirelessly argued against the speciousness of linking AIDS and homosexuality (the two issues are decidedly not convertible), the consequence of this sophistic equation, on *Melrose Place* at least, is the pathologization of Matt and Jeffrey's relationship and, a fortiori, gay sexuality as such. More generally, even as the aggressive rearticulation of the discourse of gay sexuality and AIDS confirms the malignant, ideologically fraught notion that homosexuality is sick, *Melrose Place* mobilizes this very same notion to produce the "real" of soap opera: *affect*. In other words, if it's true that emotional excess is the "surplus-enjoyment" of soap opera, on *Melrose Place* AIDS becomes, like sex itself, the stuff of melodrama.[37]

This said, it's worth reinvoking the issue of genre when addressing such politically charged topics as AIDS, since, to hazard an axiom, the politics of representation are never reducible to the political per se. This is especially true of the opera buffa of the later *Melrose Place*, where for certain gay spectators the flip, flamboyant discourse of camp effectively disrupts the straight, serious discourse associated with liberal gay politics.[38] As Andrew Sullivan has written, "Straight people watch [*Melrose Place*] as a fantasy of their lives; gay people watch it as a reverse fantasy of theirs."[39] Accordingly, however different it may have appeared from Spelling-produced anthology dramas such as *Fantasy Island* (ABC, 1978–84), *Melrose Place*—as, distinctly, soap opera—provided viewers with a space in which to engage in sexual fantasy as well as to negotiate, if not resolve, especially pressing cultural problems like AIDS.

The Romance of Capital: Fox, Female Address, and Postfeminism

> To this generation, Fox has always been there. They're not really going to remember [the time] before Fox was one of the networks—that's like life before computers.
>
> —Matt Roush, quoted in *Gen X TV*

> It might be a sign of the post-feminist times that the most popular female heroines today . . . such as Amanda on *Melrose Place* . . . embody—like pop singer Madonna—enlarged, excessive representations of the liberal-feminist ideal, but with a post-political twist.
>
> —Ien Ang, "Melodramatic Identifications"

Crucial as the issue of fantasy is to understanding or evaluating the representational politics of mainstream programs such as *Melrose Place*,[40] it's equally crucial to take into account, in addition to its generic conditions of possibility (say, melodrama or soap opera), the "other" of *jouir-en-plus*: surplus value or, in a word, capital.

Consider, for example, the program's primary demographic, which was viewers between the ages of eighteen and thirty-four. While one can extend this range to include slightly older boomer viewers (eighteen to thirty-four or even eighteen to forty-nine), anyone with a cursory familiarity with Fox knows that its strategy from the beginning has been to aggressively court the youth market.[41] As Rob Owen comments in *Gen X TV*, "Fox made a home for itself with in-your-face programs that mom and dad hated and the kids loved."[42] This trend, so-called youth-skewed programming, was the result of enormous historical changes in the television industry. To register just how significant the impact of cable, satellite, and VCRs has been on the television industry, one has only to recall that in 1991 (the year that *Beverly Hills 90210* debuted), two of the "big three" networks, CBS and NBC, failed to make a profit for the very first time.[43]

In fact, if "demography is destiny," the numbers behind the argument for youth-skewed programming are illustrative. Specifically, if a "mere 10 product categories account for fully half of all network television spending" and if "consumers aged 18–49 account for anywhere from two-thirds to three-quarters of all spending in [these] categories,"[44] then it's obvious where all the vaunted viewers lie. To be sure, *Melrose Place* is skewed not simply to the young but to young women—which is to say, women between the ages of eighteen and thirty-four.[45] The ideological implications of this narrowcasting are reflected in the program's complex representation of femininity: on *Melrose Place* the personal, to revise the feminist maxim, is the libidinal. This equation, in turn, has considerable implications for any gendered reading of the program because soap opera is "doubly a commodity" and, equally importantly, because a certain postfeminism, what one might call Gen-X feminism, is itself predicated on a specific understanding of power-capital.[46]

Thus, when in the 1995 season Billy refused Alison's sexual demands—advanced under the sign, as in *Disclosure* (1994), of reverse sexual harassment—the message was clear: her economic power was spurious (even though she was the titular head of the main corporate nexus on *Melrose Place*, D&D Advertising). Amanda's case, on the other hand, conveyed a different message. When she disdainfully refused Michael's marriage proposal (a refusal also backed up by the threat of sexual harassment), we knew she was ready to begin her not so slow climb back to the top. In the final analysis, it all comes down to character: power-sex is OK but romance is worse than useless, it's a character flaw.

Alison's too-good-to-be-true character is exemplary in this respect.[47] Diacritically coded from the very beginning of the show—like her masculine alter ego, Billy—as hopelessly romantic, she was ultimately no match for Amanda who, despite the occasional moment of romantic weakness, was as ruthless as they come. This, then, is the post-feminist twist of *Melrose Place*: Amanda effectively owns the house, a matriarchal emphasis that suggests that *Melrose Place* has more in common with the Jane Wyman-driven *Falcon Crest* (CBS, 1981–90) than with patriarchal serials such as *Dallas* or *Dynasty*.[48] Indeed, given the generic excess of female over male characters on *Melrose Place* (and, more importantly, of strong women over weak men), the program would appear to be a veritable text of female empowerment.[49]

Any such argument for feminist progressivity must eventually come to terms, however, not only with the way *Melrose Place* characteristically articulates sex-gender with economic success but also with its regressive representation of women: Jane's (Josie Bisset) relentless masochism, Jo's (Daphne Zuniga) abject maternalism, Sydney's (Laura Leighton) venal criminality, Alison's alcoholism, and so on. If I have omitted Amanda from this dysfunctional series (the stuff, to be sure, of which melodrama is made), I do so with the tacit understanding that given the strict binary codes of soap opera, even her strength must be seen as a weakness in its own right and, as such, entails not a little loss, a paradox that underscores the ideological limits or founding contradictions of the program. In other words, the moral of *Melrose Place* is not merely that women can't have it all (a reasonable enough proposition), but that romance and economic success are diametrically opposed.

Here, the sadomasochism of the genre and, for women, its extraordinary emotional ambivalence emerges in all its sociocultural force: in that feminine subculture of masochism which continues to exist within the larger popular culture, Amanda's economic power, uncoupled as it is from the deeply satisfying pleasures of romance, must inevitably become the object of the sadistic female gaze embodied, typically, by Dr. Kimberly Shaw (Marcia Cross). Given this specular, not to say spectacular dynamic (Kimberly, after all, would eventually go on to dynamite Melrose Place), Amanda's place within the program's intricate political-libidinal economy is necessarily tied to Kimberly's. Where Kimberly's "mad" character is a direct function of her absolute masochism, which is simultaneously pathetic and terrible,

Amanda's character is less sympathetic (and therefore must be subjected to an even stronger, more corrosive sadistic gaze) because her symbolic power is not mitigated, like Kimberly's, by the feminizing touch of romantic masochism.

A powerful ideological lesson is being proffered here about the role of women in the so-called real world: women with substantial socioeconomic power—say, doctors or corporate executives—are either monsters or bitches or, worst-case scenario, a monstrous hybrid of the two, the superphallic bitch.[50]

Melrose Space: The Fashion Mode

> Who are the members of Generation X? The media stereotype is white, middle-class kids who grew up in suburbia, went to college, and are searching for a career but end up at the Gap.
>
> —Rob Owen, *Gen X TV*

> "You know, *Melrose Place* is a really good show."
>
> —Lelaina (Winona Ryder), in *Reality Bites*

If one result of the schizophrenic representation of women on *Melrose Place* is a certain performative contradiction, this contradiction or, better yet, exorbitance can best be seen in the program's programmatic emphasis on fashion. Therefore, when, in a bit of crossover intrigue, Kelly Taylor (Jennie Garth) from *Beverly Hills 90201* made an appearance on *Melrose Place*, she was shown shopping for clothes at the Gap.

Now, the Gap may not be the couture of choice for Generation X (though one would be hard pressed to name a more representative corporation), but this intradiegetic spot underlines the extremely tight tie-in between youth-skewed programming and the generation-slanted agendas of the advertising industry.[51] As Bill Carter commented in the *New York Times*, "The gang [on *Melrose Place*] is twenty-something, newly employed, but trying to find their way, as well as the correct fashion statement, in the 1990s."[52]

The key word here is "fashion," as in the "fashion mode,"[53] insofar as fashion has become, at least in the post-scarce part of the first world targeted in *Melrose Place*, the ultimate sign of invidious distinction. In this super-conspicuous mode, the classic economies of scale associated with Fordism have been superseded by a flexible mode of production or regime of accumulation predicated on the delirious cycles of fashion and its distributive arm, retail culture: design, sign value, super-obsolescence, and so on.[54] Hence *Models, Inc.* (Fox, 1994–95), the spin-off of *Melrose Place* or a spin-off of a spin-off. If the first part of the former show's title is as generic as soap opera itself, but with a celebrity angle (not doctors or nurses but models!), the corporate tag is unequivocal as the Spelling trademark: fashion is big business, transnational capitalism writ small, like the Nike logo or the polo figure emblazoned on a Ralph Lauren shirt.

The location of the show, 4616 Melrose Place, at once particular and abstract like some Hegelian "concrete universal," is, in this context, richly evocative. While this indeterminacy is a direct function of a certain ethno-linguistic elision (the actual location of the exterior shots is 4616 Greenwood Avenue in the Los Feliz district of Los Angeles), it's also due to the fact that Melrose Avenue is associated in the popular imagination with the upscale, bohemian shops one finds there. In other words, unlike a number of other daytime and prime-time soap operas such as *Dallas* or *Santa Barbara* (NBC, 1984–93), *Melrose Place* does not take its name from a city but from a specific place within a larger metropolitan space.

Melrose Place as a space exceeds, then, its local determination as a site of consumption, evoking as it does not only Los Angeles but, beyond this realist determination, Hollywood (where Hollywood, like Benjamin's Paris, is the mythical entertainment capital of the world). The fact that *Melrose Place* is set in Los Angeles rather than, say, New York City—as in Star's short-lived prime-time series, *Central Park West* (CBS, 1995–96), or the more recent and popular *Sex and the City* (1998–2004)—is, as it were, symptomatic. Unlike New York City, which retains a certain Old-World pedestrian charm, Los Angeles embodies the brave new world of post-Fordism: in Los Angeles, that sprawl of sunlight, freeway, and smog, you are only as good as you look. And *Melrose Place*, it goes without saying, is all about the look.

Thus (to return to my original anecdote), Kelly is shopping at the Gap not merely to add to her already extensive wardrobe but to buy something to impress Jake Hanson (Grant Show). As Kelly herself opined, "I know he's older, but he needs me." Translation: unlike Matt, Jake is "someone you want to sleep with." Although the micro-generational gap between Kelly and Jake and, more generally, between *Beverly Hills 90210* and *Melrose Place* is effected here via the genre- and gender-inflected codes of heterosexual romance, the wild card in this scenario is Jake, whose original occupation as a construction worker effectively set him apart from both the nouveau-riche environs of *Beverly Hills 90210* and the proto-professional managerial milieu of *Melrose Place*. As the caption for an early *New York Times* profile put it, "Grant Show—an outsider in a sea of affluence."[55]

Consequently, while it's true that *Melrose Place* is "mostly about middle-class, college-educated kids in LA,"[56] Jake is an obvious exception as is his blue-collar brother, Jess (Dan Cortese). Indeed, it's apparent that the early incarnation of Jake as opposed to, say, the later petit-bourgeois one was a rapidly fading symptom of the economic recession that constituted the initial dramatic conditions of possibility of *Melrose Place*. This recession—symbolized by, among other things, the 1987 Stock Market crash—resulted in a rather surprising phenomenon in youth-skewed shows at the time, what one TV critic referred to as "talk about being rich and poor, even class distinctions."[57]

The issue of class—"being rich or poor"—raises a host of other issues, the most important of which, for my money, is Gen-X anxiety about *déclassement* or "downward mobility,"[58] an anxiety expressed on *Melrose Place* in, paradoxically enough, the language of *upward* mobility. Therefore, while Jake was plainly marked in the early episodes of *Melrose Place* as working class (which translates in American soaps to something like lower middle class[59]), his character's fate was also bound up with that of the dominant class fraction represented on the program, which is the middle class (and this is a crucial qualifier) with better than middle-class pretensions. Not surprisingly, the discursive stress in *Melrose Place* was eventually less on the differences between the rich and poor and more on the permutations of the so-called "professional managerial class" (PMC).[60]

Need one add that over the years the majority of the characters on the show became firmly ensconced in the recession-proof world of the PMC? Even Sydney, whose character in the course of a couple episodes went from being a lowly cocktail waitress at Jake's bar to the president of Mancini Designs, became living proof that despite capitalism's tendency to "boom and bust," reality doesn't in fact bite. In the long run, the rate of profit will rise and, with it, the faithful, the upwardly mobile middle class.

Adcult: The Commercial Supertext

> The omnipresence of pastiche is not incompatible with a certain humor . . . nor is it innocent of all passion: it is at the least compatible . . . with a world transformed into sheer images of itself.
>
> —Fredric Jameson, *Postmodernism*

> Television presents and sustains economics as an answer to the problems of everyday life. It articulates and, at the same time, dissolves the difference between the "supertext" and the "supermarket."
>
> —Nick Browne, "The Political Economy of the Television (Super) Text"

If postmodernity and its privileged class fraction, the PMC, are clearly central to the structure of feeling of *Melrose Place*, then a certain style of consumption, where Gen-X is a real phantom figure constructed by and for advertisers,[61] is an integral part of this political-libidinal mix.

In fact, as Amanda's dominant managerial position in the profession implies, *Melrose Place* ultimately revolves around neither medicine (as in *ER* [NBC, 1994–present) nor fashion (as in *Models, Inc.*) but advertising. Although advertising may not be as noble as medicine or artistic as photography (Kimberly's and Jo's métiers, respectively), it's sexy, like capital itself. In just this fashion, *Melrose Place* refunctions the generic soap-opera interest in the private sphere and the melodramatic travails of sex-romance even as it reflexively rehearses its commodity character as commercial television.

To suggest, however, that *Melrose Place* is virtually unintelligible outside its commercial context is by no means to claim that the reception of this super-popular cultural text is absolutely determined by its economic preconditions (since they are a necessary, though not sufficient, condition of possibility).[62] Rather, to propose that we watch *Melrose Place* as we would watch a commercial, at once cynical and sympathetic, engaged and alienated, is not so much to reduce the program to its political-economic axis as to speculate about the relation between promotion and content. The interest of this formulation in the present context, prime-time soap opera, is that it draws attention to the way in which advertising informs both the logic of the art-commodity (here the commercial supertext) and its very content (where, for example, D&D Advertising is the privileged space or locus of the interpersonal).

And here, for the sake of comparison, one might think of *thirtysomething* (ABC, 1981–88). Whereas *thirtysomething* is occasionally willing to subject the discourse of advertising to criticism (even if it's only the tortured, hand-wringing sort associated with Yuppie neoliberalism[63]), the effect of postmodern irony on *Melrose Place*—as in contemporary, "second wave" advertising more generally[64]—is that a critical, intradiegetic discourse on advertising has become both irrelevant and somehow inappropriate. One symptom of this trend on *Melrose Place* is the viruslike proliferation of interwoven commercials, where content dissolves into advert, and the sort of Gen-X issues broached in the diegesis of *Melrose Place* are resolved, like so many mini-melodramas, in the accompanying commercials: "Bad hair day? Your roots showing like Amanda's? No problem, buy Biolage 'until the world is a safer place for your hair'"!

Such a libidinal-economic pitch is, needless to say, wholly self-congratulatory, ritually reproducing at the level of content the commercial imperatives of the medium. This economic articulation is, in turn, at one with the dominant tonality of *Melrose Place*, which is pastiche—with the critical proviso that pastiche does not necessarily preclude affect or pathos, identification or desire.[65] Put another, more affirmative way: the happily alienated viewers of *Melrose Place* need their scrap of identification—say, Amanda's bleach-ruined hair—since it is only from just such synecdochic details that they can create a convincing, internally coherent, emotionally realistic world.

Moreover, as the word "bleach" with its detergent and hair-care connotations insinuates, this emotionally realistic world is impossible without, because economically and diegetically predicated upon, the discourse of advertising. Commercials may appear to represent a departure from the real, but the opposite scenario is in fact the case: the real today—and, consequently, the postrealism of *Melrose Place*[66]—takes its cue from the world of commercials.

Review

If the Internet represents one possible future for television, *The Spot* (1995–97), the first cybersoap, indicates what is at stake in the above postrealist turn. The brainchild of Scott Zacharin, an advertising film-maker, and Prophecy Entertainment, a division of the Los Angeles ad agency Fattal & Collins, *The Spot*—"part *Melrose Place*, part *The Real World*" (MTV, 1992–present)—featured five housemates living in a Santa Monica beach house who posted daily updates on their post-MTV lives.[67]

The novelty of episodic web sites aside, what remains memorable about *The Spot* was the spectacle of soap opera's industrial origins being replayed in another, more advanced medium. It was not unlike some future-anterior vision of the culture industries, a world where the Adornian post-subliminal message (as intoned by a simulacrum Rod Serling) is, "Television is advertising in reverse."

Still, given the rather rapid demise of cybersoaps (which vanished from the media landscape almost as soon as they materialized, only to be replaced by more genuinely interactive fare such as *The Sims*), it's now abundantly clear that privileging advertising over content is not an especially viable formula for either commerce or entertainment. Rather, the extraordinary popularity of prime-time continuing serials such as HBO's *The Sopranos* suggests that even youth-skewed, ostensibly cutting-edge networks such as Fox will be hard-pressed to compete with the sponsor-free space and cinematic perks of subscriber cable. From this economic and aesthetic standpoint, the difference between *The Sopranos* and *Melrose Place* is decisive: where *The Sopranos* has suddenly become, in an anamorphic blink, the very definition of that MTM thing, "quality TV," *Melrose Place* now appears—less than a decade after its premiere—a product of its time, a brief moment between Reagan and Bush II when it was cool to be into watching Fox for something other than its news.

6

Shot/Countershot

Sexuality, Psychoanalysis, and Postmodern Style in *The Sopranos*

lthough there would appear to be little similarity between *Melrose Place* and *The Sopranos*, each program has helped to establish its respective brand and network: *Melrose Place* was one of the first programs, together with *The Simpsons* (1989–present) and *Beverly Hills 90201*, to put Fox on the map as the "fourth" network, while *The Sopranos* (which Fox famously turned down) has now made HBO a viable, even mandatory, alternative to both mainstream cable and broadcast television.

In addition, the episodic seriality and strong female characters of *The Sopranos* not only locates it, like *Melrose Place*, in the "tradition of prime-time soaps,"[1] its pronounced deployment of self-reflexive and citational devices produces a characteristically postmodern tonality. The latter pastiche effect, which is a hallmark of soaps from *Dallas* to *Dawson's Creek* (WB, 1998–2003), ranges from oblique critiques of Fox's *Cops* (Christopher Moltisanti [Michael Imperioli]: "Like the cop would be calling this asshole 'sir' if the fucking camera weren't around") to elaborately-staged metatextual gags. So, in one of the very first episodes of the series, Tony Soprano and his wife Carmela (Edie Falco) can be seen watching a TV show where a Mafia pundit, Jeffrey Wernick (Timothy Nolen), talks about his new book, *Mafia: America's Longest Running Soap Opera*.[2]

In short, if *The Sopranos* can be said to constitute an evolutionary leap in the logic of televisuality (where this logic is predicated on TV's appropriation and displacement of cinema's aura), its extraordinary popularity is also the result of a rare telephilic synthesis of the epic and the domestic, of intimate melodrama and grand, *Godfather*-style family drama.

Shot: *The Godfather*

> [T]he relationship between the conventions which
> go to make up [the gangster] type and . . . the real
> facts of whatever situation it pretends to describe is
> only of secondary importance and does not deter-
> mine its aesthetic force. It is only in an ultimate
> sense that the type appeals to its audience's sense of
> reality; much more immediately, it appeals to a pre-
> vious experience of the type itself: it creates its own
> field of reference.
>
> —Robert Warshow,
> "The Gangster as Tragic Hero"

Let me set the scene: Vito Corleone (Marlon Brando) has been gunned
down outside a fruit stand by "The Turk" Sollozzo's men, oranges
rolling in the street like so many little heads, and Michael (Al Pacino),
steadfastly standing guard over his father at the hospital with Nazorine
the baker (Vito Scotti), has had his jaw broken by one Captain Mc-
Cluskey (Sterling Hayden).

Cut to the Don's office, interior, day. As the camera pulls in,
Michael, face puffed out, seated in a chair like the Don, announces with
a slight lisp to the assembled members of the Corleone Family—Sonny
(James Caan), Tom Hagen (Robert Duvall), Tessio (Abe Vigoda),
Clemenza (Richard L. Castellano): "[Sollozzo and McCluskey] want to
have a meeting with me, right? . . . Let's set the meeting. . . . if Clemenza
can figure a way to have a weapon planted [in the restroom] for me
then I'll kill 'em both." Sonny, standing, the Don's walking cane in one
hand, laughs, can't believe what he's hearing: "Didn't want to get
mixed up in the Family business, huh? Now you want to gun down a
police captain . . . because he slapped you in the face a little bit? . . .
What do you think this is, the army, when you shoot them a mile away?
Ya gotta get up close, like this [pointing an index finger at the left side
of Michael's head]—bada bing!"

Citationality: The Gangster as Serio-Comic Hero

It will come as no surprise to anyone who has watched even one episode
of *The Sopranos*, Home Box Office's acclaimed series that premiered in
January 1999, that Francis Ford Coppola's *Godfather* films (1972, 1974,
1990) remain the cinematic locus classicus for its own distinctive—in this
case, televisual—take on the gangster genre.[3] Tony himself, played to
pitch-perfect warts-and-all perfection by James Gandolfini, is no Vito, let

Fig. 12. Nuclear Gangster Family: Tony Soprano (James Gandolfini), Meadow (Jamie-Lynn Sigler), Anthony, Jr. (Robert Iler), and Carmela (Edie Falco).

alone Michael Corleone, while Carmela (the extraordinary Falco) bears little resemblance to either Mama Corleone (Morgana King) or Kay Adams (Diane Keaton). As for the Bada Bing!, the strip club located on Route 17 in northern New Jersey which functions as Tony's headquarters couldn't be further from the austere, Old-Masters ambience of the Don's office.

Indeed, *The Sopranos* "is the first piece of popular art to spin something entirely fresh from the crime family dynamics that Mario Puzo and . . . Coppola laid out in *The Godfather*."[4] If Ken Tucker's invocation here of popular as opposed to high art appears to be a reference to that most derogated of American arts, television, Ellen Willis makes the connection explicit, writing in "Our Mobsters, Ourselves" that *The Sopranos* is the "richest and most compelling piece of television—no, of popular culture—that I've encountered in the last twenty-five years."[5]

This said, the real point of comparison is not so much between TV and popular culture as between film and television: "In 1999 . . . word began to spread that the HBO series *The Sopranos* was not only the best television drama ever made but episode by episode as good or better than any Hollywood movie to be released in ages."[6] Maurice Yacowar's opening gambit in his episode-by-episode guide, *The Sopranos on the Couch*, represents an even more marked cinematic gloss: "For openers: it's brilliantly written, performed, and filmed. Each episode has the polish of an excellent feature film."[7]

Of course, the irony of these sorts of comparisons is that David Chase, the creator of the show, has consistently reiterated his express distaste for the medium of television: "I loathe and despise almost every second of it."[8] For Chase, whose sensibility was formed by European "art-house" films such as Fellini's *8 1/2* (1963) and Polanski's *Cul-de-sac* (1966), and who once "considered network TV to be propaganda for the corporate state," it has always been "cinema, cinema, cinema."[9] Moreover, as Chase has been at pains to point out, *The Sopranos* emerges out of a particular historical moment in the evolution of the mass media, a hegemonic moment when, as he puts it, "television [took] over American cinema."[10]

Consequently, when Lloyd Braun, a former executive at Brillstein-Grey (which went on to produce the show), asked Chase if he "would be interested in doing . . . a TV version of *The Godfather*," Chase's "movie idea" about a "mob guy [and] his mother" became—lo and behold!—the "first season of *The Sopranos*."[11] In other words, it's now apparent, especially if one remembers that Puzo "modelled Don Corleone after his mother,"[12] that there is an intimate, even originary, relation between *The Sopranos* and *The Godfather* (an intertextual relation that the program consistently foregrounds) as well as, equally importantly, between television and cinema (where the brand mantra "It's not TV. It's HBO" translates to the equation HBO = TV + film).

Still, given Chase's historically problematic relation to television, the performative paradox of the series, one that its "author" is no doubt keenly aware of, is that *The Sopranos* not only reflects the increasing hegemony of TV vis-à-vis film (where HBO has become the indisputable vanguard) but that its appropriation of cinematic codes, or at least those conventions we tend to associate with Hollywood film (for example, relatively high production values), deconstructs the formerly inviolate distinction between the two media. Put another way, the high audiovisual style of *The Sopranos* constitutes an original, subversive cannibalization of the art of cinema via parodic invocations of, among other things but most notably, *The Godfather*.

The net effect of this televisual reappropriation of one of the classic American film genres, the gangster film, is that even as the program frequently references this venerable cinematic tradition, a delectable corpus that extends from *Underworld* (1927) to *Casino* (1995) and beyond,[13] *The Sopranos* also reinvents this same tradition, albeit in the body of another, less culturally valorized medium: television.

"I'm a Man": Crossing Cultures

Consider, in this telefilmic context, a sequence from the pilot for *The Sopranos* (I, 1)—written and directed by Chase—where Tony's nephew, Christopher Moltisanti, in an effort to display some initiative and thereby impress his boss, whacks Emil Kolar (Bruce Smolanoff) so that the Soprano Family can resolve a "garbage contract problem." The last bit of information, which comes courtesy of Tony himself via voiceover, is part of an extended tale he is narrating to his psychiatrist, Dr. Jennifer Melfi (Lorraine Bracco), whom he has reluctantly come to because of a series of anxiety attacks that have left him literally flat on his back.

The dramatic irony of this sequence, a delicious one for the spectator, is that we get to see in glorious detail what Tony cannot, for ethical reasons, tell Dr. Melfi. The sequence begins with a ground-level establishing shot of Satriale's Meat Market. A jet passes noisily overhead, a neon sign blinks on and off like a beacon. Cut to the dark interior of the store—the only ghostly light coming from the meat counters glowing like tabernacles—where Christopher is practicing kung fu (a staple of gangsta rap, if not the gangster genre per se), Bo Diddley's "I'm a Man" blaring on the sound track. Emil arrives and is promptly ushered to the back of the store, at which point some comically desultory discussion about different kinds of sausage ensues. Emil: "Ever have our sausage?" Christopher: "I thought the only sausage they had was Italian and Jimmy Dean's. See what happens when you cross cultures and shit?"[14]

Although the sequence reverts to découpage for its stunning climax, mise-en-scène, which dominates the first part, reaches its apex when Christopher emerges from the walk-in fridge with two Budweisers and the camera reframes from a full to medium shot to reveal a bulletin board covered with black and white photos of celebrities. Emil's reiteration of the correct pronunciation of his name simultaneously punctuates Christopher's take on the current embattled state of the garbage business ("The garbage business is changing. You and I are the younger generation, we have issues in common") and sets up the concluding brutal action of the sequence. After bringing out a butcher knife "deployed" with lines of coke (the ostensible reason for the visit) and handing Emil a bill he has been rolling to "taste the wares," Christopher slips behind Emil's back and pulls out a gun he has hidden. The camera quickly tracks in and as the rhythmic backbeat of Diddley's song kicks in, he aims it at the back of Emil's head. Bada-bing! Emil Kolar's brains splashed all over the butcher block like a red Pollock splatter painting.

Cut to a low-angle shot of Christopher shooting Emil again followed, rat-a-tat-tat, by a montage, intercut with two more "shots," of black-and-white stills from the bulletin board: Bogie, Dino, Cagney (the last, famously, in *Little Caesar* [1930]). The ensuing shot of Christopher's face as he does a quizzical double take at the dead pig snouts that, eye-level, dumbly match his gaze in the freezer is the final cinematic flourish to a sequence that epitomizes the sort of audiovisual panache that distinguishes *The Sopranos*: the super-graphic violence, super at least for prime-time cable TV on God's day off, with a big pinch of black comedy, the bluesy sound of Bo Diddley's voice married to a shot of the King of Cool with cocktail.

Now, if part of the charge of the above sequence comes from Christopher's casual recourse to lethal force, another, comic part comes from the audience's superior "cognitive" position vis-à-vis Christopher (who has somehow never heard, such is the extent of his cosmopolitanism, of Polish sausage). In other words, if the dialogue, exemplified by Christopher's mangled syntax and casual ignorance about the geography of Eastern Europe, parodies the politically correct discourse of difference ("Czechoslovakia, what's that, that's a type of Polack, right?"), it also italicizes the narrow discursive limits that define his world, one where Poland and Czeckoslovakia might as well be located on another planet.

At the same time, to attempt to do some justice to James Wolcott's welcome reminder that "Fortunately, real life and top-rate entertainment have only a passing resemblance to each other,"[15] *The Sopranos* is textually predicated—not unlike, say, Tarantino's films—more on mass-media culture than so-called real life. From this perspective, "Chrissie," unlike his elders (for whom *The Godfather* is the Bible), hasn't even mastered the basics. Thus, when he and "Big Pussy" Bonpensiero (Vincent Pastore), a favored soldier in Tony's Family, are later unsuccessfully trying to toss Kolar's dead body into a enormous trash bin, Christopher exclaims out of the blue, "Louis Brasi sleeps with the fishes."[16] Exasperated and winded (for all its glamour, being a made man does not, as *GoodFellas* first detailed, exclude its own version of "dirty work"), Pussy retorts, "Luca! Luca Brasi! There's differences, Christopher, okay, from the Luca Brasi situation and this."

The black-comic frisson of this exchange comes from the fact that Christopher, who's on record preferring De Palma's *Scarface* (1983), badly misquotes a celebrated passage from *The Godfather* (something of a crime in this crew); it also derives from the fact that Christopher somehow misconstrues the meaning of this famously Sicilian message (one, in the original, lost on Sonny and Michael but not on the immigrant Italian American, Clemenza).[17] In this case, as Big Pussy points out, it's better that Kolar's uncle, not to mention the police, find out later rather than sooner, if at all. To wit, Christopher desperately wants to be a made man, but as the two pick up his dead-heavy body to restash in the car trunk, the old man is the real wise guy: "Take 'im to Staten Island and cut 'im up."

Psycho-Gangster TV: Seriality and Self-Reflexivity

"Twelve episodes (and three prescriptions, two murders, a restaurant 'torch job,' and innumerable *Godfather* references) later," as the authors of an *Entertainment Weekly* article recap the first season of *The Sopranos*, "a battle-scarred Tony concedes, 'psychiatry and cunnilingus have brought us to this.'"[18] If this now notorious epigram represents Tony's demotic verdict on *La Cosa Nostra*, it also highlights two of the main motifs of the show: psychoanalysis and sexuality. While the play of both of these discourses in Chase's series throws not a little light, however allusively or perversely, on current attitudes about therapy and sex-gender, the representation or, better yet, performance of psychoanalysis and sexuality in *The Sopranos* can be seen to problematize received critical wisdom about, respectively, television as "psychoanalysis in reverse" and postmodern pastiche as devoid of affect.[19]

Thus, against the first proposition, which is tightly bound up with the Frankfurt School stigmatization of TV and the mass-culture industry, it's possible to argue that *The Sopranos,* by creatively marrying the mob genre with the sort of analytic interiority associated with the late bourgeois novel (itself closely related to the discourse of psychoanalysis), does not so much reverse as advance, via various serial and self-reflexive devices, the case of psychoanalysis and its pop-cultural articulation of sex and death, affect and aggressivity. Indeed, I don't think it's too much to say that *The Sopranos'* dialogical deployment of psychoanalytic discourse—the way, for example, it plays action off reflection, psychopathic behavior off serial analysis—gives the show its distinctive profile, which amounts to something like a psychic X-ray, in the person of the extended Soprano Family, of the American body politic at the advent of the twenty-first century.

À la Recherche du temps perdu

Although *The Sopranos'* substantial, even visceral kick is obviously a consequence of its frequent, calculated but not, I think, wholly gratuitous recourse to nudity, violence, and graphic language, the very real "aesthetic force" (Warshow) of the program is also a result of its uncanny ability to mobilize both irony and affect, pastiche and melodrama, or, as one critic encapsulates it, "satire and realism."[20]

Consider in this dual hybridic context an episode from early in the third season, "Fortunate Son" (III, 3)—written by Todd Kessler and directed by Henry Bronchtein—which revolves around Tony's progress in psychotherapy. In the previous episode, the sight of a box of Uncle Ben's rice had sent Tony to the kitchen floor for the long count, apparently all because Meadow's (Jamie-Lynn Sigler) new boyfriend from NYU, Noah Tannenbaum (Patrick Sully), just happened to be both Jewish and African American. (Tony, baring his '50s racist mentality, boasts to Melfi, "I had a frank talk with Buckwheat.") If this weren't bad enough, Tony's archest enemy, his mother Livia—the late Nancy Marchand—finally passed away after a massive stroke, leaving Tony with a burden of guilt that only a good son gone bad can appreciate.

Dissolve from a medium shot of Tony, in the present, eating a piece of gabagool in his dead mother's house to a zoom-in long shot of Tony, age eleven (Mark Damiano II), sitting in the back seat of his father

Johnny Boy's (Joseph Siravo) red Caddy convertible parked in front of
Satriale's. The Notre Dame-USC game plays on the radio, leaves swirl in
the background on this "perfect football afternoon." Just as Tony's father
with the help of his brother, Junior (Rocco Sisto), is about to escort Mr.
Satriale (Lou Bonacki) to the back of his butcher shop for a talk, his son
appears at the front door: "Anthony, I told you to wait in the car." Moments later, Mr. Satriale, having been hit in the side of the face by Johnny
Boy because he's unable to meet his gambling debts, holds a hand to his
bruised cheek and pleads for mercy: "Your wife's weekly order is ready.
There's gotta be thirty dollars' worth of meat there—gabagool, chops,
and a beautiful standing roast." Unmoved, Johnny Boy holds Mr. Satriale's hand down on a butcher block next to an order of capicola while
Junior covers his mouth to muffle his screams. Cut to a close-up of a
meat cleaver poised in midair like a guillotine.

When the camera suddenly zooms out to the door where Anthony
has been standing, surreptitiously watching his father cut off Mr. Satriale's pinkie finger ("Anthony, what I fuckin' tell you?"), we the audience begin to understand, like Melfi, some of the traumatic root causes
of Tony's "spells." True to the show's mock-tragic tone, though, when
the scene shifts back to Melfi's office, Tony's reaction to her look of
compassion is classically nonplussed: "What? Your father never cut off
anybody's pinkie?"

Flash back again to a slow pan of Johnny Boy, set to Hugh Mon-
tenegro's spaghetti-Western-themed "The Good, The Bad, and The
Ugly," asleep on a recliner with the sports page. Waking for dinner, he
calls Anthony over for a little talk: "What you seen today, Anthony, [is] a
very sad thing." However, rather than scolding his son for earlier dis-
obeying his order, he compliments him instead and, in the process,
schools him in a certain code of masculinity: "A lot of boys your age
would have run like a little girl, but you stayed." Johnny Boy's hands-on-
cheeks lesson to his impressionable, if not exactly fortunate, son: "[Mr.
Satriale] owed me money and he refused to pay. . . . What was I supposed
to do? That's my livelihood. That's how I put food on the table."

Cut to a beaming Livia, Tony's mother (Laila Robins), a picture of
domesticity straight out of a Connie Francis film, admiring a roast as
she carries it to the dinner table: "Beautiful cut he sent." Johnny Boy, in
turn, to his wife: "You like it standing with the bone in it, huh?" The air
thick with sexual innuendo, Livia murmurs "Look at those juices," then
places a pinkie finger dipped in juice in her husband's mouth. When
Johnny Boy breaks into a Sinatra-like version of "All of Me" ("Go,
Wayne Newton," Janice [Juliet Fox] snorts), they start to slow dance. As

Tony's father squeezes his mother's ass, Tony gazes, mesmerized. Cut again to a close-up of a blood-red roast being sliced ("The lady loves her meat"), followed by a low-angle shot of Anthony falling over like a tree, "short-circuited," as Melfi later comments, by the sight of sex crossed with a rare Satriale-free roast beef.[21]

Primal Scene: Capicola as Proustian "Tea Cookie"

Later, in an analytic session set in Melfi's office, we learn that the imme-diate catalyst of Tony's most recent anxiety attack wasn't his mother's death or even the logo on the Uncle Ben's box (for Tony, an association with Meadow's boyfriend by way of The Little Rascals' "Buckwheat") but meat or, more precisely, capicola. Dr. Melfi, good-enough analyst that she is, connects the dots. Tony's first attack occurred just as he was about to grill some steak and sausages. The immediate catalyst: the family of wild ducks that had been nesting in his pool abruptly flew off. As Melfi explains, Tony's panic attacks are less about the "fuckin' ducks" than about Tony's fears about losing his family (in both senses of the word).

Similarly, the capicola-induced attack is not so much about foul play as what Freud calls "family romance"—about, according to Melfi's letter-perfect Freudian interpretation, Tony "witnessing not only [his] mother and father's sexuality but also the violence and blood connected to the food" he consumed as a child. Melfi in fact concludes her analy-sis of Tony's vivid, reverie-rich recollections by patiently explaining to him, not without wit, that behind them lies the very real dread that one day he might be called upon, "like [his] father," to "bring home the bacon." The coup de grâce of the sequence, however, is her comparison of Tony's capicola to Proust's madeleine.

Now, if one of the wonderful things about this high-cultural allu-sion is that it "robs hundreds of critics nationwide of the chance to parade their knowledge of superficial literary references,"[22] it must also be said—to attend to the clinical rather than literary aspect of this se-quence—that the brand of psychoanalysis featured on The Sopranos can best be characterized by what Richard, Melfi's husband (Richard Ro-manus), calls "Freud by numbers."[23] Most people, even perhaps Tony (who at one point informs Melfi that he became acquainted with Freud in his semester and a half at Seton Hall!), can put two and two together. For example, the amputation of Mr. Satriale's pinkie finger, which is the obvious source of the dream that Tony recounts at the end of the pilot episode about a bird flying off with his penis in its beak, has castration anxiety written all over it, a recurring theme of the series wittily refigured in "Fortunate Son" when Tony's sister, Janice (Aida Turturro), steals Livia's Russian caretaker Svetlana's (Alla Kliouka) prosthetic leg. In fine, this is pop-cultural psychoanalysis with the emphasis on the word "pop!"

Accordingly, to rack-focus on the representation of psychoanalysis in *The Sopranos* (Is it true to clinical practice?) is to radically misrecognize its real function, which is more a matter of form than content. In other words, the progressive character of this discourse in *The Sopranos* is at once medium and genre specific (TV and the gangster type, respectively) and has everything to do with seriality and self-reflexivity, of which psychoanalysis is a determinate signifier.

A comparison with *The Godfather* is instructive here. Fredric Jameson has argued that Coppola's films are, like *Chinatown* (1974), an example of postmodern "nostalgia,"[24] but however one periodizes the history of the gangster genre, *The Godfather*—not least because of its relation to the high European musical and cinematic tradition of Verdi and Mascagni, Visconti and Bertolucci, as well as its conservative revision of, inter alia, *Bonnie and Clyde* (1967)—represents a classical moment in the genre.[25] Hence the familiar historical effect whereby later films such as, to invoke a certain parodic strain in the genre, *Prizzi's Honor* (1985), *Married to the Mob* (1988), *The Freshman* (1991), and, most recently, *Analyze This* (1999) and *Analyze That* (2002) appear in hindsight as so many minor variations on Coppola's monumental, grand-operatic achievement. (Need one add that this sort of parodic revisionism is decidedly not new and is at least as old as *Little Giant*, the 1933 spoof of *Little Caesar*?)

Still, the difference between the above films and Chase's series is that for all its deadpan humor and "late" generic reflexivity (*The Sopranos* as ultimate indice of the "exhaustion of the gangster *film*"[26]), the program is frequently marked by moments of real pathos and sentiment that reveal its substantial debt to the other, dramatic strain of the gangster genre. In other words, if psychoanalysis on *The Sopranos* can be said to be a signifier of the gangster genre in its current super-self-conscious phase (of which Scorsese's *GoodFellas*, with its virtuoso display of music and montage, is the cinematic archetype[27]), psychoanalysis understood as, say, analysis terminable and interminable operates both as a structural device in the show and as a rich formal analogue for its episodic seriality.

In sum, *The Sopranos*, precisely because of its freedom from commercial breaks and its adoption of, for example par excellence, letter-boxing, mimes the experience of the theatrical feature-length film even as it mines the dramatic and ritualistic resources associated with television in the cable and satellite age.

Countershot: Case Study

> *Silvio:* "My daughter's been giving me all this feminist shit about this place [Bada Bing!]—'objectifies women.'"
>
> *Big Pussy:* "Boys are different from girls."
>
> —*The Sopranos*, "Down Neck" (1, 7)

From the very first moment of *The Sopranos*, a reverse crotch shot of Tony looking up bewildered at a nude female statue (a Klimt reproduction, no less), the series has been structured around a series of oppositions: action versus reflection, silence versus speech, the public versus the domestic sphere (where the first term of the last opposition must be understood as what happens when covert illicit behavior becomes overt, as in *Public Enemy* [1931]).[28] That Dr. Melfi is a woman, a female doctor or psychiatrist, also intimates that many of the oppositions that drive the series are gendered ones.

Indeed, the psychoanalytic scenario in *The Sopranos*, which is built on shot/countershot sequences between Dr. Melfi and Tony, is coded as distinctly feminine. Take, for instance, the title of the show. A soprano is a woman who sings with a high-pitched voice. Now, given the blood oath of *omertà* that binds, via the threat of death, the "boys" who make up a Family (e.g., the Soprano Family), to willingly engage in the "talking cure" is to "sing." In just this sense, Tony's proper name reflects his fractured identity, since in the particular criminal subculture he inhabits, to be a man is to eschew words, to remain strong and silent like Gary Cooper, not to engage in the sort of affective dialogue that defines psychoanalysis.

Hence the truth of Tony's equation of psychiatry and cunnilingus, an equation that he employed in the first season to describe the bitter intrafamilial feud between himself and Corrado "Junior" Soprano (Dominic Chianese) fueled by Tony's Machiavellian mother, Livia, who suggested to Junior in no uncertain terms that it might be in his interest to whack her son. Moreover, while Tony, in direct violation of the male codes of conduct that underwrite *La Cosa Nostra*, is privately seeing a woman doctor, Junior's secret, which is revealed in the "Boca" episode (I, 9), is that he is a "great artist" at cunnilingus. Consequently, while Tony is mortified to discover that his associates know that he is "spilling his guts" in therapy, so too Junior is mercilessly ribbed about his penchant for "kissing down there."

Fig. 13. The Other Soprano Family: "Big Pussy" Bonpensiero (Vincent Pastore), Tony Soprano, Christopher Moltisanti (Michael Imperioli), Paulie "Walnuts" Gaultieri (Tony Sirico), Hesh Rabkin (Jerry Adler), Silvio Dante (Steven van Zandt), and Furio Giunta (Federico Castelluccio) in front of Satriale's Pork Store.

The difference, of course, is that while Junior, after shoving lemon meringue pie in Roberta's face like James Cagney in *Public Enemy*, feels compelled to end his long-standing relationship with "Bobbie" (calling her, in a caustic parting shot, a "blabbermouth cunt"), Tony continues, despite the local publicity and debilitating moments of self-doubt, his twice-weekly visits to Dr. Melfi's office. Still, the consequences of feminization for a man, especially a made one, can be dire in *The Sopranos*. The attendant loss of face is not the only price one might have to pay, one can end up dead like Big Pussy, who, for singing to the Feds, must "sleep with the fishes." In fact, one might argue that death itself is feminizing. So, in "The Legend of Tennessee Moltisanti" (I, 8), Christopher and Georgie (Frank Santorelli) are digging up Emil Kolar's fast-decomposing body and Georgie says, right before vomiting, "Look at those fingernails!," to which grisly directive Christopher responds, "Oh, fuck, they're like a woman's!"

Black and Blue: Puzo's Women

If there's little doubt that the ur-text for male-male violence in *The Sopranos* is *The Godfather*, it's equally clear that the main model for violence against women derives from this very same text. If one difference is that the women in *The Sopranos* "have read the books and seen the films,"[29] it's also safe to say that, as a partial inventory of the sorts of gross objectification to which the female characters are submitted in Puzo's *Godfather* testifies, the negative representation of women in his novel is even more pronounced than it is in the film.[30] Some highlights: Michael, after returning from Italy where his first wife, Apollonia, has been blown up in a car, proposes to Kay by flatly stating, "You'll be my wife but you won't be . . . an equal partner" (360); Dr. Jules Segal, introduced in the fourth book of *The Godfather*, chides Lucy Mancini, Sonny Corleone's former *goomah*, to "stop thinking [that she] has a big box that no man can love" ("because it won't give his penis the necessary friction") before beginning surgery to repair her vagina: "He was building a new snatch as easily as a carpenter nails together two-by-four studs" (309); and Johnny Fontane, a notoriously thinly veiled portrait of Frank Sinatra, meditates at one point on his "square," "old, guinea taste for virgins," then thinks, "What could be greater than a girl who was tasting her first dick and loving it?" (172). The men in Puzo's novel even get touchy when the casual sex doesn't come with the requisite dinner and flowers. For example, Nino Valenti, an obvious double for Dean Martin, having survived being fellated in the dark by Deanna Dunn, the "object of his adolescent dreams" (and a fictional match for Deanna

Durbin), somehow feels that his masculinity has been "insulted": "she treated him like a goddamn whore" (183).

However, the most sustained physical violence against women is reserved, as in the first *Godfather* film, for the Don's only daughter. Indeed, given that the following primal scene occurs in the wake of the wedding between Connie Corleone and Carlo Rizzo that initiates the narrative, it's a constitutive aspect of the novel's libidinal economy: "He had started her off just right. She had tried to keep that purse full of money presents for herself and he had given her a nice blue eye" (238). This violent act, of course, is only a pretext for the later, more vicious beating that Connie receives at the hands of Carlo.

Since the author retrospectively emphasizes the fact that Carlo takes real sadistic pleasure in beating his pregnant wife ("slapping the spoiled bitch around always made him feel good" [238]), I quote Puzo in full: "You lousy little guinea bitch, don't talk to me or I'll beat that kid right out of your belly. She looked frightened and this enraged him even more. He sprang from his chair and slapped her across the face, the blow leaving a red welt. With quick precision he slapped her three more times. He saw her upper lip split bloody and puff up. That stopped him. He didn't want to leave a mark" (237). When Connie later asks her father, the Don, if he ever hit his wife, he says, "She never gave me reason to beat her," to which explanation Mrs. Corleone gives her immediate, unqualified, and, crucially, silent assent: "And her mother had nodded and smiled" (238). That Carlo's beating of Connie is stamped with a maternal imprimatur speaks volumes not only about Mama Corleone's submissive role in the family but about the extraordinarily oppressive burden of representation that women in Puzo's novel bear.

Repetition Compulsion: From *The Godfather* to *The Sopranos*

I have rehearsed the above incidents from Puzo's novel because *The Sopranos*, as I observed earlier, itself rehearses *The Godfather*, albeit from a substantially different perspective. In this regard, the most spectacular as well as controversial moment in the series so far, at least in terms of the female characters, transpires in the "University" episode (III, 6), where Tracee (Ariel Kelly), one of the regular dancers at the Bada Bing!, is beaten to death by Ralph Cifaretto (Joe Pantoliano). The fact that Tracee is pregnant, like Connie Corleone, insinuates that the subtext is, again, *The Godfather* even as her special status raises the critical question of why pregnant women like Connie and Tracee seem to "make particularly inviting victims in both *The Godfather* and *The Sopranos*."[31]

Certainly, Tracee's death, even more so than the beatings that are ritually administered to Connie in the first *Godfather* film, foregrounds not only the highly charged relation between men and women in *The Sopranos* but the gendered divisions that subtend the familial world of the Mafia. The most basic division—immortalized in the oft-repeated line, "It's not personal, it's business"—is the split between the private domestic sphere, frequently represented in both *The Sopranos* and *The Godfather* by the classic spaces of the kitchen and dining room, and the public, male-dominated sphere associated with Satriale's and the Bada Bing! Though these two worlds are supposed to remain separate (since the whole point of just such "splits built into the social system" is to "protect the family from the brutality of business"[32]), sometimes, not to put too fine a point on it, they bleed into one another.

A subtle, comic instance of the conflation rather than separation between family and Family happens in the very first episode of the third season, "Mr. Ruggerio's Neighborhood" (III, 1)—written by Chase and directed by Allen Coulter—when FBI agents refer to the Sopranos as the "Bings" with Tony as "Der Bingle" (a reference to Bing Crosby), Meadow as "Princess Bing," and Anthony, Jr., as "Baby Bing." If this wordplay suggests that the Feds have way too much time on their hands, at a more fundamental level it reflects the deep connection between the ostensibly separate worlds of family and business: in this case, between the suburban upper-middle-class space of the Soprano home and the urban industrial space of the Bada Bing!

Of course, like Satriale's (which traumatic location we see Tony pass at the beginning of each show in his peregrination from the city to the suburbs), the Bada Bing! is one of the main places where the men do business. However, where Satriale's represents the bloody interface between the violence that is an occupational imperative for made men and (to remember Johnny Boy) the food they put on the table for their families, the Bada Bing! signifies the sometimes deadly conjunction between sex and death or, as elaborated in Freud's *Beyond the Pleasure Principle*, the erotic and aggressive drives. The issue that the "University" episode poses with exceptional force is whether one can in fact get "Beyond the Bada Bing!"[33]

Beyond the University

Writing about Livia, Carmela, Janice, and Meadow, Cindy Donatelli and Sharon Alward propose, referencing the finale of the first *Godfather* film where Michael closes the door in Kay's face, in the process definitively excluding her from his world, that "no one is ever going to slam the door in the face of these powerful, angry women."[34] While this claim is, I think, moot (Janice, for example, is badly beaten up by Russian thugs to the point of hospitalization for stealing Svetlana's leg in "Employee of the Month"), it's not surprising that doors, which both close off as well as allow access from one space to another, assume a key symbolic role in the "University" episode.

Thus, in a sequence set at the Bada Bing!, the camera pans slowly right from a couple of girls pole dancing to a female bartender giving change to a patron, then pans slowly back past a man and woman to Georgie opening a door to the VIP room. Another dancer, Debbie (Kelly Kole), wants in, but first, as Georgie makes plain, there is the price of admission: "VIP work, VIP prices. Fifty bucks to me plus a blowjob later on." After a shot of Tony ignoring Tracee and heading straight to one of the private rooms with another girl ("Wanna show you where the horse bit me"), Georgie opens the door to Ralphie, who has come flush with grandiose visions of *Gladiator* (2000) running through his head: "I have come to reclaim Rome for my people." When Georgie doesn't get the allusion ("Fuckin' *Gladiator*, ya fuck. The movie!"), Ralphie turns his attention to Tracee, who is dressed in an extremely revealing red dress. However, when she tries to kiss him hello, he spurns her advances: "Don't fuckin' kiss me. How many cocks you suck tonight?"

The *Gladiator* as opposed to *Spartacus* (1960) or *Dementia 13* (1963) reference is no passing allusion: Ralphie is spoiling for action, sexual or otherwise, and the Bada Bing! is his Coliseum.[35] Later, stubbing a cigar out on Georgie's chest ("Get the video. There'll be a quiz next week"), he announces to the room while mimicking Russell Crowe in *Gladiator*, "You're all dead men," before picking up a pool cue and repeatedly spearing him. The climax of the sequence occurs when the camera cuts on action from a traveling shot of Ralphie swinging a heavy padlock chain menacingly at Georgie to a shot of Tony in the midst of getting a very vigorous blowjob (this, too, is a form of labor) back to Georgie in the foreground holding his eye, crying "I'm blind!" In the background, meanwhile, Ralphie is trying to cover his mouth to keep from laughing hysterically. The contrast between Tony and Ralphie is striking: If Tony is intent, before he is rudely interrupted by Ralphie's antics, on enjoying the sexual perks that come with being a mob boss, Ralphie gets off on publicly emasculating Georgie, reducing him to a "cry baby" and "pussy boy."

Once Ralphie has been dispatched to the hospital with Georgie, Tracee, now that her man has left, approaches Tony to ask about the "breakfast" date-nut bread she made for him as "thanks" for advising her about her sick son, Danny. Tony, though, rebuffs her again. The last shot of the sequence, which shows Tracee walking all alone toward the door of the VIP room, and the ensuing bridge shot of Meadow coming through the door of her dorm room at Columbia University, visually connects the two women even as it emphasizes the very different lives they lead: while Meadow is ensconced in a dorm room at an exclusive Ivy League university, studying or having safe sex with Noah, Tracee is a working girl, stripping on the main stage at the Bada Bing! or dispensing sexual favors in the VIP room.

If doors are a recurring spatial motif throughout "University," "bread," which is the final word of the opening sequence, is a significant thematic one.[36] In fact, Tracee poses a problem for Tony precisely because she comes bearing bread, which is a gift that could potentially involve him in an overly familiar rather than, as he reminds her, strictly impersonal, "employer/employee thing." Moreover, if one understands "bread" as slang for money, Tony cannot accept Tracee's thank-you ("You can't be doin' stuff like this") since to do so would be to reverse the terms of their relationship, one where he receives his "taste" from Tracee only indirectly, via the mediated hierarchical chain of command that, like the imperial Roman army on which it is based, defines the Mafia. Silvio (Steven van Zandt), her immediate boss, stresses this, the verboten character of her goodwill gesture, chastising her: "No good."

Tragically, Tracee never really seems to comprehend this unwritten rule. Later, approaching Tony again in the main room of the Bada Bing!, dressed this time only in a g-string, she asks him about her new braces: "Well, what do you think?" However, because Tracee is completely defined by her physical assets (here, her breasts) Tony has absolutely no idea what she is talking about: "What am I looking at?" Tony's reflexive recourse to the visual register, coupled with the dual male point of view (Tony's and Silvio's), accents her abject status as an object to looked at, as does Silvio's firm, repeated reprimands against "fraternizing": "I didn't shell out three crackers for you to be modelling your teeth. Get to work." In a poignant refrain (consider, for instance, Meadow's casual disregard of her dental appointments), the camera frames Tracee as she walks, alone, to the stage to start dancing.

That Tracee is only the sum of her body parts is made crystal clear by the dialogue that Tony and Silvio exchange as they stand at the bar:

Silvio: Usually it's fake tits they want.

Tony: She don't need those—that's for sure.

Silvio: The kid's a thoroughbred.

Silvio's casual reference to Tracee as a domesticated animal, one used for sport, suggests that the Bada Bing! "girls" are "something less than human," their "body parts, whether silicon boobs or braces," mere "investments."[37] In other words, Tracee is valuable and to be respected precisely to the extent that, like a racehorse, she embodies and exhibits her status as a commodity-body. Inasmuch as Silvio is also "juicing" her by way of a loan for her braces, better teeth or breasts basically means more money for him and (this is pivotal) for Tony as well.

To be sure, Tony does not have sex with Tracee, as we later see Ralphie doing, from behind, in a private part of the VIP room: "What, are you cryin'? I'll give you something to cry about." However, the brief scene that immediately precedes this one, where we see a police officer receiving a "free" blowjob from her ("Watch the braces, honey"), reveals, since we earlier saw Tony in the very same situation, that he's not above or beyond the base circuit of exploitation that enslaves Tracee. One cannot, perhaps, emphasize this point enough—that is to say, Tony's complicity in Tracee's fate—since in the "University" episode as a whole, he appears distinctly more sympathetic to her than either Silvio or Ralphie. For example, when Tracee shows up one bright breezy morning in the parking lot of the Bada Bing! to tell Tony she's pregnant with Ralphie's baby (significantly, Tony is shown exiting the building counting money), he initially tries to beg off: "I don't get involved in affairs of the heart." Once she confesses she's got no one else to talk to, though (dialogue that resonates with numerous scenes in the episode, in particular one where we see Meadow snuggling up to Carmela in bed to talk about her problems with Noah), Tony counsels her against keeping the baby since Ralphie, as he understates the matter, is no "Father Knows Best."

Still, Tony's other, no doubt well-intentioned bit of advice for Tracee—"You're young, you've still got your figure, you're making money"—effectively recondemns her to her dead-end life. Thus, when Tracee doesn't show up for work at the Bada Bing! because she's been sick, Silvio goes to Ralphie's place and forcibly retrieves her ("You know how many girls would kill for the opportunity you got?"), then slaps her around for talking back to him: "Listen to me, you little fuck. Until you pay what you owe, that shaved twat of yours belongs to me." The combination of physical violence and abusive epithet exposes Silvio for the misogynist character that he is. The last shot of the sequence, a long shot of Ralphie framed in a window laughing convulsively, not only harkens back to his blinding of Georgie but looks forward to Tracee's imminent demise.

Post-Mortem: Bad Love

Tracee's death, to cite the "Amour Fou" (III, 2) episode of *The Sopranos*, is not "cinematic."[38] Or perhaps, as Laura Mulvey was the first to demonstrate, such sadistic scopophilia remains central to the sorts of visual pleasure that propel mainstream narrative film and television.[39] For if it's true that the women of *The Sopranos* are familiar with the "patriarchal script" of the *Godfather* series and *GoodFellas*,[40] the same can also be said for the men. Consequently, although Ralphie's continuing mimicry of Russell Crowe in *Gladiator* is at odds with the modern gangster figure favored by Tony and his soldiers, for Ralphie the hyper-masculinity associated with gladiatorial combat remains the prototype.

Therefore, when Tracee tells Ralphie to fuck off in the VIP room of the Bada Bing!, right after he has finished telling a Custer-and-Indians joke to an audience of made men, he retorts, "That's how you talk to a man in front of his friends?" Though Tracee's rejoinder ("What man?") echoes her earlier response to Silvio's lecture about "opportunity" ("What? Working for you?"), Ralphie momentarily appears to take her remark comically in stride: "Women, women, women." In fact, following Tracee outside, he not only tells her he's going to take care of her when she's "nine months pregnant," he even reciprocates her declaration of love: "I love you too, baby."

The key word here is "baby," which not unlike "bread" in the first sequence, has powerful subtextual reverberations in the episode as a whole. So, after promising Tracee that if their baby is a girl, they'll name it after her, Ralphie's gloss on this happy-ever-after domestic scenario— "This way, she can grow up to be a cocksuckin' slob just like her mother"—brings savagely home both his sadistic character and the pathetic nature of Tracee's romantic illusions. Humiliated, Tracee spits in his face ("That's right. Get it all out, you little whore"), then slaps him, drawing blood. Ralphie, in turn, slaps her with the back of his hand, at which point Tracee, who's been backed up against a guardrail, exclaims, "Make you feel good? You feel like a man?" With this direct affront against his masculinity, Ralphie punches Tracee in the face, the stomach, then—as the camera cuts to a low-angle shot that accentuates his dominance and Tracee's defenselessness—hits her again and again and again.

The prolonged duration of this scene, together with the fact that Tracee is pregnant and does not resist, makes it an especially wrenching one to watch. Earlier in the same episode, Caitlin, Meadow's roommate (Ari Gaynor), had queried, apropos of Tod Browning's *Freaks* (1932), "Why is other people's pain a source of amusement?"[41] If Ralphie is not exactly amused by Tracee's death, his blasé demeanor, reinforced by the cocktail music playing in the Bada Bing! when he goes back inside (Dean Martin's "Powder Your Face with Sunshine"), suggests that it won't cause him much pain either. One is reminded of Tom Hagen's response to the death of a Las Vegas working girl in the second *Godfather* film: "It'll be as though she never existed."[42]

Though Tony's first question to Ralphie after he has seen Tracee's battered and bloodied body—"How fuckin' dare you?"—is rife with ambiguity, his immediate response to Tracee's death is not. After knocking a drink out of Ralphie's hand, Tony punches him repeatedly, as if to make him pay somehow for his outrageous behavior. At the same time, if the close-up of Tony's face through a chain-link fence as he pummels Ralphie recalls the chain used on Georgie, it also signals that, blinded by rage, Tony has violated a cardinal rule of his subculture (which is that made men like Ralphie can't be touched), a serious violation of the rules that puts Tony himself in a precarious position. Hence Ralphie's first question to Tony after being attacked by him: "Are you out of your fuckin' mind, layin' your hands on me?"

The appropriateness of Tony's own violent response to Tracee's death is, however, confirmed by Paulie (Tony Sirico), who says of Ralphie, "Cocksucker was way out of line." More importantly, whereas Tony's epitaph on Tracee's life—"Twenty years old, this girl"—reflects a pained awareness of how abridged her youth was, Paulie's reaction ("That too") hints that for him as well as the other executive members of the Bada Bing!, Ralphie's real act of transgression was not so much beating a young woman to death as having disrespected the Bing! The closing shot of the sequence, a long shot of the rear of the Bada Bing! with an open sewer pipe in the foreground and Tracee's lifeless body lost somewhere in the shadows of the background, puts a distinctly grim twist on Meadow's earlier comment to Noah's father at dinner, at a chic restaurant in Manhattan, that her own father's métier is "waste management" or, as she hastily amends it, "environmental clean-up."

D-I-S-R-E-S-P-E-C-T: Tele-Psychoanalytic Metatext

If the psychoanalytic shot/countershot between Tony and Dr. Melfi is the "central structuring device" of *The Sopranos*,[43] the fact that there is only one such encounter in the "University" episode denotes its significance. In the wake of Tracee's death, Tony has come—not, as it were, heavy but with a heavy heart—to Melfi's office with his wife, Carmela. When Melfi comments that he is "being particularly quiet," Tony replies, "A young man who worked for us . . . died a work-related death. Sad when they go so young."

Tony's considered response to Melfi's question belies, of course, the real facts, facts he intuitively knows he cannot share with his wife: that the "young man" is in fact a young woman, and that her death is only "work-related" in the most euphemistic sense. Tony's repeated stress on the word "work" also betrays his inability to come to terms with the utter senselessness of Tracee's death, which he was unable to prevent and for which he feels personally responsible. From another, gendered perspective, the importance of the scene, abbreviated as it is, derives from its amplification of Tony's overdetermined relation vis-à-vis women. He may not be, relative to someone like Tracee, a "vulnerable object" of the gaze,[44] but sitting there in Melfi's office between his wife and therapist, caught between the mandates of the "talking cure" and the imperatives of the personal sphere, he looks, despite his obvious physical size, small, diminished.

This said, it would be a mistake I think to argue that the actions of Tony and his friends are framed by a "*feminist* metatext."[45] The conclusion to the "University" episode appears, for instance, to invite a totally opposed reading. In the penultimate scene, set in the main room at the Bada Bing!, two dancers speculate about Tracee's whereabouts: "I heard she went outside with Ralphie and never came back." "Who knows, maybe she quit." Debbie, who's been listening in on the conversation, advises, however, silence, invoking the code of *omertà* that constrains her bosses: "Do yourself a favor. Keep what you hear to yourself."

The final scene of the episode, which reprises the Kinks' "Livin' on a Thin Line," provides a classical, if unambiguously downbeat, resolution. Georgie is initiating another new girl into the ground rules of the VIP room: "Lotta high rollers, lotta big tips. You want in . . . 50 bucks to me plus a blowjob later on." A young woman has been beaten to death, but it's business as usual at the Bada Bing! Indeed, if Tony's sadness, simultaneously articulated and masked in the reasonably safe, therapeutic space of Melfi's office, suggests that he, at least, remains haunted by Tracee's death, the lyrics from "Livin' on a Thin Line" allow little hope for change in the base male order of things: "I see change / But inside we're the same as we ever were."

An exchange between Tony and Ralphie in "He Is Risen" (III, 8) confirms this dispiriting dénouement. Ralphie, reiterating Tony's own initial reaction to Tracee's death, finally offers an apology, admitting that he "disrespected the Bing and the girl," an equation that reduces Tracee's death to a serious, if passing, violation of the sacred male space of the Bada Bing! Johnny "Sack" Sacrimoni's (Vincent Curatola) response to Tony's palpable remorse ("You know what he did? That poor girl just had her twentieth birthday") is even more dismissive: "But she was a whore, Tony." Against the last categorical judgment (where to be a whore is to be beyond contempt[46]), there is only the unspoken eloquence of the visual register: a shot of Meadow approaching Tony, like some ghostly apparition of Tracee, with a cake. This private moment exposes, like a raw nerve, the deep paternal and familial sources of Tony's empathy for Tracee; it also touches on one of the hard, ugly truths of *The Godfather*: that sometimes the battle lines between family and business break down, sometimes "civilians" such as "problem" women like Tracee get hurt.

Analysis Interminable

Any analysis of *The Sopranos* must, at least at this moment, remain provisional. In a larger, more profound sense, analysis itself, as Freud famously insisted, is interminable, and the primary "text" of the series, which now runs to sixty-five episodes, makes it, combined with its rich array of self-reflexive and citational devices, an especially complex object.

Given the latter formal aspects, it should come as no surprise that even content as disturbing as Tracee's death by beating in the "University" episode is subjected, true to the dialectical shot/countershot structure of *The Sopranos*, to self-reflexive stratagems. So, earlier in the episode, entertainment lawyer Len Tannenbaum (Michael Garfield) corrects Meadow at dinner, politely informing her that one of his clients, Dick Wolf, is not a "sportscaster" but the producer of *Law & Order: Special Victims Unit* (USA, 1999–present). The citation of the NBC prime-time spinoff cuts both ways: even as it presents an oblique commentary on Tracee's status (she is no "special victim" and her anonymous death will fall well below the radar of the forces of law and order), it satirizes broadcast television's generic attempts to realistically capture, among other things, the physical abuse of women.

The Sopranos' programmatic appropriation of the medium of cinema is a crucial component of this punctual, intricate sense of citationality. Thus, when Noah and Meadow are discussing Caitlin's inability to reconcile her small-town Oklahoma upbringing with everyday life in New York City (represented in the "University" episode by a black bag lady with newspaper for underwear), Noah blithely says, invoking his and Meadow's Los Angeles and New Jersey roots, respectively, "We're kind of used to the mean streets." Here, the invocation of *Mean Streets* (1973) not only explicitly references Scorsese's seminal film as a principal source of *The Sopranos'* graphic depiction of mob violence, the allusion mirrors Noah's own smug, film-pervasive take on reality, one constitutionally incapable of comprehending the sorts of economically derived problems that beset someone like Tracee.

Still, in the context of Tracee's death, the most significant example of citationality and self-reflexivity is undoubtedly Tony's impromptu but highly motivated killing of Ralphie in "Whoever Did This" (written, like "Employee of the Month" [III, 4], by Robin Green and Mitchell Burgess [IV, 9]). In this episode, Tony confronts Ralphie at his house after having learned that their horse, Pie-O-My (which earlier we had seen Tony sitting up with late into the night like a concerned parent), had to be put down after an "accidental" stable fire. Ralphie's improvident remark about Pie-O-My's painful demise—"It's an animal. This is a hundred grand apiece"—sends Tony into a murderous rage. Though the climatic action derives its visceral force from its extended deferment (the audience having long been primed for the whacking of Ralphie), it derives not a little signification from its ravelling of a number of intertextual threads.

In other words, if Tony's seemingly irrational love for Pie-O-My ("beautiful, innocent creature") recalls the stereotype of the tough guy with a soft spot for animals, the figure of the racehorse reminds us, via displacement, of Silvio's pointed designation of Tracee as a "thoroughbred." Moreover, while Tony's killing of Ralphie by repeatedly knocking his head against a kitchen floor echoes the latter's battering of Tracee, the consequences of Tony's violent act narratively resolves Ralphie's obsessive oratorical sampling of *Gladiator* first introduced in "Employee of the Month" ("What we do in life echoes in eternity") since Ralphie ends up beheaded and Tony gets his revenge for Tracee's death in *this* life. The grace note that concludes "Whoever Did This" is at once powerful and subtle: having separately disposed, with Christopher's aid, of Ralphie's head and body, Tony stops to reflect—for a brief, pregnant moment—before a picture of Tracee posted on a bulletin board in the women's dressing room at the Bada Bing!

Finally, both Tracee's and Ralphie's deaths are subject to the complicated logic of seriality. For instance, while the rape of Melfi in the "Employee of the Month" episode (directed by John Patterson) precedes the above events, it also retroactively inflects our reading of them. More specifically, in the aforementioned episode, Melfi is brutally raped in the stairwell of her office parking garage. However, even though the perpetrator, Jesus Rossi (Mario Polit), an "employee of the month" at a local sandwich shop, WrapNation,[47] is identified, he's released on a "legal thing" (a misplaced evidence kit has "fouled up the chain of custody").

Later, Melfi has an empowering dream, which she subsequently recounts to Dr. Kupferberg (Peter Bogdanovich), in which she is saved from being raped again by Rossi by a Rottweiler, a dog that is a "direct descendent," according to Melfi, of the one used by "Roman armies to guard their camps." In the course of her session with Dr. Kupferberg, Melfi herself eventually comes to the realization that the Rottweiler is a stand-in for Tony (whom we've previously seen wielding an ax), though she's also compelled to admit that despite the fact that she's not about to "break the social contract," she took a "certain satisfaction"[48] in seeing her assailant get what was coming to him—if only in a dream: "No feeling has ever been so sweet as to see that pig beg and plead and scream for his life."

The critical moment in the episode—and, arguably, one of the most revelatory moments in the series so far—occurs when Melfi must choose between yielding to the temptation to tell Tony about the rape (and thereby satisfy her violent desire for revenge) or respect the flawed but indispensable protocols of what Dr. Kupferberg calls "civilization." In this, the second session of the episode, Melfi, sans cane, manages to maintain her professional demeanor until Tony announces that he's willing to try behavior modification therapy. After an exchange of portentous exchanges, Melfi suddenly breaks down and, as Tony walks over to comfort her, the scene shifts from shot/countershot to a master two-shot marked by a severe asymmetrical imbalance, with both Melfi and Tony positioned to the far left of the screen. The psychoanalytic relation—and, more profoundly, the value of cultural controls versus the forbidden wish for vengeance, for vigilante justice—hangs, for a moment, in the balance.

The resolution turns on a dialogue-prompted return to the compositional principle at the psychoanalytic heart of *The Sopranos*. As the camera reframes to a medium two-shot, Tony, his hand overlaid on Melfi's, gently repeats over and over again like a lullaby, "Tell me, what's the matter?" It's not until Melfi tells him—"Go sit over there. We'll do this. It's OK, go on"—that he finally retreats, confused, to his seat opposite her. The episode climaxes with another charged series of shot/reverse shots between the two, the last of which, a tight close-up of Melfi, is punctuated by her emphatic refusal of the savage aggressivity behind Tracee's beating and her own rape[49] as well as Tony's understandable but ultimately retributive killing of Ralphie. To Tony's closing impassioned question, "You want to say something?," Melfi's answer is a simple and definitive "No."

Fig. 14. *Et Tu*, Tony: Dr. Jennifer Melfi (Lorraine Bracco), Tony Soprano's psychoanalytical "better self," in her office.

Martini Shot: "Hall Hath No Fury"

With the conclusion of season five of *The Sopranos*, the devices that distinguished the series in the first four seasons remain central to its televisual vitality. While the titles of individual episodes ("All Happy Families" [V, 4], "Sentimental Education" [V, 6], etc.) reference high culture as embodied in canonical Western literature (here, Tolstoy and Flaubert, respectively), the show's penchant for self-reflexivity is evident in episodes such as "Test Dream" (V, 11) where the mise-en-scène is dominated by television screens.

Seriality, however, remains the one indispensable element of the program if only because it necessitates change at the level of plot and character. Thus, Tony Blundetto's (Steve Buscemi) release from prison in the "Two Tonys" (V, 1) precipitates the conflicted, interfamilial dynamics between Tony and Johnny Sack that constitute one of the dominant narrative arcs of the season. Climactic events, especially in conjunction with "cliffhangers," are also, of course, a staple of continuing series, satisfying audiences' desire for moments of intense emotionality. Hence the "terror and pity" that resulted from the sudden execution-style death of Adriana, whose character, beloved by many for her Jimmy Choos and ever-changing coiffure, was killed off for "ratting out" Christopher to the Feds.

Still, the link between seriality and audiences ultimately begs the question, Why do viewers tune in to a show week after week, season after season? There are any number of reasons why *The Sopranos* continues to be must-see TV (filmic look, gangster genre, and so forth), but I would be remiss if I did not mention that one of the indubitable pleasures of the show is its overt refusal of so-called political correctness. In fact, the series' real jouissance derives in no small part from the friction between two competing impulses: its fidelity to the characteristic, if regressive, behavior of the Mafia subculture it so faithfully documents and its ostensibly ironic cognizance of the discursive, distinctly liberal protocols that govern contemporary American social life. The result is a guilty—or, I suppose, not so guilty—pleasure where the audience's ethical-libidinal itch is at once inflamed and scratched.

The Sopranos' frequent, and flagrant, violation of politically correct codes is also inextricable from its insistent employment of stereotypes. For example, it's not simply that the show draws on stereotypical notions of ethnicity (in this case, Italian American or, more precisely, Sicilian American identity) but that the main characters consistently define themselves in stereotypical opposition to other, non-Sicilian groups and subcultures. This identitarian difference can be seen in the way that race—in particular, African American culture—is performed in the series. A crucial episode in this context is "Unidentified Black Males" (V, 9) where Tony B. explains why he's favoring his right foot which he injured while shooting, against Tony S.'s express wishes, Joe Peeps (Joe Maruzzo) and an unnamed prostitute: "Two black guys jumped me outside a bar." On one hand, Tony B.'s lie—which doesn't fool anyone, least of all Tony—highlights how pathetic and dim-witted he is, as if all the years in the pen have irreparably dulled his imagination. On the other hand, his generic invocation of "two black guys" reinforces stereotypical notions about African Americans (e.g., blacks are the primary cause of inner-city violence against whites).

It probably goes without saying that the above racial conceit—"unidentified black males"—is not an isolated one; indeed, it effectively structures season five as a whole. In "Long-Term Parking," the penultimate episode of the season, Tony S. calls "TB"—he's hiding somewhere in upstate New York after having killed Billy Leotardo (Chris Caldovino) and injured his brother, Phil (Frank Vincent)—and confesses that the night his cousin was arrested, he passed out and injured his head after a heated argument with Livia. Tony S.'s admission that the real cause of his absence that fateful night wasn't certain "unidentified black males" but his mother (which he has earlier admitted to Melfi in therapy) suggests a deep libidinal connection in *The Sopranos* between maternality and black masculinity.

This nexus or constellation also returns us to what I take to be the series' core problem, which is not so much the external difference between, say, blacks and whites as the internal one between masculinity and femininity. Tony himself suggests as much when, in the "Two Tonys," he tells Melfi, "Forget the way Tony Soprano makes his way in the world. There's two Tony Sopranos." In other words, just as there are two Tonys (Tony B. and Tony S.), so there are two sides to Tony S.: the hyper-masculine "boss" and another, more emotionally available self. Ironically, the latter Tony is considerably more apparent in his relations with other men than with women. For example, he seems perfectly willing to threaten the welfare of his family (in both senses of the word) for the sake of his friend from childhood, "TB," whom he unconditionally protects like a brother or sister: like, that is, his other, more vulnerable self.

The final two episodes of the season rehearse the ongoing battle between the sexes, a war that is arguably the repressed "other" of Tony's feud with the New York Family represented by Carmine Lupertazzi (Tony Lip) and, later, upon his death, Johnny Sack. In "Long-Term Parking," Adriana, as noted earlier, is executed by Silvio for talking to the Feds and, in the final episode, "All Due Respect" (V, 13), Tony S. finally kills Tony B. with a shotgun blast to the head. In the former episode, Ade's fleeting fantasy of escape, driving west away from New Jersey in her Thunderbird with only her red suitcase in the backseat to accompany her, epitomizes just how restricted her sense of agency is. She can no more leave the life she has made with Chris, however miserable, than her fiancé can escape, on penalty of death, his fate as a solider in the Soprano Family.

Significantly, we do not see Adriana's death as it transpires in a secluded, wooded area off the highway. One imagines that the two shots, preceded by Silvio's and his subculture's preferred valediction for such women ("cunt"), are to the head and are not, to recite "Amour Fou," "cinematic." However, after Tony S. has killed his cousin, the shot stays on Tony B.'s blood-spattered face, as if to tangibly italicize the brutal code that rules their Family.

And yet, for all of Tony S.'s hand wringing about having to whack his cousin (Tony to Johnny in the waning moments of season five: "I paid enough, I paid a lot"), Tony B.'s death, curiously enough, is devoid of the pathos that marks Adriana's: Ade's is the one that feels like a death in the family. Consequently, Tony's later talk with Chris, who is holed up in a cheap hotel room and who bitterly laments Adriana's betrayal of him to the Feds, bespeaks subtle undercurrents of fear and rage. Tony S.'s final word about Adriana (whom at one point, in the drug-fueled throes of his divorce, he befriended) is as abusive as it is abbreviated: "cunt." The fact that this is the exact same word that Tony used earlier in the season with Melfi (when it finally sank in that she would have nothing to do with him) cements the deadly subterranean link in *The Sopranos* between sexuality and violence. Cunts get killed.

In the end, Tony himself is forced to run from the law when the Feds raid Johnny Sack's home where the two have met to discuss the post–Tony B. state of things. Tony S.'s concluding peroration on *la règle du jeu* oratorically punctuates the season even as it marks, in absentia, the constitutive "other" role and place of women: "What we are here for in the end is to put food on the table for our families, our *sons*, our future."

Emphasis mine.

Reprise

Tony Soprano, Meet Buffy
the Vampire Slayer

Light art as such . . . is not a decadent form.

> —Theodor Adorno and Max Horkheimer,
> "The Culture Industry"

The work of art still has something in common
with enchantment.

> —Adorno and Horkheimer,
> "The Culture Industry"

Who can say this ended well
All those secrets you've been concealing
Say you're happy now—once more with feeling.

> —Sweet, "Once More with Feeling,"
> *Buffy the Vampire Slayer* (VI, 7)

Telephilia is frequently affiliated with the ineluctable dynamics of the family romance. There were six siblings in my immediate family, and most of my enduring memories of television, whether it was the eagerly awaited fall prime-time shows or Saturday morning cartoons, special annual screenings of *The Wizard of Oz* or *The Ten Commandments*, cannot be separated from my childhood and adolescence growing up in western New York, first in Niagara Falls, then in Lewiston, a suburb of the "honeymoon capital of the world."

This autohistorical telephilia is not confined, though, to the distant past, nor does it survive solely in the form of those habits and rituals we adopt early on as spectators, but lives on in current TV passions and predilections. For example, I know that my enthusiasm for *The Sopranos* has not a little to do with the fact that "Don" Stefano Magaddino lived right around the corner from me, on "Mafia Row," on a "posh street in the northern suburb of Lewiston."[1] ("Posh"? Nice maybe, but definitely not posh.) Although my parents were and are devout Irish Austrian Catholics (of the liberal Vatican II variety), I spent my adolescence running, sometimes literally, with Mafia kids, playing penny-ante poker night and day and, later, in high school, acting as a two-bit bookie during football season.

To be frank, my "Mafia" friends never talked explicitly about La Cosa Nostra, but they were not above joking about the "black hand," and we all knew, just as certainly as there would be fish sticks and french fries on Friday, that Magaddino was the boss of the Buffalo Family. The Don himself (whom I cannot disassociate from the long black Cadillac limousines he was chauffeured in) was a mythical figure in my neighborhood, so much so that I can't remember whether, playing hard ball in the street, I actually saw a line drive bounce off the picture window of his house as if it were made of rubber, or if it's a secondhand story I've repeated so many times over the years that it's acquired the certainty of truth. (The fact that, in 1936, a bomb intended for Magaddino detonated in the wrong house, killing his sister, or that, in 1958, a hand grenade hurled through his kitchen window failed to kill him only because it did not explode suggests, however, that my memory may not be entirely unreliable.)

What I do know for certain is that the only time I saw the Don— a man who was an original member of the National Commission, who arranged the famous summit meeting of Mob bosses at Apalachin in 1957 (which forced J. Edgar Hoover to recant his claim that there was no such thing as organized crime), and who had the longest tenure as a crime boss (fifty-two years)—he looked as wrinkled and harmless as any other octogenarian, even if he was the "grand old man of La Cosa Nostra."[2]

Yet as *The Sopranos* regularly illustrates with extraordinary wit and acuity, you can be a stone-cold killer, as both Tony is and Don Magaddino no doubt once was, and still seem like a nice enough ("wise") guy. Moreover, just as the history of Niagara Falls and, to some extent, that of my family is intertwined with that of the Mafia (the day the Feds closed off Dana Drive, which bordered our backyard, and arrested the Don for racketeering remains etched in my memory as if it happened yesterday), so *The Sopranos*, which is the definitive contemporary expression of the gangster genre, is not without its share of familiar soap-operatic moments.

This hybridity, where genres are recombined and retrofitted to "attract niche markets and coalitional audiences" (soap opera + gangster genre = *The Sopranos*),[3] is in fact a dominant feature of television in the cable and satellite age and also describes cult programs such as *Buffy the Vampire Slayer*. While the extensive, albeit stylized, martial-arts violence on *Buffy* would appear to distinguish it from the more natural-istic sort featured on *The Sopranos*, the series' frequent recourse to the "conventions of the soap opera, horror, comedy, music video, action and sci-fi genres,"[4] ally it with, in addition to its steady employment of citational and self-reflexive devices, the televisual logic of postmodern TV. These traits—in particular, generic hybridity—are, in turn, a prod-uct not only of the disintegration of the canonical difference between film and TV (*Buffy*, of course, derives from the 1992 film of the same name) but of the historical antithesis between high and pop culture.

Thus, Tony Soprano and his crew, like the "reservoir dogs" in Tarantino's début film (think "Madonna"), do not exist in some wholly self-contained world apart from our postmodern, mass-mediated condi-tion. As Patricia Pender remarks in the course of arguing about whether Buffy is a slayer or "girly girl," "Buffy is strong, sexy, and subversive, not despite her immersion in popular culture but because of it."[5] Indeed, it is only within just such a context, where TV both is a part of and comments on popular culture, that the most compelling political and aesthetic issues raised by shows such as *The Sopranos* and *Buffy* can be posed: Is Tony So-prano a loving, devoted family man or a heartless monster, a mobster or a mensch? Is Buffy feminist or femme, demon-dusting warrior woman or yet another cleavage-baring embodiment of femme-inanity?[6]

Buffy the Vampire Slayer first aired on The WB from 1997 to 2001, then on UPN from 2001 to 2003 with Sarah Michelle Gellar in the lead role as Buffy Anne Summers, the Slayer of Sunnydale. She is aided in her daily battle to keep the omnipresent demons and vampires at bay by her Watcher, Rupert Giles (Anthony S. Head), and the members of the Scooby gang, the Slayerettes, composed, in season six, of Willow (Alyson Hannigan), Xander (Nicholas Brendon), Tara (Amber Benson), Anya (Emma Caulfield), and Buffy's sister, Dawn (Michelle Trachtenberg). With its high production values, its "glossy visual style, fluid camera-work and artistically choreographed fight sequences," *Buffy* is a prime example, like *The Sopranos*, of "quality prime-time programming."[7]

Although the series' episodes were typically written and directed by various hands and season six was coexecutive produced by Marti Noxon (who assumed dual control with creator Joss Whedon when the show moved to UPN), "Once More With Feeling" (VI, 7) stands out among *Buffy* episodes because it was written and directed by Whedon (with music by Christophe Beck and Jesse Tobias). It also stands out from other critically acclaimed episodes such as "Hush" (IV, 10) and "The Body" (V, 16) because it does not simply "break the established format"—as, for example, in "Hush" where the characters are mute—but represents a radical generic transformation.[8]

Fig. 15. The Scooby Gang: Spike (James Marsters), Anya (Emma Caulfield), Tara (Amber Benson), Rupert Giles (Anthony S. Head), Buffy Summers (Sarah Michelle Gellar), Xander (Nicholas Brendon), and Willow (Alyson Hannigan) ponder the future of demon slaying in *Buffy the Vampire Slayer*.

The genre in question is the musical, and Whedon has talked both passionately and knowledgably about the influence of this genre on the production of "Once More with Feeling," which ranges from classic '50s MGM films such as *The Band Wagon* (1952) to the work of Stephen Sondheim ("I'm a Stephen Sondheim fanatic, born and bred. I know every show of his backward!"[9]). The other, more immediate influence on Whedon's decision to mount a musical episode of the show (and one that speaks to its recurrent scrambling of high- and popular-cultural codes) is Shakespeare.[10] Hence the opening verse of Buffy's climactic song set in the Bronze where the episode's nemesis, Sweet (Hinton Battle), sits in regal, zoot-suited splendor with his "queen," Dawn: "Life's a show and we all play our parts."[11]

The main premise of "Once More with Feeling" is that under the spell of Sweet (who has been summoned, innocently enough, by Xander—"Just thought there would be music and songs"), the main characters' secrets and feelings are revealed. The external problem is not so much that overnight all the world has turned into a musical sound stage, Sunnydale as Avon with music and lyrics by Sondheim, but that certain people, once dancing, can't stop. Consequently, there is a smash cut from Dawn at the Magic Box questioning the gang's anxiety—"Come on, songs, dancing. . . . What's wrong with that?"—to an alley at night where a man dances, *"Red Shoe*-like," faster and faster until he spontaneously combusts.

Whedon's passing reference to "The Red Shoes," the conceit of which tale provides the underlying dramatic impetus of the episode, is typical of *Buffy*'s hyperallusiveness. Hans Christian Andersen's "The Red Shoes" has, of course, long since entered into "theatrical mythology,"[12] but the complex intertextuality of "Once More With Feeling" is apparent in more subtle ways as well. For example, the dialogue, true to Whedon's interest in the film and Broadway musical, references everything from Carmen Miranda movies ("dance with coconuts") to *The Music Man* ("Seventy-six bloody trombones"), while the dance numbers recall such varied films as *Singin' in the Rain* (1952), *West Side Story* (1961), and *Absolute Beginners* (1986).

This pervasive citationality is coupled with an equally pervasive sense of ironic reflexivity that has been a staple of the series and a fan favorite since its inception. So, in an establishing scene at the Magic Box after the members of the gang confess that they've all recently "burst into song," Giles replies, referring to his own experience the night before in his hotel room, "That would explain the huge backing orchestra I couldn't see" (an allusion to the use of nondiegetic orchestral scores in musicals).

Still, the paradigmatic postmodern line in "Once More with Feeling" (and my personal favorite) occurs when Anya, reflecting on "I'll Never Tell," her prenuptial, Noel Coward-like musical duet with Xander, says, "Our number was clearly a retro pastiche that's never gonna be a breakaway hit." If this quip reflects Whedon's disappointment that Buffy never became a blockbuster program with the attendant Top-20 Nielsen ratings, it also sounds remarkably like postmodern theory. And, in fact, the episode dramatizes the play of theory in the first musical number set in the Magic Box when each member of the gang speculates about what's causing all the commotion: Giles ("I've got a theory / That it's . . . a dancing demon"), Willow ("I've got a theory / Some kid's dreamin'"), Anya ("I've got a theory / It could be bunnies"[13]), and, finally, Buffy ("I've got a theory / It doesn't matter").

"Once More with Feeling" may be a musical or, more properly, a "retro pastiche" of a Broadway/Hollywood musical complete with all the televisual touches (including wide-screen photography), but as the note of world weariness in Buffy's verses suggests, the episode, like the series as a whole, is not without its serious (melo-) dramatic aspects. The most serious subplot, outside of Buffy's dismay at having to learn how to live in this world after having come back from the dead, involves Willow and her partner, Tara. Previously on Buffy, Willow had tried to cast a spell to make Tara forget the argument the two had had about Willow's growing addiction to magic ("All the Way" [VI, 6]).[14]

In "Once More with Feeling," both the power dynamics and sexual-romantic elements of the latter relationship (the two first met at a Wiccan meeting) are explored. First, while the gang is assembled at the Magic Box trying to solve the mystery behind all the singing and dancing, Willow and Tara fabricate an excuse to go off by themselves, cutting through a park on their way to the house (where, importantly, the first scene of the episode is set and where Tara finds, under her pillow, what she takes to be a flower left for her by Willow). Just as it is Willow's idea to escape the Magic Box, so too she uses some boys' passing gaze at Tara to express her sexual desire. Tara: "What are they looking at?" Willow: "The hotness of you, doofus." The rhetorical combination of sexiness ("hotness") and geek speak ("doofus") is classic Buffy.

The light comic banter—including Tara pretending that she's suddenly been converted ("Oh my god. I'm cured. I want the boys")—is, however, prelude to a musical number, "Under Your Spell," that glimmers darkly with ambiguity and uncertainty. Thus, the deep amorousness reflected in the lovers' final, presong exchange—Willow: "You can't imagine what [those boys] see in you" / Tara: "I know what they see in me. You"[15]—almost immediately modulates in the second verse of "Under Your Spell" to troubling feelings of doubt and fear: "Now I'm bathed in light / Something just ain't right."

Fig. 16. Spellbound: Tara and Willow study each other in "Once More with Feeling."

With its play on the closeted darkness of Tara's life before she met Willow ("I've lived my life in shadow / Never the sun on my face"),[16] "Under Your Spell" draws, in fact, on the long-standing association between love and magic, one that is amplified in the context of Tara and Willow's relationship by the additional popular-cultural association between witchcraft and lesbianism. Accordingly, the following lyrics, which seem wholly placid, hint at strong, even dangerous undercurrents swirling right below the surface of their romance:

> Am I under your spell
> How else can it be
> Anyone would notice me
> It's magic I can tell
> How you set me free

Nevertheless, when Tara takes Willow's hand, her concern about her partner's possible misuse of her magical powers momentarily evaporates. The glittering dust that Tara scatters as, singing, she traces her hand through the air mimes the liberatory power of Willow's magic.

If the fairy-tale special effects represent the romantic apex of "Under Your Spell," the ensuing scene shift from the park to the bedroom in Buffy's house is at once more cinematic and magical, magical because cinematic, effecting a subsumptive return—albeit on a less playful, more profound note—to the discourse of power and sexual desire with which the sequence begins. Though Willow has earlier remarked, in response to Tara's abrupt expression of heterosexuality, that she's "not large with the butch," when she repeats Tara's fairy-dust gesture, her light trail is even grander. Moreover, though Tara dominates the sequence in terms of performance (she sings and dances while Willow watches and listens), it is Willow who, spinning her round and round, transports her from the park to the bedroom.

The verses of "Under Your Spell" before Tara falls back onto the bed not only invoke the periodic rhythms of the moon and sea, not to mention those of a woman's body (Willow came out to Buffy in "New Moon Rising" [IV, 19]), but position Willow as the more dominant figure. Hence the brief suggestive shot, before she withdraws from the frame, of Willow on top of Tara. The succeeding line sung by Tara, "Spread beneath my willow tree," is wonderfully graphic, but the most spectacular moment in the sequence, audiovisually speaking, occurs when, on the word "believe" ("You make me believe"), Tara's body slowly begins to levitate, then floats in midair as she repeats the final verse of the number:

You make me complete
You make me complete
You make me complete

While the sentiment of these lyrics is conventional enough, not to say clichéd (the Platonic, *Symposium*-derived notion that lovers complement each other), Amber Benson's phrasing, which accents the first syllable of the last spellbinding word, "complete," imbues the lines with a powerful sexual charge: under Willow's spell, Tara's body breaks over and over again in waves of pleasure until it levitates.

"Under Your Spell," a simple but lyrically rich ballad with drums and electric guitar, is one of the musical highlights of "Once More with Feeling." Its intense sexual and emotional lyricism must be situated, however, within the episode as a whole which, like Sondheim's musicals, is surprisingly dark. (As Tara declares as the Scoobies stride en masse toward the final confrontation with the tap-dancing demon, Sweet, "Everything's turning out so dark.") So, later, in act 3, when Dawn makes an offhand comment to Tara about the fight Willow and she had about magic, Tara, perturbed, consults an occult book and realizes that the "little weed" Willow left for her is, in fact, Lethe's Bramble.[17] That it is used not only to cast "spells of forgetfulness" but "mind control" (the latter of which Tara is all too familiar with—see "Tough Love" [V, 19]) alarms her, as the brief musical reprise of "Under Your Spell" intimates:

I'm under your spell
God, how can this be
Playing with my memory
You know I've been through hell

This stanza not only foreshadows Tara's impending break from Willow ("We're done") but, as illustrated by the fact that her lament is also a duet with Giles (who is struggling with the realization that he must leave Buffy so that she can better assume her adult responsibilities), reiterates one of the central motifs of "Once More with Feeling": loss. (Given the controversial death of Tara in "Seeing Red" [VI, 19] as well as Willow's violent, revengeful reaction, abandonment, loss' dark twin, is arguably the dramatic pivot on which the season as a whole turns.[18])

This thematic is most forcefully articulated in the penultimate sequence of "Once More with Feeling" when Buffy must confront the demon Sweet whose puppet henchmen have kidnapped her sister. Since Sweet wants Dawn for his queen, Buffy, in an echo of the end of season five when she sacrificed herself for her sister, first tries to cut a deal with him: "You take me to hellsville in her place." However, when he tells her that her perspective is "gloomy" (to quote Anya, Buffy has come back from the grave "much graver"), she answers with a song—set to drums, piano, and electric guitar—that puts a dark, ironic twist on the musical convention of turning life's misery into melody. Reluctantly, Buffy sings:

> When the music starts
> We open up our hearts
> It's all right if something's come out wrong
> We'll sing a happy song

Then, looking directly into the camera, she adds, "And you can sing along."

After this spell-breaking wink at the audience, Buffy attacks Sweet's henchmen, punctuating the sort of happy platitudes that virtually define Disney animated musicals such as *Snow White* ("Whistle while you work") with a kick or a blow. As in "Under Your Spell," though, the cool irony, tough attitude, and kick-ass action give way to the somber and sobering recognition that not "every day's a gift": "So hard / All day / To be like other girls / To fit into this glittering world." These lines, which can be said to recapitulate in musical terms the overarching theme of *Buffy the Vampire Slayer* (the dilemma of being both the Chosen One and a normal young woman) is made especially poignant in "Once More with Feeling" because Buffy, unbeknownst to her friends—save Spike (James Marsters), who learned about her secret in "After Life" (VI, 3)— has been brought back not from some "hell dimension" but heaven.

Hence, when the gang finally arrives at the Bronze to back her up (and, in an especially witty bit, Anya and Tara heed Giles's order and take their place as Buffy's backup singers), Buffy acknowledges in song that she did not want to be saved:

> There was no pain
> No fear, no doubt
> Til they pulled me out of heaven
> So that's my refrain
> I live in hell
> 'Cause I was expelled from heaven

The chiasmatic reversals that structure season six of *Buffy the Vampire Slayer* are encapsulated in these lines (sung in a slightly off-key "blue" register by Gellar): what the gang thought was hell was, for Buffy, heaven and therefore living, day-to-day life in all its petty and not so petty pain and disappointment, is a kind of death in life.

The climax occurs when Spike (who, of course, as a centuries-old vampire knows about which she speaks) physically stops Buffy from surrendering to her desire to dance faster and faster until she combusts. His response, like Buffy's plea, is pretty strong stuff for a TV musical, not to mention teen soap in the wake of the Columbine massacre: "Life's not a song / Life isn't bliss / Life is just this: it's living."[19] Dawn seconds Spike's sentiment, parroting, with all the toughness and affection of a younger sister, Buffy's earlier advice to her in "The Gift" (V, 22): "The hardest thing in the world is to live in it."

Now, if it's fair to say that the Big Bad of season six is life itself (i.e., "Life sucks"),[20] Buffy has reached a turning point in hers. Her mother, Joyce, has died; Giles, who has effectively functioned as her surrogate father, has left and returned only to realize that he's "standing in her way"; Dawn has resorted to stealing to get her and the other Scoobies' attention (in act 2 she pockets a talisman from the Magic Box); and now Willow is shattered to learn that Buffy did not want to be resurrected. The happy ending of "Once More with Feeling" is, appropriately enough, a qualified one. After the gang recommunes to sing "Where Do We Go From Here" (a reprise of act 1's chorus, "What Can't We Face If We're Together"), Buffy and Spike—after a brief duet ("I touch the fire and it freezes me" / "I died so many years ago but you can make me feel")—passionately kiss as the orchestral music swells.[21]

And so it would appear that we in fact get, as Xander hoped when he first summoned Sweet, the wished-for happy ending. Yet despite the big Hollywood finale, the retro Twentieth Century Fox logo and the closing curtain, the audience is quite aware, since this is the very nature of serial, soap-operatic TV such as *Buffy*, that this is not "The End," that there will be new vampires to slay and different demons to dust.

Indeed, the larger interest as well as not inconsiderable achievement of "Once More with Feeling" is the way it freezes or reframes the episodic logic of the series and thereby formalizes it. From this meta-episodic perspective, "Once More with Feeling," as the title indicates, is not so much or only about Buffy's awareness that she's merely "going through the motions" but about the life, the artistic and commercial longevity, of the show itself (which had already been on the air for five seasons, a classic transitional point in prime-time network programming). Whedon's decision to stage a musical version of *Buffy* can therefore be seen as an especially inspired creative solution to one of the main problems inherent in continuing nighttime series, what one might call, in Buffy's lyrical parlance, the pitfalls of the "same arrangement" where "nothing seems to penetrate the heart."

Here, the double *double entendre* on musical scoring and vampire staking epitomizes the televisual genius of Joss Whedon and, *Cop Rock*

(ABC, 1991) be damned, the singular ingenuity of "Once More with Feeling": pop-musical TV with heart, soul, and not a little wit.

⚜

The action of "Once More with Feeling" occurs in the long wake of the conclusion to season five when in "The Gift" (V, 22) Buffy sacrifices her life to save her sister's. The final shot marks Buffy's dramatic demise:

BUFFY ANNE SUMMERS
1997–2001
BELOVED SISTER
DEVOTED FRIEND
SHE SAVED THE WORLD
A LOT

The premiere episode of season six, "Bargaining, Part 1" (VI, 1), picks up where the previous season leaves off and concludes with Buffy's resurrection: "Cut to a half-decayed body in a coffin; the body is renewed and suddenly we see it's Buffy. Buffy, like Spike, like the vampires she has slain, has just 'woken up in a box,' reborn."[22] The mise-en-scène could not be more suggestive: Buffy, like the Vamp Willow showcased in "Doppelgangland" (III, 16), is herself a vampire, haunting the inky nooks and crannies of Sunnydale.

If Buffy can be seen as a vamp in her own right (as Spike says in "Once More with Feeling" when she visits his crypt: "Sun sets, and she appears"), the location of Sunnydale in that vale of sun called Southern California[23] elicits another, equally uncanny double: Adorno as the Slayer of popular-cultural icons such as Buffy. In this context, the signatory date of *Dialectic of Enlightenment*—Adorno and Horkheimer's meditation on the dialectical dance between myth and enlightenment or vampires and reason (see Goya)—acquires a certain retrospective irony: May 1944, Los Angeles, California. "California," of course, is shorthand for that source or local anti-genie that inspired the authors' renowned critique of mass culture.

With these elements constellated, one has only to recollect Marx's reading of capital as "vampire-like" ("which lives only by sucking living labour, and lives the more, the more labour it sucks"[24]) to begin to appreciate the global condemnation of post-*Tristan* integrated TV broached in "The Culture Industry":

> Television aims at a synthesis of radio and film. . . . Its consequences will be quite enormous and promise to intensify the

impoverishment of aesthetic matter so drastically, that by tomorrow the thinly veiled identity of all industrial culture can come tri-
umphantly out into the open, derisively fulfilling the Wagnerian
dream of the *Gesamtkunstwerk*. . . . The alliance of word, image and
music is all the more perfect because the sensuous elements . . . are
in principle embodied in [a] technical process [that] integrates all
the elements of the production. . . . It is the triumph of invested
capital, whose title as absolute master is etched deep into the
hearts of the dispossessed in the employment line.[25]

Tomorrow is today. Which is to say that the genealogy of "Once More
with Feeling"—from opera to operetta, operetta to music theatre, music
theatre to film musical, and, finally, film musical to TV—emblematizes
the utter decadence of popular culture. In this admittedly rather grim
scenario, Buffy is ritually slain by Adorno, her body laid to rest on the
high altar of *Kultur*.

There is, of course, another, alternative scenario, one where Adorno
has always already rolled over in his grave and has risen up like the
undead, feeding voraciously every night on the passive, blood-warm
corpus of mass culture. In other words, in the clash between "Old World"
values and "New World consumer culture," Adorno is a double of sorts of
Giles where the antagonism is between "heavy-handed patriarchal and
anachronistic European culture (embodied in the heartless . . . Watchers'
Council) and lighter . . . if not safer . . . America."[26] The gender stakes
of this continental trope, especially if one considers Buffy as a provocative
incarnation of girl culture, couldn't be sharper.

Still, one cannot help but wonder (Tony Soprano aside): In hand-
to-hand, if not mano-a-mano combat, who would win, Buffy or Adorno?
The Slayer or the Übervamp? Pop culture or *Kulturkritik*? "Kitsch de-
lights" or the sublime pleasures of Beethoven?[27]

There is, truth be told, no end to this dialectic. Just as Adornian
critique will continue to represent the return of the repressed of popular culture, so popular culture in its various and particular media guises
will continue to actively resist the demonizing tendencies of this very
same critique. Equally importantly, Adorno and Horkheimer's critique
is not identical to itself, as can be gleaned from the following all too
often neglected passage from "The Culture Industry": "Light art has
been the shadow of autonomous art. It is the social bad conscience of
serious art. . . . The division itself is the truth."[28]

And yet, for all the prescience of *Dialectic of Enlightenment* (which
remains an unusually spooky text), it must be said that today is not yesterday nor, for that matter, the dystopian tomorrow—signified by the

word "television"—espied in the distance by Adorno and Horkheimer while living, no doubt unhappily expatriated, in the indubitable here and now of la-la land. While there's still some truth to the claim that the division between high and low culture expresses the "negativity of the culture which the different spheres constitute,"[29] 2004 is not, in fine, 1944.

Chuck Berry's speculations about "America" in the postwar period throw, for instance, a different sort of illumination on the whole notion of "light art" as well as, perhaps, on where we've been and where we're going: "No white person can conceive the feeling of obtaining Caucasian respect in the wake of a world of dark denial, simply because it is impossible to view the dark side when faced with brilliance."[30] The historical dialectic between myth and enlightenment that Berry gestures toward here, the enforced division or segregation between the races in 1950s American society, constitutes one implicit, affirmative counter to the relentlessly disenchanting argument of *Dialectic of Enlightenment*.

Finally, "light art"—if this term is not merely honorific ("lite art") and can be applied to popular-cultural texts like "Once More with Feeling"—is not quite as light or meretricious as one might imagine. Popular culture is serious in its own postmodern, relatively autonomous fashion. (Buffy in act 1: "Well I'm not exactly quaking in my stylish but affordable boots but there's definitely something unnatural going on.") In fact, given its extraordinary popularity on the Internet,[31] *Buffy* cannot be written off simply as a cult thing but can, instead, be seen as a model of mass culture in the best populist sense.

Frankly, it's also unabashedly utopian and, as such, may well be, if one were wont to reinflect Adorno and Horkheimer's ethical rhetoric, the "*good* social conscience" of a lot of other, ostensibly better art. This, at least, is how I choose to read Buffy's magically empowering address to her fellow potential slayers in the final, seventh season of the series:

> In every generation one Slayer is born because a bunch of guys that died thousands of years ago made up that rule. . . . So I say we change the rules. . . . From now on, every girl in the world who might be a Slayer will be a Slayer. Every girl who could have the power will have the power. Who can stand up will stand up. Every one of you, and girls we've never known, and generations to come . . . they will have strength they never dreamed of, they will have each other.

Slayers of the world unite!

Notes

Introduction

1. Dwight Macdonald, "A Theory of Mass Culture," in *Mass Culture: The Popular Arts in America*, ed. Bernard Rosenberg and David Manning White (Glencoe, IL: Free Press, 1957), p. 59.

2. Ibid., p. 61.

3. For some sense of this historical moment, see Michael Wreszin, introduction to *Interviews with Dwight Macdonald* (Jackson: University Press of Mississippi, 2003), pp. x–xx.

4. Raymond Chandler, *Farewell, My Lovely* (New York: Vintage Crime/Black Lizard, 1992), p. 41.

5. Macdonald, "A Theory of Mass Culture," p. 59.

6. See, for example, Nino Frank's "The Crime Adventure Story: A New Kind of Detective Film" (1946) and Pierre Chartier, "The Americans Are Making Dark Films Too" (1946) in *Perspectives on Film Noir*, ed. R. Burton Palmer (New York: G. K. Hall, 1996), pp. 21–24 and 25–27, respectively.

7. See, for example, Alain Silver, "*Kiss Me Deadly*: Evidence of a Style," in *Film Noir Reader*, ed. Silver and James Ursini (New York: Limelight Editions, 2000), pp. 209–35; Robert Lang, "Looking for the 'Great Whatzit': *Kiss Me Deadly* and Film Noir," in Palmer, *Perspectives on Film Noir*, pp. 171–84; Jack Shadoian, "*Kiss Me Deadly*," in *Dreams and Dead Ends: The American Gangster/Crime Film* (Cambridge, MA: MIT Press, 1977), pp. 265–84.

8. See Volker R. Berghan, "European Elitism, American Money, and Popular Culture," in *The American Century in Europe*, ed. R. Laurence Moore and Maurizio Vaudagna (Ithaca, NY: Cornell University Press, 2003), pp. 117–30.

9. On the intimate link between politics and aesthetics in this period, see Francis Stonor Saunders, *The Cultural Cold War: The CIA and the World of Arts and Letters* (New York: New Press, 2000).

10. Louis Menand, "Culture Club: The Short, Happy Life of an American Highbrow," *The New Yorker*, October 15, 2000, p. 210.

11. Ibid.

12. On the popularization of opera, see "'Expecting Rain': Opera as Popular Culture?," in *High Pop: Making Culture into Mass Entertainment*, ed. Jim Collins (Oxford: Blackwell, 2002), pp. 32–55.

13. See, for example, the opening to "Defining Popular Culture," in Henry Jenkins, Tara McPherson, and Jane Shattuc, *Hop on Pop: The Politics and Pleasures of Popular Culture* (Durham, NC: Duke University Press, 2003), p. 45.

14. Jim Collins, "High Pop: An Introduction," in Collins, *High Pop*, p. 19.

15. Robert Fink, "Elvis Everywhere: Musicology and Popular Music Studies at the Twilight of the Canon," in *Rock Over the Edge: Transformations in Popular Music Culture*, ed. Roger Beebe, Denise Fulbrook, and Ben Saunders (Durham, NC: Duke University Press, 2002), p. 64.

16. Ibid., p. 66.

17. Ibid., p. 65.

18. Ibid., p. 64.

19. Alex Ross, "Pop 101: Academia Tunes In," *The New Yorker*, July 14 and 21, 2003, p. 97.

20. Ibid., p. 93.

21. Chuck Berry, quoted in Fred Rothwell's *Long Distance Information: Chuck Berry's Recorded Legacy* (York, England: Music Mentor Press, 2001), p. 34.

22. See Jenny Eliscu, "2002's Music Biz Disaster," *Rolling Stone*, February 6, 2003, pp. 11–12. See also John Seabrook, who reports that CD sales "declined in 2001, by six per cent, and then dropped 9 percent in 2002" ("The Money Note: Can the Record Business Survive?," *The New Yorker*, July 7, 2003, p. 50).

23. Steven Daly and David Kamp, "The Rock Snob Dictionary, Volume 3," *Vanity Fair*, November 2000, p. 297.

24. "Top 25 Albums," Nielsen Soundscan, cited in Chris Willman, "Beautiful South," *Entertainment Weekly*, January 17, 2003, p. 77.

25. Lawrence Grossberg, "Reflections of a Disappointed Popular Music Scholar," in Beebe, Fulbrook, and Saunders, *Rock Over the Edge*, pp. 40–41.

26. Francesco Casetti, *Theories of Cinema, 1945–1995*, trans. Francesca Chiostri and Elizabeth Gard Bartolini-Salimbeni with Thomas Kelso (Austin: University of Texas Press, 1999), p. 197.

27. Kathryn Kalinak, "The Language of Music: A Brief Analysis of *Vertigo*," in *Movie Music: The Film Reader*, ed. Kay Dickinson (New York: Routledge, 2003), pp. 15–23.

28. Theodor Adorno and Hans Eisler, "Prejudices and Bad Habits," in Dickinson, *Movie Music*, pp. 27–31.

29. Ibid., p. 25. On *Dialectic of Enlightenment* as well as, inter alia, the distinction in German between "*the* culture industry" ("the media and their factories") and "culture industry" ("the principle of commodity-form cultural activity"), see Heinz Steinert, *Culture Industry*, trans. Sally-Ann Spencer (Malden, MA: Polity, 2003).

30. Macdonald, "A Theory of Mass Culture," pp. 34–35.

31. Michel Chion, *Audio-Vision: Sound on Screen*, ed. and trans. Claudia Gorbman (New York: Columbia University Press), p. 141.

32. Ibid., pp. 153–54.

33. Adorno and Eisler, "Prejudices and Bad Habits," p. 29.

34. Ibid.

35. This is, needless to say, a commonplace of American film reviewers as evidenced by a recent Q&A in *Entertainment Weekly*: "Which director has achieved the greatest success both commercially and critically in the past 25 years?" Lisa Schwarzbaum's answer: "Spielberg" (August 8, 2003, p. 54).

36. Dana Polan, *Pulp Fiction* (London: British Film Institute, 2000), p. 78.

37. Tarantino, quoted in *Tarantino, A to Zed*, ed. Alan Barnes and Marcus Hearn (London: B. T. Batsford, 1996), p. 162.

38. Barnes and Hearn, *Tarantino, A to Zed*, p. 102.

39. Hilary De Vries, "Quentin Tarantino, Master of Mayhem," in *Quentin Tarantino: Interviews*, ed. Gerald Peary (Jackson: University of Mississippi Press, 1998), p. 116.

40. Clement Greenberg, "Avant-Garde and Kitsch," in Rosenberg and White, *Mass Culture*, p. 102.

41. Tarantino, quoted in "Television," in Barnes and Hearn, *Tarantino, A to Zed*, p. 141.

42. See Toby Miller's *Avengers* (London: British Film Institute, 1997).

43. Chris Lehmann, *Revolt of the Masscult* (Chicago: Prickly Paradigm Press, 2003), p. 55.

44. Ibid., pp. 54 and 55.

45. Ibid., p. 55.

46. See, in this context, the cover of the revised and updated edition of Herbert J. Gans's *Popular and High Culture: An Analysis and Evaluation of Taste* (New York: Basic Books, 1999).

47. Lehmann, *Revolt of the Masscult*, p. 39.

48. Andreas Huyssen, "Adorno in Reverse," in *Adorno: A Critical Reader*, ed. Nigel Gibson and Andrew Rubin (Oxford: Blackwell, 2002), p. 52.

49. Andrew Lockett, "Cultural Studies and Television," in *Television Studies*, ed. Toby Miller (London: British Film Institute, 2002), p. 24.

50. Lehmann, *Revolt of the Masscult*, p. 3.

51. Adorno, "Television and Patterns of Mass Culture," in Rosenberg and White, *Mass Culture*, p. 474. See also, in general, Douglas Kellner, "Television and the Frankfurt School (T. W. Adorno)," in Miller, *Television Studies*, pp. 17–20.

52. Macdonald, "A Theory of Mass Culture," p. 31.

53. For one take on this difference, see Todd Boyd, "The Pimp Stick or the Pulpit," in *The New H.N.I.C.: The Death of Civil Rights and the Rise of Hip Hop* (New York: New York University Press, 2002), pp. 48–56.

54. Dwight Macdonald, "Masscult and Midcult," *Against the American Grain* (New York: Random House, 1962), p. 74.

55. Mark L. Rogers, Michael Epstein, and Jimmie L. Reeves, "*The Sopranos* as HBO Brand Equity: The Art of Commerce in the Age of Digital Reproduction," in *This Thing of Ours: Investigating* The Sopranos, ed. David Lavery (New York: Columbia University Press, 2002), p. 49.

56. Ibid., p. 46.

57. For my sense of televisuality, see, for example, "The Film Look," in John Thornton Caldwell's *Televisuality: Style, Crisis, and Authority in American Television* (New Brunswick, NJ: Rutgers University Press, 1995), pp. 84–88.

58. Rogers, Epstein, and Reeves, "*The Sopranos* as HBO Brand Equity," p. 45.

59. Alan McKee, "Fandom," in Miller, *Television Studies*, p. 24.

60. Rogers, Epstein, and Reeves, "*The Sopranos* as HBO Brand Equity," p. 46.

61. Casetti, "Semiotics/Materialism/Psychoanalysis," in *Theories of Cinema*, p. 200.

62. Ien Ang, "Popular Culture, Populism, and the Ideology of Mass Culture," in *Watching "Dallas": Television and the Melodramatic Imagination* (New York: Routledge, 1985), p. 116.

63. On the Melrose Place Project, see "MP Art—Art by the GALA Committee as Seen on Melrose Place," http://www.arts.ucsb/projects/mpart/about/about.html.

64. Ibid.

65. Ibid.

66. Ibid.

67. Dorothy Hobson, *Soap Opera* (London: Polity, 2003), p. 212.

1. Rock 'n' Theory

1. Robert Palmer, *Rock & Roll: An Unruly History* (New York: Harmony Books, 1995), p. 11.

2. Robert Palmer, "Rock Begins," *The Rolling Stone Illustrated History of Rock & Roll*, ed. Jim Miller (New York: Random House/Rolling Stone Press, 1980), p. 12.

3. Ibid.

4. Greil Marcus, "The Girl Groups," in Miller, *The Rolling Stone Illustrated History of Rock & Roll*, p. 160. However, for the girls' point of view, see Barbara Bradby's "Do-Talk and Don't-Talk: The Division of the Subject in Girl Group Music," in *On Record: Rock, Pop, and the Written Word*, ed. Simon Frith and Andrew Goodwin (New York: Pantheon, 1990), pp. 341–68.

5. Marcus, "The Girl Groups," p. 160.

6. Lester Bangs, "The British Invasion," in Miller, *The Rolling Stone Illustrated History of Rock & Roll*, p. 169.

7. Peter Guralnick, "Elvis Presley," in Miller, *The Rolling Stone Illustrated History of Rock & Roll*, p. 34.

8. For my sense of this song, see Shiela Whiteley, "The Rolling Stones," in *The Space Between the Notes: Rock and the Counter-Culture* (New York: Routledge, 1992), pp. 88–89.

9. Robert Christgau, "The Rolling Stones," in Miller, *The Rolling Stone Illustrated History of Rock & Roll*, p. 192.

10. Dick Bradley, *Understanding Rock 'n' Roll: Popular Music in Britain, 1955–1964* (Buckingham, UK: Open University Press, 1992), pp. 13 and 15–16.

11. Keith Richards, "Glimmer of Youth," interview conducted by David Browne, *Entertainment Weekly*, October 3, 1997, p. 31.

12. For an informative and critical overview of this period of British cultural studies, see Richard Middleton, "Subcultural Theory," in *Studying Popular Music* (Buckingham, UK: Open University Press, 1990), pp. 155–66.

13. Neil Nehring, *Popular Music, Gender, and Postmodernism: Anger Is an Energy* (Thousand Oaks, CA: Sage, 1997), pp. 47 and 67. On Lawrence Grossberg's intellectual itinerary, see "Another Story," in *Bringing It All Back Home* (Durham, NC: Duke University Press, 1997), pp. 22–29.

14. Grossberg, *Dancing in Spite of Myself: Essays on Popular Culture* (Durham, NC: Duke University Press, 1997), p. 9, hereafter referred to in parentheses as "D." For Grossberg's critique of neoconservatism, see the second section of *We Gotta Get Out of This Place*, "Another Boring Day in . . . Paradise: A Rock Formation" (New York: Routledge, 1992), pp. 131–239, hereafter referred to in parentheses as "W."

15. On the "body in dance," see the introduction to my *From Hegel to Madonna: Towards a General Economy of "Commodity Fetishism"* (Albany: State University of New York Press, 1998), pp. 9–36.

16. Marcus, "Four More Years," *Ranters & Crowd Pleasers: Punk in Pop Music, 1977–92* (New York: Anchor, 1994), p. 269.

17. Simon Frith, "The Real Thing—Bruce Springsteen," *Music for Pleasure: Essays in the Sociology of Pop* (New York: Routledge, 1988), pp. 98 and 101.

18. Grossberg, "Is Anybody Listening? Does Anybody Care? On 'The State of Rock,'" in *Microphone Fiends: Youth Music and Youth Culture*, ed. Andrew Ross and Tricia Rose (New York: Routledge, 1994), pp. 41–58; reprinted in *Dancing in Spite of Myself*, pp. 102–21.

19. In "The Sound Begins," Charlie Gillett argues that in "tracing the history of rock and roll, it is useful to distinguish *rock 'n' roll*—the particular kind of music to which the term first applied—both from *rock and roll*—the music that has been classified as such since rock 'n' roll petered out around 1958—and from *rock*, which describes post-1964 derivations of rock 'n' roll." *The Sound of the City* (London: Sphere Books Limited, 1971), p. 1.

20. Frith, *Music for Pleasure*, p. 1.

21. Dave Harker, "Blood on the Tracks: Popular Music in the 1970s," in *The Arts in the 1970s: Cultural Closure?*, ed. Bart Moore-Gilbert (New York: Routledge, 1994), pp. 240–58.

22. On, for instance, Ice-T and Time-Warner, see Andrew Ross's piece on "Cop Killer" (1992) and Madonna's *Sex* (1992) in "This Bridge Called My Pussy," in *Madonnarama*, ed. Lisa Frank and Paul Smith (Pittsburgh: Cleis Press, 1993), pp. 47–54. With respect to the rhetoric of the "death of rock," it's worth noting that after Ice-T decided to pull "Cop Killer" from *Body Count* (Sire/1992), "it was only a matter of time," as Ross notes, "before an organ of record [i.e., the *Source*] announced the death of rap." *Microphone Fiends*, p. 3.

23. Keith Negus, *Popular Music in Theory* (Hanover, NH: Wesleyan/ University Press of New England, 1997), p. 118.

24. On social consumption and copyright revenue, see Keith Negus, *Producing Pop: Culture and Conflict in the Popular Music Industry* (London: Edward Arnold, 1992), pp. 12–14.

25. See, for example, "Affect and the Popular" in *We Gotta Get Out of This Place* and "Postmodernity and Affect" in *Dancing in Spite of Myself*, pp. 79–87

and 145–65, respectively. As Grossberg comments in the introduction to the former text, "My studies of rock convinced me of the importance of passion (affect) in contemporary life" (p. 2). Grossberg provides a concise and popular-cultural gloss on his sense of affect in "Rockin' in Conservative Times," the penultimate essay in *Dancing in Spite of Myself*: "The affective logic, which I have described . . . as being at the center of rock culture, . . . is being reorganized and redeveloped in the service of a specific agenda [i.e., neoconservatism]. What was . . . an empowering machine is turned (as in *Star Wars*' image of 'the force' being turned to the dark side) into the service of a disempowering machine" (p. 257). For a restatement of his understanding of affect, see the introduction to *Bringing It All Back Home*, p. 28.

26. Grossberg, *Bringing It All Back Home*, pp. 16 and 27. For a more elaborate take on the "detour of theory" (Marx), see Grossberg, "Cultural Studies: What's in a Name?" (1995), in *Bringing It All Back Home*, pp. 262–64. For the Marx, see the *Grundrisse*, in *Selected Writings*, ed. David McLellan (Oxford: Oxford University Press, 1985), p. 352.

27. Grossberg is adamant on this point: "In truth, I do have theoretical reservations about theories of identity and difference and strategic concerns about the efficacy of a politics organized around investment in cultural identities. Nevertheless, the mere absence of a topic from a discussion, however important, does not, in my opinion, necessarily constitute a serious weakness" (*Dancing in Spite of Myself*, 25). For Grossberg's sense of identity politics, see, for example, "Identity and Difference," in *Bringing It All Back Home*, pp. 356–63; and "Difference and the Politics of Identity," in *We Gotta Get Out of This Place*, pp. 364–69.

28. See Angela McRobbie, "Settling Accounts with Subcultures: A Feminist Critique," first published in *Screen Education* (1980), in Frith and Goodwin, *On Record*, pp. 66–80; for the Gill critique, which is in part a response to Richard Dyer's "In Defense of Disco" (1979), see, for example, "Nightclubbing," in *Queer Noises: Male and Female Homosexuality in Twentieth-Century Music* (Minneapolis: University of Minnesota Press, 1995), pp. 134–42. For a succinct overview of these issues, see Keith Negus, "Identities," in *Popular Music in Theory*, pp. 99–135, esp. 123–30.

29. Robert Walser, "Forging Masculinity: Heavy Metal Sounds and Images of Gender," in *Running with the Devil: Power, Gender, and Madness in Heavy Metal Music* (Hanover, NH: Wesleyan/University Press of New England, 1993), pp. 108–36. On the Riot Grrrl movement, see Emily White, "Revolution Girl Style Now" (1992), reprinted in *Rock She Wrote*, ed. Evelyn McDonnell and Ann Powers (New York: Delta, 1995), pp. 396–408; and Joanne Gottlieb and Gayle Wald, "Smells Like Teen Spirit: Riot Grrrls, Revolution and Women in Independent Rock," in Ross and Rose, *Microphone Fiends*, pp. 250–74; Nehring, "Riot Grrrls and Carnival," *Popular Music, Gender, and Postmodernism*, pp. 150–79; and Evelyn McDonnell, "Rebel Girls," in *Trouble Girls: The Rolling Stone Book of Women in Rock*, ed. Barbara O'Dair (New York: Random House/Rolling Stone Press, 1997), pp. 453–63.

30. On The Fatback Band's "King Tim III," see David Toop, *Rap Attack 2: African Rap and Global Hip Hop* (London: Serpent's Tail, 1991), pp. 81–82. For an update on the Sugarhill Gang's "Rapper's Delight," see Rob Brunner, "Birth of Rap," *Entertainment Weekly*, January 9, 1998, p. 84.

31. Tricia Rose, "Soul Sonic Forces," *Black Noise: Rap Music and Black Culture in Contemporary America* (Hanover, NH: University Press of New England, 1994), pp. 51–52. I might add that in terms of what one might call the semiautonomy of rap with respect to rock music, Nelson George has pointed out that although Run-DMC "recaptured a piece of the rock audience" with "Walk This Way," they were able to do so "without dissolving themselves . . . into white culture." *The Death of Rhythm & Blues* (New York: Pantheon, 1988), p. 194.

32. Africa Bambaataa on the Bronx hip-hop scene in 1984: "I used to catch the people who'd say, 'I don't like rock. . . .' I'd throw on Mick Jagger—you'd see the blacks and the Spanish just *throwing* down, dancing crazy. I'd say, 'I thought you don't like rock!' They'd say, 'Get out of here!' I'd say, 'Well, you just danced to the Rolling Stones.'" Cited in Toop, *Rap Attack 2*, p. 66. On "Payoff Mix," Double D and Steinski's mastermix of, inter alia, G.L.O.B.E. and Whiz Kid's "Play That Beat, Mr. DJ," see Toop, *Rap Attack 2*, pp. 153–54.

33. Roland Barthes, "Myth Today," in *Mythologies*, trans. Annette Lavers (New York: Noonday Press, 1990 [1972]), p. 12.

34. See, for example, Midddleton, "'Change Gonna Come'? Popular Music and Musicology," in *Studying Popular Music*, pp. 103–26; and the section on musicology and semiotics in Frith and Goodwin's *On Record*, in particular Susan McClary and Robert Walser's "Start Making Sense! Musicology Wrestles with Rock," pp. 277–92.

35. Robert Palmer, *Rock & Roll*, p. 9.

36. Negus, *Popular Music in Theory*, p. 162.

37. Ibid., p. 101.

38. Paul Friedlander, *Rock and Roll: A Social History* (Boulder, CO: Westview Press, 1996), p. 2.

39. Timothy D. Taylor, *Global Pop: World Music, World Markets* (New York: Routledge, 1997), p. 20.

40. Ibid., p. 23.

41. Ibid., p. 201.

42. Negus, "Culture of Production," in *Popular Music in Theory*, pp. 61–64. The seminal text for the "production of culture" perspective is Richard Peterson, *The Production of Culture* (Thousand Oaks, CA: Sage, 1976).

43. Negus, *Producing Pop*, p. 153.

44. Ibid., p. vii.

45. Negus, "Histories," in *Popular Music in Theory*, p. 163.

46. On rock and capitalism, see Timothy D. Taylor, "Popular Musics and Globalization," in *Global Pop: World Music, World Markets* (New York: Routledge, 1997), pp. 1–38. For a survey of rock with respect to media and cultural imperialism, see Negus, "Geographies," in *Popular Music in Theory*, in particular "Music and the Modes of Media Imperialism" and "Feeling the Effect: Cultural

Imperialism and Globalization," pp. 168–71 and 171–80, respectively; and *Music at the Margins: Popular Music and Global Diversity*, ed. Deanna Campbell Robinson, Elizabeth B. Buck, and Marlene Cuthbert (Newbury Park, CA: Sage, 1991).

47. On Cuba, see Humberto Manduley López, "Rock in Cuba: History of a Wayward Son," in *Bridging Enigmas: Cubans on Cuba*, ed. Ambrosio Fornet, Special Issue of *South Atlantic Quarterly* 96, no. 1 (Winter 1997): 135–41. On China, Argentina and South Africa, see, respectively, Tim Brace and Paul Friedlander, "Rock and Roll on the New Long March: Popular Music, Cultural Identity, and Political Opposition in the People's Republic of China"; Pablo Vila, "*Rock Nacional* and Dictatorship in Argentina"; and Denis-Constant Martin, "Music beyond Apartheid?," trans. Val Morrison, in *Rockin' the Boat: Mass Music and Mass Movements*, ed. Reebee Garofalo (Boston: South End Press, 1992), pp. 115–27, 209–29, and 195–207. On Eastern Europe and the former Soviet Union, see Timothy W. Ryback, *Rock Around the Bloc: A History of Rock Music in Eastern Europe and the Soviet Union* and *Rocking the State*, ed. Sabrina Petra Ramet (Boulder, CO: Westview, 1994). More generally, see Robin Denselow, *When the Music's Over: The Story of Political Pop* (London: Faber and Faber, 1989).

48. Donna Gaines, "The Local Economy of Suburban Scenes," *Adolescents and Their Music: If It's Too Loud, You're Too Old*, ed. Jonathon S. Epstein (New York: Garland, 1994), pp. 47–65.

49. Donna Weinstein, "Expendable Youth: The Rise and Fall of Youth Culture," in Gaines, *Adolescents and Their Music*, p. 82.

50. Ibid., p. 20.

51. Ibid., p. 73.

52. Ibid., pp. 69 and 75, respectively.

53. Negus, *Producing Pop*, p. 100. Data on consumption patterns in fact indicate that while the "purchase of rock music declines with age," this decline is "gradual across ages 25–44." Negus, *Producing Pop*, p. 100.

54. Weinstein, "Expendable Youth," p. 83.

55. Ibid., p. 82.

56. Before the advent of the British Invasion (which is to say, pre-Beatles and pre–JFK assassination), "total industry sales were under $1 billion" (Goodman, "So How'd We Keep Score?," *Entertainment Weekly*, May 3, 1996, p. 29); now, it's well over 40 times this figure.

57. Negus, "Histories," p. 148.

58. But for a very witty, critical take on this sort of historicizing ("punk rose with the Pistols in 1977 and ended with Sid in 1979"), see John Strausbaugh, *Rock Til You Drop: The Decline from Rebellion to Nostalgia* (London: Verso, 2002), pp. 197–205.

59. Negus, "Histories," p. 139.

2. Roll Over Adorno

1. For a thorough analysis of the politics of rave culture, see Jeremy Gilbert and Ewan Pearson, *Discographies: Dance Music Culture and the Politics of Sound* (London: Routledge, 1999).

2. Jürgen Habermas, cited by Brian O'Connor in introduction to *The Adorno Reader*, ed. O'Connor (Oxford, UK: Blackwell, 2000), p. 1.

3. Noël Carroll, "Philosophical Resistance to Mass Art," in *A Philosophy of Mass Art* (Oxford, UK: Clarendon, 1998), p. 105.

4. Ibid., p. 104.

5. Theodore Gracyk, "Adorno, Jazz, and Popular Music," *Rhythm and Noise: An Aesthetics of Rock* (Durham, NC: Duke University Press, 1996), p. 156.

6. For this point, see Gracyk, *Rhythm and Noise*, p. 173.

7. See my "The Commodity-Body-Sign," *From Hegel to Madonna: Towards a "General Economy" of Commodity Fetishism* (Albany: State University of New York Press, 1998), pp. 61–95.

8. For the author's sense of this term, see Gracyk, *Rhythm and Noise*, p. 166.

9. For the author's own definitions of these terms, see Raymond Williams, *Marxism and Literature* (Oxford, UK: Oxford University Press, 1977), pp. 121–27.

10. For Adorno's reading of the relation between Beethoven and the "revolutionary bourgeoisie," see "Society," in *Beethoven: The Philosophy of Music*, ed. Rolf Tiedemann and trans. Edmund Jephcott (Stanford, CA: Stanford University Press, 1998), pp. 29–48.

11. Ibid., p. 29.

12. Adorno, "Music and Concept," *Beethoven*, p. 10. *Resistance Through Rituals: Youth Subcultures in Post-War Britain*, ed. Stuart Hall and Tony Jefferson (London: Routledge, 1976); Dick Hebdige, *Subculture: The Meaning of Style* (London: Methuen, 1979).

13. Adorno, "Prelude," *Beethoven*, p. 6.

14. Ibid.

15. Adorno, *Philosophy of Modern Music*, trans. Anne G. Mitchell and Wesley V. Blomster (New York: Seabury Press, 1973), p. 129.

16. I might add that I have chosen this particular comparison because the *Eroica* for Adorno is "Beethoven's most 'classical' symphony" whereas the Ninth, for example, is a "reconstruction of the *classical* Beethoven." *Beethoven*, pp. 101 and 97, respectively. As for the Stravinsky, *L'histoire du soldat* is, according to Adorno, "Stravinsky's pivotal work." *Philosophy of Modern Music*, p. 175. In the latter context, see also Adorno's comments on *L'histoire du soldat* and "commercial" jazz in the same volume—e.g., "Stravinsky reveals, by means of distortion, the shabby and worn-out aspects of a dance music which has . . . given in completely to the demands of the market." Ibid., p. 171, note 25.

17. Adorno, "Schoenberg and Progress," *Philosophy of Modern Music*, p. 126, note 55.

18. Ibid., p. 126, note 58.

19. Walter Benjamin, *One-Way Street*, cited by Tiedemann in *Beethoven*, p. vii.

20. Tiedemann, *Beethoven*, p. viii.

21. Ibid.

22. Adorno, "Scientific Experiences of a European Scholar in America," in *Critical Models: Interventions and Catchwords*, trans. Henry W. Pickford (New York: Columbia University Press, 1999), p. 228.

23. Adorno, *Philosophy of Modern Music*, p. xiii.

24. Adorno, "Scientific Experiences," p. 226.

25. Adorno, "The Fetish Character in Music and the Regression in Listening," in *The Essential Frankfurt School Reader*, ed. Andrew Arato and Eike Gebhardt (New York: Urizen Books, 1978), p. 278.

26. Adorno, "Scientific Experiences," p. 220; Adorno, "A Social Critique of Radio Music" (1945), cited by Gracyk in *Rhythm and Noise*, p. 169.

27. Adorno, "Prelude," p. 3.

28. Adorno, "Society," p. 31.

29. Adorno, "Types of Musical Conduct," in *Introduction to the Sociology of Music*, trans. E. B. Ashton (New York: Seabury Press, 1976), p. 4.

30. Ibid., pp. 5 and 17.

31. Ibid., pp. 15–16.

32. Gracyk, *Rhythm and Noise*, p. 167.

33. Ibid., p. 173.

34. James Miller, "October 29, 1949: Red Hot and Blue," *Flowers in the Dustbin: The Rise of Rock and Roll, 1947–1987* (New York: Simon and Schuster, 1999), p. 34.

35. Ibid., p. 37.

36. Ibid., p. 38.

37. Ibid.

38. Ibid.

39. Ibid., p. 39.

40. Ibid. Chuck Berry seconds this in his *Autobiography*: "It seems to me that the white teenagers of the forties and fifties helped launch black artists nationally into the main line of popular music. . . . [T]hese transistor-radio teenagers exercised great liberty in following their musical tastes" ([New York: Harmony, 1987], p. 95).

41. On Chuck Berry ("architect" and "poet laureate"), see, respectively, Michael Campbell and James Brody, *Rock and Roll: An Introduction* (New York: Schirmer Books, 1999), pp. 82; and Paul Friedlander, "Classic Rockers—The First Generation: Just Give Me Some of That Rock and Roll Music," *Rock and Roll: A Social History* (Boulder, CO: Westview Press, 1996), p. 34. For the phrase "fast-car fantasy," see Charlie Gillett, "Five Styles of Rock 'n' Roll," in *The Sound of the City* (London: Sphere Books, 1971), p. 40. For the music of Chuck Berry, see the two-volume Chess compilation, *Chuck Berry: The Best* (Chess, 1997).

42. Gracyk, *Rhythm and Noise*, p. 159.

43. Ibid.

44. Friedlander, *Rock and Roll*, p. 33.

45. Ibid., p. 35.

46. Berry, *The Autobiography*, p. 149.

47. Nick Cohn, "Classic Rock," *The Penguin Book of Rock and Roll Writing*, ed. Clinton Heylin (New York: Viking, 1992), p. 46.

48. Peter Wicke, "'Roll Over Beethoven': New Experiences in Art," in *Rock Music: Culture, Aesthetics, Sociology*, trans. Rachel Fogg (Cambridge: Cambridge University Press, 1990), p. 8.

49. Adorno, "On Popular Music," in *On Record: Rock, Pop, and the Written Word*, ed. Simon Frith and Andrew Goodwin (New York: Pantheon, 1990), p. 306.

50. Chuck Berry's retrospective remarks on magnetic tape recording are especially interesting in light of Adorno's "pessimistic" perspective on reproduction: "During the summer of '51 I bought a secondhand reel-to-reel magnetic wire recorder from a friend who recorded me singing on it at his house. I think I would have stolen it if he hadn't sold it as I was completely fascinated by its reproduction qualities. It was that inspiration that started me to recording the first of my original improvisations, both poetical and melodical." *The Autobiography*, p. 87.

51. Jerry Leiber and Mike Stoller, cited in Wicke, *Rock Music*, p. 13. On the difference between writing songs and "sketching the charts of the track sessions for a record," Wicke writes, "Conventional pop songs, the Tin Pan Alley hits, existed primarily within such musical parameters as melody, harmony and formal structure, which could be best worked out in musical notation. In contrast, the human voice, with its timbre and register, the niceties of intonation and phrasing, the sound characteristics of the instruments and the physical presence of metre and rhythm could now be controlled by technical means and could therefore be used increasingly consciously as a separate plane of expression." *Rock Music*, p. 13.

52. Wicke, *Rock Music*, p. 11.

53. Max Paddison, *Adorno's Aesthetics of Music* (Cambridge: Cambridge University Press, 1993), p. 214.

54. Adorno, *Aesthetic Theory*, trans. Christian Lenhardt (London: Routledge and Kegan Paul, 1984), p. 177.

55. Adorno, "On Popular Music," p. 301.

56. Adorno, "Postscript—Sociology of Music," in *Introduction to the Sociology of Music*, p. 224. See also Adorno's famous comment in a letter to Benjamin about the dialectic of the "highest" and the "lowest": "Both bear the stigmata of capitalism, both contain elements of change. . . . Both are torn halves of an integral freedom, to which however they do not add up." "Presentation III," trans. Harry Zohn, in Bloch et al., *Aesthetics and Politics* (London: Verso, 1977), p. 123.

57. Ibid., p. 224.

58. Adorno, "On Popular Music," p. 302.

59. Adorno, "Scientific Experiences," p. 239.

60. Ibid., pp. 239 and 241, respectively.

61. Fredric Jameson, "The Parable of the Oarsman," in *Late Marxism, or the Persistence of the Dialectic* (London, Verso: 1990), p. 148.

62. Adorno, "The Culture Industry Reconsidered," trans. Anson G. Rabinbach, in O'Connor, *The Adorno Reader*, p. 25.

63. The "first legitimate, paid alternatives" to Napster et al.—RealOne Music (sponsored by Warner Music, EMI, and BMG), Rhapsody (Listen.com), and Pressplay (Sony and Universal)—began to appear late in 2001. "Music Services Ready for Business," *USA Today*, December 3, 2001, p. 3D. I would only add that, not surprisingly, record companies (e.g., Universal Music Group) have also begun to produce copy-protected CDs.

64. Gracyk writes, "The 'alternative' musician who genuinely scorns and avoids commerce is the anomaly. . . . Even Fugazi has a national distributor that keeps their CDs in stock at the local outlet." *Rhythm and Noise*, p. 154.

65. Fred Goodman, "The Most Dangerous Man in the Music Business," *Rolling Stone*, July 6–20, 2000, p. 42.

66. In the very near future, "the catalog-rich but user-unfriendly service Pressplay will morph into a new, legal Napster—courtesy of tech firm Roxio, which now owns both Pressplay and the Napster name." Brian Hiatt and Evan Serpick, "The 99 Cent Solution," *Entertainment Weekly*, June 6, 2003, pp. 12–13.

67. John Seabrook, "The Money Note: Can the Record Business Survive?," *New Yorker*, July 7, 2003, p. 51.

68. Ibid., p. 52.

Reprise: Beethoven's Hair

1. Russell Martin, *Beethoven's Hair* (New York: Broadway Books, 2000), p. 36.

2. Ibid., p. 271.

3. Alex Ross, "Listen to This," *New Yorker*, February 16 and 23, 2004, p. 155.

4. Ibid., 150.

5. Ibid., p. 155.

6. Ibid. In the context of hair, see as well the Coen brothers' *The Man Who Wasn't There* (2001) which features the sonatas of Beethoven, including the *Moonlight* and *Pathétique*.

7. Edward Said, in Daniel Barenboim and Said, *Parallels and Paradoxes: Explorations in Music and Society* (New York: Pantheon, 2002), pp. 131–32. Said has observed that "what people respond to in Beethoven" is the "aesthetic as an indictment of the political." This aesthetic indictment is, for both Said and Adorno, the very antipode of so-called politically committed art.

8. Ibid., p. 135.

9. Theodor Adorno, *Beethoven: The Philosophy of Music*, ed. Rolf Tiedemann and trans. Edmund Jephcott (Stanford, CA: Stanford University Press, 1998), p. 77.

10. Ibid., p. 78.

11. Adorno, "On Popular Music," in *Essays on Music*, ed. Richard Leppert (Berkeley: University of California Press, 2002), p. 462.

12. Ibid., p. 462.

13. See, in general, Henry Cooper, "On *Über Jazz*: Replaying Adorno with the Grain," *October* 75 (Winter 1996): 99–133.

14. Richard Leppert, "Commentary: Music and Mass Culture," *Essays on Music*, p. 347.

15. Adorno, "The Radio Symphony," in Leppert, *Essays on Music*, p. 268.

16. Adorno, "Little Heresy," in Leppert, *Essays on Music*, p. 319.

17. Robert B. Crease, "Jazz and Dance," in *Cambridge Companion to Jazz*, ed. Mervyn Cooke and David Horn (Cambridge: Cambridge University Press, 2002), pp. 75–76.

18. Whiteman, from Whiteman and McBride's *Jazz* (1926), quoted by Leppert, "Music and Mass Culture," p. 354.

19. Leppert, "Music and Mass Culture," p. 354.

20. Gary Giddens, *Bing Crosby: A Pocketful of Dreams, The Early Years, 1903–1940* (Boston: Little, Brown & Co., 2001), p. 142.

21. Bruce Johnson, "The Jazz Diaspora," in Cooke and Horn, *The Cambridge Companion to Jazz*, pp. 38–39.

22. Ibid., p. 50.

23. Ibid.

24. Giddens, *A Pocketful of Dreams*, pp. 142 and 230.

25. Ibid., p. 142.

26. Cooper, "On *Über Jazz*," p. 129.

27. Ibid.

3. The Suture Scenario

1. Slavoj Žižek, "Back to the Suture," *The Fright of Real Tears* (London: British Film Institute, 2000), p. 31.

2. Noël Carroll, *Mystifying Movies: Fads and Fallacies in Film Theory* (New York: Columbia University Press, 1988), p. 1; Jacques-Alain Miller, "La suture," *Cahiers pour l'analyse* 1 (1966): 39–51.

3. Jean-Pierre Oudart, "La suture," *Cahiers du cinéma* 211 (1969): 36–39; Oudart, "La suture," *Cahiers du cinéma* 212 (1969): 50–55; Miller, "Suture: Elements of the Logic of the Signifier," trans. Jacqueline Rose, *Screen* 18, no. 4 (1977): 35–47; Oudart, "Cinema and Suture," trans. Kari Hanet, *Screen* 18, no. 44 (1977): 35–47. For the Heath essay, see "Notes on Suture," *Screen* 18, no. 4 (1977): 48–76; reprinted in Heath's *Questions of Cinema* (Bloomington: Indiana University Press, 1981) as "On Suture," pp. 76–112.

4. Daniel Dayan, "The Tutor-Code of Classical Cinema," *Film Quarterly* 28, no. 1 (Fall 1974): 22–31, reprinted in *Movies and Methods*, ed. Bill Nichols (Berkeley: University of California Press, 1976), p. 439; William Rothman, "Against 'The System of the Suture,'" *Film Quarterly* 29, no. 1 (1975): 45–50; reprinted in Nichols, *Movies and Methods*, pp. 451–59.

5. Ernesto Laclau and Chantal Mouffe, *Hegemony and Socialist Strategy: Towards a Radical Democratic Politics* (London: Verso, 1985), p. 85, note 1.

6. Heath, "On Suture," p. 106.

7. Ibid., p. 83.

8. Jacques Lacan, "What Is a Picture?," *The Four Fundamental Concepts of Psycho-Analysis*, trans. Alan Sheridan (New York: Norton, 1981), p. 117.

9. Heath, "On Suture," pp. 83 and 86.

10. Ibid., p. 83.

11. Lacan, "What Is a Picture?," p. 117.

12. David Bordwell, "Contemporary Film Studies," in *Post-Theory*, ed. Bordwell and Noël Carroll (Madison: University of Wisconsin Press, 1996), p. 6.

13. For the Rothman article, see note 4 above; for the Salt, see "Film Style and Technology in the Forties," *Film Quarterly* 31 (Fall 1977): 46–57.

14. "Quilting point" is a translation of the Lacanian notion of the *point de capiton*, a "button" that "sutures" the *glissement* or "sliding" associated with the signifying chain.

15. Bordwell, preface to *Making Meaning: Inference and Rhetoric in the Interpretation of Cinema* (Cambridge: Harvard University Press), p. xiv.

16. Elizabeth Cowie, "Identifying in the Cinema," in *Representing the Woman: Cinema and Psychoanalysis* (Minneapolis: University of Minnesota Press, 1998), p. 116.

17. Homi Bhabha, "The Other Question," *Screen* 24, no. 6 (1983): 312–31; reprinted in *The Sexual Subject: A Screen Reader in Sexuality*, ed. Mandy Merck et al. (London: Routledge, 1992), pp. 312–31.

18. Kaja Silverman, "Suture," in *The Subject of Semiotics* (New York: Oxford University Press, 1983), p. 233.

19. Ibid., pp. 212–13.

20. Ibid., pp. 231–32.

21. Žižek, "Short Circuit," in *The Fright of Real Tears*, p. 58.

22. Cowie, "Identifying in the Cinema," p. 116.

23. Jeff Smith, "Unheard Melodies: A Critique," in Bordwell and Carroll, *Post-Theory*, pp. 230–47. In my analyses of audiovisuality in *Tongues Untied* and *Set It Off*, I presuppose that the significance of any given popular-musical song within a film is dependent, as Smith observes in *The Sounds of Commerce*, "upon the meaning of pop music in the larger sphere of society and culture" ([New York: Columbia University Press, 1998,] p. 5). I also share Smith's methodological assumption that "musical allusions serve to underline the subtext of a scene, offer critical comment on a dramatic situation, or even foreshadow later developments in the narrative" (172).

24. Ibid., p. 233.

25. Marlon Riggs, "*Tongues Untied*: An Interview with Marlon Riggs," interview conducted by Ron Simmons, in *Brother to Brother: Collected Writings by Black Gay Men*, ed. Essex Hemphill (Los Angeles: Alyson Books, 1991), p. 193. See also David Van Leer, "Visible Silence: Spectatorship in Black Gay and Lesbian Film," in *Representing Blackness: Issues in Film and Video*, ed. Valerie Smith (New Brunswick, NJ: Rutgers University Press, 1997), pp. 157–81.

26. Smith, "Unheard Melodies," p. 237.

27. For a slightly different, prose version of Riggs's voice-over narration in *Tongues Untied* (which I cite here), see "Tongues Untied," in Hemphill, *Brother to Brother*, pp. 200–05.

28. See Billie Holiday (with William Dufty), *Lady Sings the Blues* (New York: Penguin, 1956).

29. On the parallels between the image of Holiday propagated in her autobiography and in the film version of the book, *Lady Sings the Blues*, see Krin Gabbard, "Black and Tan Fantasies: The Jazz Biopic," in *Jammin' at the Margins: Jazz and the American Cinema* (Chicago: University of Chicago Press, 1996), pp. 95–99.

30. On the turn to the pop-oriented sound of the early Decca recordings, see also Donald Clarke, "The War Years," in *Wishing on the Moon: The Life and Times of Billie Holiday* (New York: Viking, 1994), pp. 234–35. The 1944 version of

"Lover Man (Oh, Where Can You Be?)" can be found on the first cut on disc 1 of *Billie Holiday: The Complete Decca Recordings, 1944–1950* (MCA, 1991).

31. Nicholson, *Billie Holiday* (Boston: Northeastern University Press, 1995), p. 141.

32. John Simmons, a well-regarded Swing-era bassist, recalls, "If someone introduced [Billie Holiday] to a woman and she had eyes, 'I'm William'—she'd introduce herself as a man, 'I'm William.'" Clarke, "The War Years," *Wishing on the* Moon, p. 174. As for the cross between form and content, in "When a Woman Loves a Man" Angela Y. Davis argues that Holiday's later style challenges the "social condition implied by the lyrics" of her love songs "through the musical form—the *aesthetic* dimension." *Blues Legacies and Black Feminism* (New York: Pantheon, 1998), p. 170.

33. Riggs, "Black Macho Revisited: Reflections of a Snap Queen," in Hemphill, *Brother to Brother*, pp. 253–57.

34. Riggs, "*Tongues Untied*: An Interview," p. 190.

35. Ibid., p. 194.

36. Davis, *Blues Legacies and Black Feminism*, p. 161.

37. Ibid.

38. Chuck Kleinhans, "*Ethnic Notions, Tongues Untied*: Mainstreams and Margins," *Jump Cut* 36 (May 1991): 115.

39. Nicholson, *Billie Holiday*, p. 141.

40. Valerie Smith, "Intersectionality and Experiments in Black Documentary," *Not Just Race, Not Just Gender* (New York: Routledge, 1998), p. 101.

41. Kobena Mercer, "Dark and Lovely Too: Black Gay Men in Independent Film," *Queer Looks: Perspectives on Lesbian and Gay Film and Video*, ed. Martha Gever, Pratibha Parmar, and John Greyson (New York: Routledge, 1993), p. 247.

42. Andrew Ross, "The Gangsta and the Diva," in *Real Love: In Pursuit of Cultural Justice* (New York: New York University Press, 1998), p. 76.

43. Queen Latifah (with Karen Hunter), *Ladies First: Revelations of a Strong Woman* (New York: William Morrow, 1999), p. 19. See also Tricia Rose, "One Queen, One Tribe, One Destiny," in *Rock She Wrote*, ed. Evelyn McDonnell and Ann Powers (New York: Delta, 1995), p. 316. Queen Latifah's discography includes *All Hail the Queen* (Tommy Boy, 1989), *Nature of a Sista* (Tommy Boy, 1991), *Black Reign* (Motown, 1993), and *Order in the Court* (Motown, 1998).

44. Tricia Rose, "'All Aboard the Night Train,'" in *Black Noise: Rap Music and Black Culture in Contemporary America* (Hanover: Wesleyan/New England University Press, 1994), p. 105.

45. Queen Latifah, *Ladies First*, p. 3.

46. Nelson George, "Too Live," *Hip Hop America* (New York: Viking, 1998), p. 184.

47. Queen Latifah, *Ladies First*, p. 3.

48. Judith Halberstam, "An Introduction to Female Masculinity" and "A Rough Guide to Butches on Film," in *Female Masculinity* (Durham, NC: Duke University Press, 1998), pp. 29 and 228, respectively.

49. "*Set It Off*," in *The Motion Picture Guide*, ed. Edmond Grant (New York: CineBooks, 1997), p. 332. For a number of the mostly new songs featured

in *Set It Off* (but excluding, alas, Yo-Yo, Eric B. & Rakim, and The Geto Boys), listen to *Set It Off: Music from the New Line Cinema Motion Picture* (Electra/East West Records, 1996).

50. George, *Hip Hop America*, p. 106.

51. For "Flash Light," consult Parliament's *Funkentelechy vs. the Placebo Syndrome* (Casablanca, 1977).

52. Indeed, in an interview, Dr. Dre recalled that, pre–World Class Wreckin' Cru, he worked as a DJ playing a lot of "P-funk stuff" and that the "strongest influence" on his own gangsta-funk style was George Clinton. Brian Cross, *It's Not About a Salary . . . : Rap, Race, Resistance and Los Angeles* (New York: Verso, 1993), p. 196.

53. George, "Where My Eyes Can See," in *Hip Hop America*, p. 106. For a revealing portrait of Dr. Dre, see Ronin Ro, "Moving Target," in *Gangsta: Merchandising the Rhymes of Violence* (New York: St. Martin's Press, 1996), pp. 145–56. More recently, Dr. Dre—in addition to releasing *2001* (1999, Aftermath)—has served as the mentor of Eminem, executive producing for example the latter's *The Marshall Mathers LP* (Interscope, 2000).

54. There's also something of an audiovisual pun to the use of The Geto Boys' "Point of No Return" here, since even as their sound reverberates with the Parliamentary grooves of the original West-Coast gangsta group, NWA, their cop-killer ethos is embodied in the cinematic posturings of their Capone-styled MC, Brad Jordan (aka "Scarface"). For "Point of No Return," listen to *The Resurrection* (Rap-A-Lot/Noo Trybe Records, 1996).

55. Cleo's refusal of Black Sam's request for Frankie as sexual interest also recollects the scene early on in *Set It Off* when Stony prostitutes herself to Nate Andrews (Charlie Robinson) in order to help her brother Stevie.

56. Halberstam, *Female Masculinity*, p. 29.

57. Dr. Dre, "Dr. Dre (Interview)," in Cross, *It's Not About a Salary*, p. 197.

58. On the topic of female automobility, see Kathleen McHugh, "Women in Traffic: LA Autobiography," *South Atlantic Quarterly* 97, no. 2 (Spring 1998): 391–412, esp. 405–08.

59. Yo-Yo's "Bonnie and Clyde II" (featuring Ice Cube) references, of course, not only the Arthur Penn film *Bonnie and Clyde* (1967) but, in the person of Yolanda "Yo-Yo" Whitaker herself, early West Coast female gangsta rap. For the Yo-Yo CD on which "Bonnie and Clyde II" appears, see *Total Control* (Electra/East West Records, 1996).

60. Queen Latifah, *Ladies First*, p. 123.

4. Audiophilia

1. Stephen Heath, "Cinema and Psychoanalysis: Parallel Histories," in *Endless Night: Cinema and Psychoanalysis, Parallel Histories*, ed. Janet Bergstrom (Berkeley: University of California Press, 1999), p. 33.

2. Laura Mulvey, "Visual Pleasure and Narrative Cinema," in *The Sexual Subject: A* Screen *Reader in Sexuality* (London: Routledge, 1992), p. 33.

3. Meaghan Morris, *Too Soon, Too Late: History in Popular Culture* (Bloomington: Indiana University Press, 1998), pp. xiii–xxiii.

4. Mulvey, "Visual Pleasure," p. 33.

5. Fredric Jameson, "Pleasure: A Political Issue," in *The Ideologies of Theory: Essays 1971–1986* (Minneapolis: University of Minnesota Press, 1988), p. 74. The original appears in *Formations of Pleasure*, ed. Formations Editorial Collective (London: Routledge and Kegan Paul, 1983), pp. 1–14.

6. Michel Chion, *Audio-Vision: Sound on Screen*, trans. Claudia Gorbman (New York: Columbia University Press, 1994).

7. By "musical imaginary" I mean the whole gamut of social and affective effects associated with sound cinema, which is itself the product of a particular, historically specific technology and mode of representation. The term "imaginary" has in the context of this chapter (and opposed to its usual pejorative valence in, say, Lacan) a relatively neutral status, as does the related notion of fantasy. To paraphrase Adorno, fantasy or the imaginary—that is to say, the sensuous play of appearances—is indispensable to the work of art.

8. My sense of the acoustic signifier derives from Metz's notion of the cinema as imaginary signifier. More specifically, the term "acoustic signifier" is intended to suggest that sound can, depending on its function (fidelity, intelligibility, expressivity) refer to a signified (say, a diegetic image) or another signifier (say, another acoustic signifier, so that the sound track can be said to exist apart from the diegesis or image track). This, the ambiguity or undecidability of the acoustic signifier is partly what gives it its extraordinary plasticity. With respect to Chion's claim that "there is no sound track," see Rick Altman et al. who argue in their brief for a notion of *mise-en-bande* that sounds in cinema need not be defined through their "relation to diegetic events" but can be defined "through internal sound-to-sound coherence." "Inventing the Cinema Sound Track," in *Music and Cinema*, ed. James Buhler, Caryl Flinn, and James Neumeyer (Hanover, NH: Wesleyan University Press, 2000), p. 341. For the most nuanced reading of the relation between the image and sound tracks, see James Buhler, "Analytical and Interpretive Aproaches to Film Music (II)," in *Film Music: Critical Approaches*, ed. J. K. Donnelly (New York: Continuum, 2001), pp. 39–61, especially "The Ontology of the Soundtrack" (53–55).

9. Christian Metz, *The Imaginary Signifier: Psychoanalysis and the Cinema*, trans. Celia Britton, Annwyl Williams, Ben Brewster, and Alfred Guzzetti (Bloomington: Indiana University Press, 1982), p. 7.

10. Ibid.

11. Ibid.

12. Paul Willemen, "Cinephilia Reconsidered," in *Looks and Frictions: Essays in Cultural Studies and Film Theory* (Bloomington: Indiana University Press, 1994), p. 232.

13. Ibid., p. 225.

14. On Metz as the originary figure of contemporary film theory, see chapter 3.

15. Stephen Heath, "Difference," in *The Sexual Subject*, pp. 47–106.

16. Metz, *The Imaginary Signifier*, pp. 14–15.

17. Mulvey, "Visual Pleasure," p. 24.

18. Ibid.

19. Ibid.

20. See, respectively, in *The Sexual Subject*: Mary Ann Doane, "Film and Masquerade: Theorizing the Female Spectator" (1982), pp. 227–43; Steve Neale, "Masculinity as Spectacle" (1983), pp. 277–94; and Jackie Stacey, "Desperately Seeking Difference" (1987), pp. 244–64.

21. Richard Dyer, "Don't Look Now: The Male Pin-Up" (1982), in *The Sexual Subject*, pp. 265–76.

22. D. A. Miller, "Visual Pleasure in 1959," *Out Takes: Essays on Queer Theory and Film*, ed. Ellis Hanson (Durham, NC: Duke University Press, 1999), p. 117.

23. Ibid., p. 122.

24. Hanson, introduction to *Out Takes*, p. 8.

25. Ibid., p. 2.

26. Ibid., p. 5.

27. Homi Bhabha, "The Other Question: The Stereotype and Colonial Discourse," in *The Sexual Subject*, pp. 213–31; for "The Last Special Issue of Race," see *Screen* 29, no. 4 (1988).

28. bell hooks, "Oppositional Gaze," and Slavoj Žižek, "Looking Awry," in *Film and Theory*, ed. Robert Stam and Toby Miller (New York: Blackwell, 2000), pp. 529 and 514, respectively.

29. Ibid., p. 515 and p. 529, respectively.

30. hooks, "Cool Cynicism: *Pulp Fiction*," in *Reel to Real: Race, Sex and Class at the Movies* (New York: Routledge, 1996), pp. 46–47.

31. Sharon Willis, "Borrowed 'Style': Quentin Tarantino's Figures of Masculinity," in *High Contrast: Race and Gender in Contemporary Hollywood Film* (Durham, NC: Duke University Press, 1997), p. 216.

32. Ibid.

33. Kaja Silverman, *Male Subjectivity at the Margins* (New York: Routledge, 1992), p. 130.

34. Willis, "Borrowed 'Style,'" p. 217. For a reading that focuses more on other elements of the sound track such as, inter alia, effects, see my "Real Fantasies: Connie Stevens, *Silencio*, and Other Sonic Phenomena in *Mulholland Drive*," in *Lowering the Boom*, ed. Jay Beck and Tony Grajeda (forthcoming).

35. Quentin Tarantino, Jackie Brown: *A Screenplay* (New York: Hyperion, 1997), p. 1. All further references to the published version of the screenplay will be cited in parentheses. For the sound track, refer to *Jackie Brown: Music From the Motion Picture* (A Band Apart/Maverick, 1997). The popular-musical imaginary of *Jackie Brown* is mainly a function of '70s music—whether it's the electric blues of Elvin Bishop ("She Puts Me in the Mood") or the down-home New Orleans funk of The Meters ("Cissy Strut"), Germaine Jackson's post–Jackson Five "My Touch of Madness" or the Vampire Sound Inc.'s raucous "Lion and the Cucumber" from Jesús Franco's sexploitation classic, *Vampyros Lesbos* (1970). However, the musical imaginary of *Jackie Brown* also encompasses historically heterogeneous music such as the Supremes' mid-'60s number-one Motown hit, "Baby Love," Johnny Cash's '90s alt-folk/country rendition of "Tennessee Stud," and,

most significantly perhaps, Foxy Brown's mid-'90s rap anthem, "Letter to the Firm." The live Viper-Room version of Cash's "Tennessee Stud" is from the celebrated, Rick Rubin-produced *American Recordings* (1994, Universal).

36. I am playing here on the French terms *le regard* (which can be translated as either the "look" or the "gaze") and its aural equivalent, *l'écoute* (Chion, *Audio-Vision*, p. 216, note 1). I should add that the relation between diegetic and nondiegetic sound is, as Buhler and David Neumeyer note, "highly complex": "the simplest situation, in which the types are strictly isolated in their respective . . . spheres, is an extreme case; in practice, music can and does routinely cross the membrane that separates them" ("Analytical and Interpretive Approaches to Film Music (I)," in Donnelly, *Film Music*, p. 17). My working notion here derives from Buhler's observation that "Non-diegetic music . . . always speaks from a position of discursive authority" ("Analytical and Interpretive Approaches to Film Music (II)," p. 52).

37. Tarantino, "Interview with Quentin Tarantino" (1994), interview conducted by Joshua Mooney, in *Quentin Tarantino: Interviews*, ed. Gerald Peary (Jackson: University of Mississippi Press, 1998), p. 77.

38. Fred Botting and Scott Wilson, *The Tarantinian Ethics* (London: Sage, 2001), p. 165.

39. Jackie's musical point of view is also audible in the scenes where Max listens to the Delfonics while driving to and from the Del Amo Mall. For an instructive reading of the scene where Jackie selects the Delfonics to play for Max, see Ken Garner, "Would You Like to Hear Some Music?: In-and-Out-of-Control in the Films of Quentin Tarantino," in Donnelly, *Film Music*, p. 160.

40. The Delfonics, who recorded for Stan "The Man" Watson's Philly Groove Records, drew on, among other things, the doo-wop sound of Frankie Lymon and Little Anthony and the Imperials to produce '60s and '70s hits such as "La-La Means I Love You" (1968) and "Didn't I Blow Your Mind This Time," both of which appear on the sound track of *Jackie Brown*. For a sampler, see *The Delfonics: La-La Means I Love You: The Definitive Collection* (Arista, 1997).

41. Tarantino, "Press Conference on *Jackie Brown*" (1997), transcribed by Peter Keough, in Peary, *Quentin Tarantino*, p. 199.

42. Ibid., p. 195.

43. See the entry on "Music" in Alan Barnes and Marcus Hearn, *Tarantino, A to Zed: The Films of Quentin Tarantino* (London: Batsford, 1996), p. 102.

44. In *Pulp Fiction* Bonnie Dimmich (Vanessa Valentino)—Jimmy's badass black wife who in turn appears to be modelled on Pam Grier in *Coffy*—and Alabama Whitman in *True Romance* ("Sounds like a Pam Grier movie!") are, of course, the precursors in Tarantino's own densely intertextual corpus. For Tarantino's conception of blaxploitation, see "Blaxploitation: What It Is . . . What It Was!," in *The Film Geek Files*, ed. Paul A. Woods (London: Plexus, 2000), pp. 138–43.

45. Botting and Wilson, *Tarantinian Ethics*, p. 165.

46. "Empathetic sound," for Chion, is music that "directly express[es] its participation in the feelings of the scene, by taking on the scene's rhythm, tone, and phrasing" (*Audio-Vision*, p. 8).

47. In fact, this ambiguity or plasticity is implicit in the whole notion of nondiegetic sound, where the latter is predicated on the diegesis understood in its most reductive form not so much as narrative but image. The acoustic signifier's undecidability is also what accounts for the ambiguous status of diegetic or nondiegetic sound in general as well as "acousmatic" off-screen sound. For a resonant example of the latter (I bracket here the equally significant Max-motivated toilet flush that bookends *Jackie Brown*), note the scene where we are first introduced to the character of Max Cherry: although the camera stays with Ordell and Louis as they enter his office, the acoustic space is dominated by the sound of Max talking off-screen on the phone. The resonance of this acousmatic moment derives from the way in which it foreshadows the conclusion of the film when Max breaks his clinch with Jackie in order to take another phone call (from, appropriately, a mother whose son is "still in school"): unlike, it appears, Jackie, Max cannot escape that inverted prison which is his job as a bailbondsman.

48. On "musical 'point of view,'" see David Cooper, *Bernard Hermann's Vertigo: A Film Score Handbook* (Westport, CT: Greenwood Press, 2001), pp. 67–68. The problem with the notion of musical point of view—in addition to the fact that it pertains only to music and not sound in general—is, of course, its rhetorical valorization of point of view, which has the conceptual effect of reinstituting the primacy of the visual axis. Hence my recourse, however loose with respect to the industrial definition, of "point of audition." In subjective point of audition, according to Chion, "we find the same phenomenon as that which operates for vision. . . . It is the visual representation of a character in closeup that, in simultaneous association with the hearing of sound, identifies this sound as being heard by the character shown" (*Audio-Vision*, p. 91).

49. For a more comprehensive reading of this key sequence, see Garner, "Would You Like to Hear Some Music?," pp. 198–99. For the Ayers's tracks, check out *Coffy* (1973, Polydor).

50. By "idiosyncratic" diegetic sound, which is to be distinguished from both Chion's restricted understanding of point of audition and so-called musical point of view, I mean sound and musical effects that are associated with a single character or set of characters. Thus, although Louis also "beeps" Ordell's car, this sonic act says more about Ordell than Louis (i.e., Ordell dominates Louis). In this context (and according to the above logic), one can also speak of "objective" diegetic as well as "subjective" and "objective" nondiegetic sound.

51. The fact that the only music associated with Louis is the Supremes' "Baby Love" (which is playing in the background of Simone's apartment while she stripteases for him) musically connotes just how out of touch he is. Tarantino's introductory description of his character in the screenplay captures this musically obtuse aspect of his character: "While acutely aware of the rhythm of life inside a correctional facility, in the real world [Louis's] timing is thrown. It's like a song he doesn't know the lyrics to but attempts to sing along [to] anyway" (4).

52. The music played at Jackie's haunt, the Cockatoo Inn, in the various scenes located there—in particular, Ayers's "Exotic Dance" (Jackie/Max) and Minnie Ripperton's "Inside My Love" (Jackie/Ordell)—resound with the per-

formative complexity of Jackie's character. For example, the sublime "Inside my Love," which features the extraordinary range and grain of Ripperton's soprano voice, echoes Ordell's strategic paen to Jackie: "I bet you come here on a Saturday night, you need nigga repellent keep 'em off your ass."

53. See, for example, Foster Hirsch, "The Boys in the Back Room," *Detours and Lost Highways: A Map of Neo-Noirs* (New York: Limelight, 1999), pp. 138–39.

54. Chion: "An inherent quality of the *acousmêtre* is that it can be instantly dispossessed of its mysterious powers (seeing all, omniscience, omnipotence, ubiquity) when it is de-acousmatized, when the film reveals the face, that is the source of the voice." *Audio-Vision*, p. 130.

55. Ibid., p. 131.

56. Ibid., p. 130.

57. Willemen, "Cinephilia Reconsidered," p. 251.

58. Ibid.

59. Bauer, "The Mouth and the Method," *Sight and Sound* 8, no. 3 (March 1996): 9.

60. Ibid.

61. Ibid.

62. See the entry for "Stuck in the Middle with You," in Barnes and Hearn, *Tarantino, A to Zed*, p. 138.

63. However, if only Jackie Burke's hair color is marked in Leonard's novel ("dark blond" [p. 36]), both Ordell's and Louis's race is explicitly registered: "a light-skinned black guy and a dark-skinned white guy," respectively. *Rum Punch* (New York: Delacorte, 1992), p. 3. This registration has an added kick given the context: a neo-Nazi "white power demonstration in downtown Palm Beach" (p. 1).

64. The Guess Who (1964), the Grass Roots (1964), and the Delfonics (1965) were all founded at roughly the same time. However, while the sound of the Grass Roots could be characterized as soul, albeit white pop-soul, the difference couldn't be greater between the classic, hard album-rock of the Guess Who—epitomized by the guitar work of Randy Bachman—and the anti-Stax, horn-and-strings Philly sound of the Delfonics featuring the high tenor of William Hart.

65. When Ordell visits Jackie's apartment after she's been released from jail and he puts his hands around her throat, she presses Max's gun against Ordell's "dick." Jackie's command to Ordell is also noteworthy for its sarcastic reiteration of his demotic patois: "Now take your hands from around my throat, nigga" (p. 79). This moment is reiterated when Ordell, talking to Louis about the bungled money exchange, realizes that Jackie Brown is the "architect" (162) of the double-cross: "Gotcha, nigga" (198).

66. See "Ears," in Barnes and Hearn, *Tarantino, A to Zed*, pp. 49–51.

67. Quoted in Barnes and Hearn, *Tarantino, A to Zed*, p. 81.

68. The song in question, Foxy Brown's "Letter to the Firm" (sample lyric: "I'm married to the Firm . . . you gotta understand / I'll die for 'em, gimme a chair and then I'll fry for 'em") provides a striking counterpoint to Max's, not to mention Jackie's and Ordell's, musical tastes; it also prefigures

Tarantino's extensive use of the RZA in the first volume of *Kill Bill* (2003). For the Foxy Brown tune—which, appropriately enough, samples Isaac Hayes's "Ike's Mood, Part 1" (*To be Continued* [1970, Stax])—consult her début album, *Ill Na Na* (1996, Def Jam).

69. Tarantino, "Interview" (1998), interviewed by Adrian Wootton. http://film.guardian.co.uk/Guardian_NFT/interview.

70. Ibid.

Reprise: Alex's "Lovely Ludwig van" and Marty McFly's White Rock Minstrel Show

1. Stephen Heath, "On Suture," *Questions of Cinema* (Bloomington: Indiana University Press, 1981), pp. 107–08.

2. See, for example, *Narrative, Apparatus, Ideology: A Film Theory Reader*, ed. Philip Rosen (New York: Columbia University Press, 1986).

3. For an incisive reading of the relation between fantasy and reality in *A Clockwork Orange*, see Mario Falsetto's *Stanley Kubrick: A Narrative and Stylistic Analysis* (Westport, CT: Praeger, 2001), p. 121. Thomas Allen Nelson also notes in *Kubrick: Inside a Film Artist's Maze* that Alex does not recognize the "difference between his fantasies and those projected on a movie screen." (Bloomington: Indiana University Press, 2000), p. 159.

4. As Rasmussen writes, "Alex is reduced to [being] a captive audience at someone else's horrorshow, just as Mr. Alexander was forced, for Alex's edification, to watch the rape of his wife" (Adrienne Corri). *Stanley Kubrick: Seven Films Analyzed* (Jefferson, NC: McFarland, 2001), p. 147. On the sexual politics of *A Clockwork Orange* (which are, to say the least, complicated, if not problematic as such), see Margaret DeRosia, "An Erotics of Violence: Violence and (Homo) Sexuality in Stanley Kubrick's *A Clockwork Orange*," in *Stanley Kubrick's* A Clockwork Orange, ed. Stuart Y. McDougal (New York: Cambridge University Press, 2003), pp. 61–84.

5. For Burgess's version of this passage (which features Alex listening to Geoffrey Plautus as "played by Odysseus Choerilos with the Macon [Georgia] Philharmonic," then, post sex, Mozart's "Jupiter" and J. S. Bach's "Brandenburg Concerto"), see *A Clockwork Orange* (New York: Ballantine, 1963), pp. 38 and 40. The locution "kitsch music-box" comes from Alexander Walker's reading of *A Clockwork Orange* in his *Stanley Kubrick: Director* (New York: Norton, 1999), p. 218.

6. In the novel, Alex listens not to Beethoven's Ninth but his Fifth Symphony. Not so incidentally, the fate theme from the Fifth also appears as a door chime in *A Clockwork Orange* when Alex first goes with his gang to the home of the Alexanders.

7. Both the "dancing Jesus" and "Roman solider" sequences also appear to ironically echo the dramatic orchestral conclusion to *Spartacus* (1960).

8. The Christian thematics of *A Clockwork Orange* are complex and intricate. The Chaplain's description of Alex, post conditioning, as a "true Christian . . . ready to be crucified rather than crucify" suggests something of its import.

9. Of course, the Cat Lady also wields a bust of Beethoven when Alex attacks her in her house with her penis sculpture, and there is, as well, a bust of Beethoven in Alex's cell.

10. Kubrick, "Modern Times: An Interview with Stanley Kubrick" (1972), interviewed by Philip Strick and Penelope Houston, in *Stanley Kubrick: Interviews*, ed. Gene D. Phillips (Jackson: University of Mississippi Press, 2001), p. 130.

11. Kubrick, "Kubrick Country," interview by Penelope Houston in Phillips, *Stanley Kubrick: Interviews*, p. 110.

12. Schiller's ode is first heard when a "sophisto" breaks into it at the Korova Milkbar to the astonishment of Alex and the consternation of Dim (Warren Clarke).

13. On, for example, the critical reception of Kubrick's film in the United States, including the feminist response, see Janet Staiger, "The Cultural Productions of *A Clockwork Orange*," in *Perverse Spectators: The Practices of Film Reception* (New York: New York University Press, 2000), pp. 93–111. For critical responses to the music used in the film, see Krin Gabbard and Shailja Sharma, "Stanley Kubrick and the Art of Cinema" and, in particular, Peter Rabinowitz, "'A Bird of Like Rarest Spun Heavenmetal': Music in *A Clockwork Orange*," in McDougal, *Stanley Kubrick's* A Clockwork Orange, pp. 85–108 and 109–30, respectively.

14. Huey Lewis and the News' Top 40, bar-rock music, which was inescapable in the mid-1980s (represented in *Back to the Future* by "The Power of Love" and "Back in Time"), is, of course, central to the musical imaginary of the film. This musical imaginary also comprises other contemporary audio tracks such as Eric Clapton's "Heaven Is One Step Away" and Lindsay Buckingham's "Time Bomb Town" as well as period songs such as the Four Aces' "Mr. Sandman" (1954) and Fess Parker's "Ballad of David Crockett" (1955). In this context, see also the record store next to Lou's café, whose shop window features album cover art for Nat King Cole's *Unforgettable* (1953), Patti Page's *In the Land of Hi-Fi* (1956), and Eydie Gorme's *Eydie in Dixieland* (1960).

15. For an analysis of the dynamics of shame and humiliation in *Back to the Future*, see Warren Buckland and Thomas Elsaesser, "Oedipal Narratives and the Post-Oedipal," in *Studying Contemporary American Film: A Guide to Movie Analysis* (London: Arnold, 2002), pp. 240–42.

16. At the beginning of the film, before Marty travels back in time, George half-heartedly makes a fist while talking to his son after finding out from Biff that his car has been trashed: "I'm afraid I'm just not very good at confrontations."

17. Buckland and Elsaesser, "Oedipal Narratives and the Post-Oedipal," p. 236.

18. Fred Rothwell, *Long Distance Information: Chuck Berry's Recording Legacy* (York, UK: Music Mentor Books, 2001), p. 87.

19. John Collis, *Chuck Berry: The Biography* (London: Arum Press, 2002), p. 81.

20. Chuck Berry, quoted in Bruce Pegg, *Brown Eyed Handsome Man: The Life and Hard Times of Chuck Berry* (New York: Routledge, 2002), p. 87

21. Berry, *The Autobiography* (New York: Harmony Books, 1987), p. 157.

22. Booker T. Washington, *Up From Slavery* (New York: Signet, 2000), p. 154. In this, the "Atlanta Compromise Speech" chapter of *Up From Slavery*, see the play of the figure of hands in Washington's prose: "nearly sixteen millions of hands will aid you in pulling the load upward" (p. 155). See also Pegg, *Brown Eyed Handsome Man*, p. 88.

23. Fred Pfeil, "Plot and Patriarchy in the Age of Reagan: Reading *Back to the Future* and *Brazil*," in *Another Tale to Tell* (London: Verso, 1990), p. 235.

24. The phrases cited are from the following authors: "stopped string bends": Pegg, *Brown Eyed Handsome Man*, p. 89; "chicken-pecking": Collis, *Chuck Berry*, p. 81; "note for note": Rothwell, *Long Distance Information*, p. 54.

25. Berry: "The gateway . . . was somewhere 'close to New Orleans,' where most Africans were sorted through and sold." *The Autobiography*, p. 156. About New Orleans Berry also notes that it was a place he'd "longed to visit ever since hearing Muddy Waters's lyrics, 'Going down in Louisiana, way down behind the sun'" (p. 126).

5. Gen-X TV

1. Given the critical consensus that *Melrose Place* began its downward spiral during the 1995–96 season, this chapter will focus on its heyday—from, that is, 1993 to 1995. For this consensus (which was shared by the producers), see, for example, Bruce Fretts, "Spelling Lessons," *Entertainment Weekly* 317, March 8, 1996, pp. 50–52; Kristen Baldwin et al., "Fall TV Preview," *Entertainment Weekly* 344, September 13, 1996, p. 52; and for what Baldwin calls the "fun-filled camp heyday from '93 to '95," see "Classic Reruns: *Melrose Place*," *Entertainment Weekly* 338, August 2, 1996, p. 51. It's worth noting, I think, that the finale of the third season involved, as fans know, the literal destruction of Melrose Place; ironically enough, this episode may have represented the apex of the show. On the last, see, for example, Gina Bellafante's "Stop the Inanity!," *Time*, May 13, 1996, p. 85. *Melrose Place* began its first syndication run on *E!* on August 5, 1996.

2. On *Melrose Place* as "*Dynasty* for Generation X," see Tom Gliatto, Tom Cunneff, and Craig Tomashoff, "Hot Property," *People Weekly*, February 21, 1994, p. 65. See also Jane Feuer, who comments that although "*Melrose* is no *Dynasty*," it is the "only nineties show truly to understand *Dynasty*'s contribution to the form of the melodramatic serial" and that the program does not "signify an historical period and Zeitgeist so much . . . as a generational awareness." *Seeing Through the Eighties* (Durham, NC: Duke University Press, 1995), pp. 130, note 4, and 147.

3. On what I call a "general" or "libidinal-political" economy, see Robert Miklitsch, *From Hegel to Madonna: Towards a General Economy of "Commodity Fetishism"* (Albany: State University of New York Press, 1998). For the standard, "regulation school" account of post-Fordism, see Michel Aglietta's *A Theory of Capitalist Regulation: The U.S. Experience*, trans. David Fernbach (London: New Left Books, 1979). For a translation of sorts, see David Harvey,

"The Political-Economic Transformation of Late-Twentieth Century Capitalism," in *The Condition of Postmodernity* (Cambridge: Blackwell, 1989), pp. 121–97. For a concise, balanced discussion of post-Fordism, see Martyn J. Lee, "Flexible Post-Fordism or Primitive Capitalism," in *Consumer Culture Reborn* (New York: Routledge, 1993), pp. 108–18. On the economics of Generation X, see, for example, Rob Nelson and Jon Cowan, "Generation Debt," in *Revolution X: A Survival Guide for Our Generation* (New York: Penguin, 1994), pp. 18–35; Alexander Abrams and David Lipsky, "The Bottom of All That Americans Do," in *Late Bloomers* (New York: Random House, 1994), pp. 51–78; Jeffrey Holtz, "The Impoverished Generation," in *Welcome to the Jungle: The Why Behind Generation X* (New York: St. Martin's, 1995), pp. 141–76; and Steven E. Shier, "Hazards Lie Ahead: Economic Prospects for Generation X," in *After the Boom: The Politics of Generation X* (Lanham, MD: Rowman and Littlefield, 1997), pp. 127–44.

4. In *Politics and Letters* Williams describes "structure of feeling" in the following terms: "It was a structure in the sense that you could perceive it operating in one work after another . . . yet it was one of feeling much more than of thought." *Politics and Letters: Interviews with New Left Review* (London: Verso, 1979), p. 159. In *Marxism and Literature*, Williams also observes that an "alternative definition" of "structures of feeling"—of, that is, those "specifically affective elements of consciousness" as well as those "characteristic elements of impulse, restraint and tone"—is "structures of *experience*." *Marxism and Literature* (London: Oxford University Press, 1977), p. 132. In other words, feeling is not so much a matter of private expression, a function of the individual subject, as a form of sociality. Less obviously but no less importantly, structure of feeling intimates that emotion, like imagination, has a history.

5. See, for example, David Wild, "*Melrose Place* Is a Really Good Show," *Rolling Stone*, May 19, 1994, p. 50. As Spelling himself remembers, "In the beginning, *Melrose* stories were structured like the early *90210* episodes, with everybody learning moral lessons about life on each show." *A Prime-Time Life* (New York: St. Martin's, 1995), p. 190.

6. Chris Willman, "Addicted to the 'Place,'" *New York Times*, March 16, 1994, sec. F, p. 1.

7. As a "high-ranking source" at Spelling Entertainment has recounted, "Look at the first episode of *Melrose Place* and look at the ratings after Heather Locklear was brought in." Cited in Mathew Tyrnauer, "Star Power!," *Vanity Fair*, May 1995, p. 173.

8. Darren Star, cited in Rick Marin, "TV Tour Guide to the New LA," *New York Times*, August 23, 1992, sec. 9, p. 8.

9. Wild, "*Melrose Place* Is a Really Good Show," p. 50.

10. Star, cited in Marin, "TV Tour Guide to the New LA," p. 8.

11. According to the Nielsen ratings for the 1994–95 season, *Melrose Place* was number four for ages 18–24 and number ten for ages 18–34. However, overall (which is to say for all ages), *Melrose Place* at the end of, for instance, the 1994–95 season was listed number seventy. For the first set of figures, see Rob Owen, *Gen X TV* (Syracuse, NY: Syracuse University Press, 1997), p. 69; for the latter, see "Ranks for the Memories," *Entertainment Weekly*, June 7, 1996, p. 23.

12. For a thorough survey of reception studies and audience research, see Virginia Nightingale, *Studying Audiences: The Shock of the Real* (New York: Routledge, 1996).

13. The literature on the relation between soap opera and melodrama is too extensive to cite; for a representative sample, see, however, Ang, "Melodramatic Identifications: Television Fiction and Women's Fantasy," in *Living Room Wars* (New York: Routledge, 1996), pp. 85–97; and Lynne Joyrich, "All That Television Allows: TV Melodrama, Postmodernism, and Consumer Culture," in *Re-Viewing Reception: Television, Gender, and Postmodern Culture* (Bloomington: Indiana University Press, 1996), pp. 45–66.

14. The issue of modalities of viewing—the fact that "we watch TV with different degrees of attention and in conjunction, often, with other activities"—is a crucial, if neglected, methodological problem. David Morley and Roger Silverstone, "Domestic Communication: Technologies and Meanings," in Morley, *Television, Audiences, and Cultural Studies* (New York: Routledge, 1992), p. 207.

15. On, inter alia, regularization in the context of soap opera, see Robert C. Allen, "Soap Opera's Mode of Production," in *Speaking of Soap Operas* (Chapel Hill: University of North Carolina Press, 1985), pp. 46–58. For the Bourdieu citation, see *Distinction*, trans. Richard Nice (Cambridge: Harvard University Press, 1984), pp. 101–02.

16. For the phrase "prime-time continuing melodramatic serial," see Feuer, *Seeing Through the Eighties*, p. 1. On the difference between "series" and "serial," see Ien Ang, *Watching "Dallas": Soap Opera and the Melodramatic Imagination* (New York: Routledge, 1982), p. 52; and on "serial narrational structure," see Robert C. Allen, introduction to *To Be Continued . . . Soap Operas Around the World*, ed. Allen (New York: Routledge, 1995), p. 1.

17. Douglas S. Cramer, cited in Andy Meisler, "A 'Soap' Mogul with an Eye for the 90's," *New York Times*, August 29, 1993, sec. 2, p. 29. See also, in general, David Marc and Robert J. Thompson, "Aaron Spelling: Crime, Punishment, and Affirmative Action," in *Prime Time, Prime Movers* (Boston: Little, Brown, 1992), p. 168. For Spelling's own take on his career (where Spelling, as Marc and Thompson suggest, "is arguably the most prolific television auteur in the history of the medium"), see *A Prime-Time Life*, p. 163.

18. Meisler, "'Soap' Mogul," p. 29.

19. For the phrase the "last of the great soap operas," see Cramer, cited in Meisler, "'Soap' Mogul," p. 29.

20. For a discussion of the politics of this period with respect to "ensemble cast serial melodramas," see Feuer, "Serial Form, Melodrama, and Reaganite Ideology in Eighties Television," in *Seeing Through the Eighties*, pp. 111–30.

21. Bruce Handy, "1600 Melrose Place," *Time*, May 30, 1994, p. 18. The pretext for this article was the sexual harassment suit filed by Paula Jones against President Clinton, the "story line" of which was echoed in the 1993–94 two-hour season finale of *Melrose Place*.

22. On *Beverly Hills 90210* as a "transitional show," see Elayne Rapping, "The Year of the Young," *The Progressive*, February 1993, p. 37.

23. Spelling, cited in Wild, "*Melrose Place* Is a Really Good Show," p. 108. For a sense of the very first episode of *Melrose Place*, which was structured around Alison trying to pay the rent, see the script excerpt in Spelling, *A Prime-Time Life*, pp. 185–88.

24. Richard Zoglin, "The Young and the Senseless," *Time*, March 28, 1994, p. 69.

25. On the incarnations of *Melrose Place*, see Owen, *Gen X TV*, p. 100.

26. Zoglin, "The Young and the Senseless," p. 69.

27. See "Change of Address," special *Melrose Place* issue, *Entertainment Weekly*, October 31, 1995, p. 98. As the authors of the above issue put it, "Rhonda Blair, the only African-American ever to live in the complex" (98). Or as the first script had it, establishing the dominant representational code of *Melrose Place*—hair: "Twenty-something, black, with hair that sends a message." Cited in Spelling, *A Prime-Time Life*, p. 186.

28. Christine Geraghty, "Sex, Race and Class: The Pressures to Change," in *Women and Soap Opera: A Study of Prime-Time Soaps* (Cambridge: Polity Press, 1991), p. 142.

29. Ibid., p. 143.

30. John O'Connor, "Once More unto the Pool, Hunks," *New York Times*, July 15, 1992, sec. C, p. 15.

31. Zoglin, "The Young and the Senseless," p. 69.

32. O'Connor, "Once More unto the Pool," p. 15.

33. While Fox ordered the producers of *Melrose Place* to alter the "same-sex smooch" scene, the Gay and Lesbian Alliance Against Defamation (GLAAD)—the Los Angles chapter of which named *Melrose Place* Best Television Drama in 1993—protested the censored kiss. The pretext for the alteration was the 1990 incident involving ABC's *thirtysomething* "when corporate sponsors withdrew more than $1 million in advertising from an episode that showed two gay men sharing a bed." Chris Bull, "Acting Gay," *Advocate*, December 27, 1994, p. 46.

34. As Savant himself said in an interview, "I don't understand the controversy. [The kiss] is very tame. It's more about Billy's reaction to finding out his best man is gay." Alan Carter, "The Hard-Bodied Men of 'Melrose Place,'" *Entertainment Weekly*, May 20, 1994, p. 17. For an incisive take on Matt Fielding as well as the hyper-heterosexual politics of *Melrose Place*, see also Stephen Tropiano, *Prime Time Closet: A History of Gays and Lesbians on TV* (New York: Applause, 2002), pp. 124–27.

35. After Jeffrey, Matt got involved with one Dr. Paul Graham (David Beecroft) of Wilshire Memorial Hospital. Though Matt and Paul were shown emerging from Matt's bedroom the morning after a date, "what the good doctor really desired," as the editors of the special *Melrose Place* issue remark, was not, say, hot sex but to "frame Matt for his wife's murder." "The Ecstasy and the Agony," special *Melrose Place* issue, p. 28.

36. On this public fiction (AIDS equals homosexuality), see Lee Edelman, "The Tank and the Mirror: 'AIDS,' Subjectivity, and the Rhetoric of Activism," in *Homographesis: Essays on Gay Literary and Cultural Theory* (New York: Routledge, 1994), pp. 93–117.

37. Consider in this context the bit of narrative *bizarrie* when Kimberly threatened to stick Matt with an HIV-infected needle because he tried to expose her plan to murder her then fiancé, Michael Mancini. The follow-up to this plot was an episode where "Matt advised Michael that it might not be a good idea to get back together with Kimberly just weeks after she had tried to kill him." Bull, "Acting Gay," 49. Michael's dumb-and-dumber response to Matt: "I don't judge your lifestyle, don't judge mine."

38. On the distinction between "camp" and "liberal gay discourse," see Mark Finch, "Sex and Address in 'Dynasty,'" in *The Media Reader*, ed. Manuel Alvarado and John O. Thompson (London: British Film Institute, 1990), pp. 65–81.

39. Andrew Sullivan, "Washington Diarist," in *The New Republic*, December 12, 1994, p. 43.

40. See in this context Ang's discussion of fantasy, "Pleasure, Fantasy, and Cultural Politics" (pp. 130–36), which for me remains one of the seminal aspects of *Watching "Dallas."*

41. On Fox's aggressive appeal to teenagers and young adults (18–34), see John O'Connor, "TV's Midterm Grade," *New York Times*, November 1, 1992, sec. 2, p. 1. See also Mike Freeman's "Spelling Entertainment on a Roll Again," which begins by pointing out—the bad news—the networks' declining interest in Spelling's "adult-skewing network series *Dynasty, Hotel,* and *The Colbys.*" *Broadcasting and Cable*, June 8, 1992, p. 14. The good news, of course, was that in a "dramatic turnaround, the company . . . reshaped its image into one of a hip, youth-oriented producer, using its Fox hit *Beverly Hills 90201* as a springboard" (p. 14).

42. Owen, "Fourth Network," *Gen X TV*, p. 56.

43. See Bill Carter, "This Fall, The Barely Adult Set Is the Object of Network Desire," *New York Times*, September 10, 1992, sec. C, p. 17. For an excellent account of the "recessionary aesthetics" of the period immediately preceding the appearance of *Beverly Hills 90210* and *Melrose Place*, see John Thornton Caldwell, *Televisuality: Style, Crisis, and Authority in American Television* (New Brunswick, NJ: Rutgers University Press, 1995), pp. 284–301, esp. 285–88.

44. On "product categories," see Bill Carter, "Three Networks Frantically Seek Fountain of Youth and Profits," *New York Times*, August 3, 1992, sec. D, p. 8.

45. On Fox's success—via *Beverly Hills 90210* and *Melrose Place*—with "female demographics that previously went unserved" as well as the "Spelling Entertainment Group's push to launch a female-skewing block" (e.g., *Savannah* [1996]), see Mike Freeman, "Spelling Pitches Prime-Time Block," *Broadcasting and Cable*, October 4, 1993, p. 16.

46. On the double-commodity status of soap operas, see Dennis Porter, "Soap Time: Thoughts on a Commodity Art Form" (1977), *Television: The Critical View*, ed. Horace Newcomb (New York: Oxford University Press, 1979), p. 96. On postfeminism in general (and Naomi Wolf and Katie Roiphe in particular) in the context of *Melrose Place*, see Elayne Rapping, "That Jane Austen Thing," *Progressive*, July 1996, p. 38.

47. For an example of this sort of reading in *Dynasty*, see the Krystle ("good")/Alexis ("bad") graph in Gabriele Kreutzner and Ellen Seiter, "Not All 'Soaps' Are Created Equal," in Allen, *To Be Continued*, p. 248.

48. On matriarchal versus patriarchal soap operas, see Geraghty, "Family Matters," in *Women and Soap Opera*, pp. 60–83.

49. The excess of strong female characters on *Melrose Place* is arguably a result not only of a particular historical moment (i.e., postfeminism) but, of course, genre.

50. On the "ultimate" or "super bitch" (i.e., "phallic bitch"), see Jostein Gripsrud, "Dimensions of Domestic Reception," in *The Dynasty Years: Hollywood, Television, and Critical Media* (New York: Routledge, 1995) p. 140.

51. On, in general, the relation between advertising and Generation X, see Karen Ritchie, *Marketing to Generation X* (New York: Lexington Books, 1995), p. 20.

52. Carter, "The Barely Adult Set," p. 17.

53. For the Barthes, see *The Fashion System*, trans. Matthew Ward and Richard Howard (New York: Hill & Wang, 1983).

54. On fashion with respect to post-Fordism and postmodernity, see, for example, Gail Faurschou, "Fashion and the Cultural Logic of Postmodernity," in *Body Invaders: Panic Sex in America*, ed. Arthur and Marilouise Kroker (New York: St. Martin's, 1987), pp. 78–93; and Malcolm Barnard, "Fashion, Clothing, and Postmodernity," in *Fashion as Communication* (New York: Routledge, 1996), pp. 145–70.

55. Betsy Sharkey, "Grant Show: The Blue-Collar Sex Symbol of 'Melrose Place,'" *New York Times*, July 26, 1992, sec. 2, p. 23.

56. Rapping, "The Year of the Young," p. 37.

57. John O'Connor, "An Emotional Subtext in the Sexy New Shows," *New York Times*, August 9, 1992, sec. 2, p. 28.

58. For an acute analysis of middle-class *déclassement*, see Barbara Ehrenreich, *Fear of Falling: The Inner Life of the Middle Class* (New York: Harper Perennial, 1989).

59. Of course, the middle class is the classic province of American soap opera. As Allen notes, "The paradigmatic function of the middle class is itself an effect of larger, essentially ideological forces. The compression of social reality in the soap opera into a middle class universe facilitates a suppression of material concerns in general." *Speaking of Soap Operas*, p. 74.

60. The classic text on the PMC is Barbara Ehrenreich and John Ehrenreich's "The Professional-Managerial Class," in *Between Labor and Capital* (Boston: South End Press, 1979), pp. 5–45.

61. Feuer, "The Yuppie Spectator," *Seeing Through the Eighties*, p. 49.

62. For something like the standard discussion of commodification in soap opera studies, see Allen, "The Soap Opera as Commodity and Commodifier," *Speaking of Soap Operas*, pp. 45–60.

63. On *thirtysomething*, see, for example, Feuer, "Yuppie Envy and Yuppie Guilt," in *Seeing Through the Eighties*, pp. 68–81.

64. On "second wave" or "reflexive" advertising, see Martyn J. Lee, *Consumer Culture Reborn* (New York: Routledge, 1993), pp. 152–56.

65. On parody versus pastiche, see Fredric Jameson, "Culture," *Postmodernism* (Durham, NC: Duke University Press, 1991), pp. 16–19. See also Feuer, who argues that postmodern pastiche (as, for instance, in the gay camp reading of *Dynasty*) "does not preclude emotional identification—attitudes normally viewed as mutually exclusive—at the same time and as part of the same sensibility" (*Seeing Through the Eighties*, p. 135).

66. On antirealism, see, for example, Sasha Torres, "Melodrama, Masculinity, and the Family: *thirtysomething* as Therapy," in *Male Trouble*, ed. Constance Penley and Sharon Willis (Minneapolis: University of Minnesota Press, 1993), pp. 283–302. On postrealism (which, according to Ien Ang and Jon Stratton, is defined by a radical excess which "fundamentally unsettles the premises of realism itself"), see "The End of Civilization As We Knew It," in Allen, *To Be Continued*, pp. 122–44.

67. On *The Spot*, see Owen, *Gen X TV*, pp. 178–82. *The Spot*, which was picked up by American Cybercast (AMCY), ended its run on July 1, 1997.

6. Shot/Countershot

1. Cindy Donatelli and Sharon Alward, "'I Dread You'?: Married to the Mob in *The Godfather*, *GoodFellas*, and *The Sopranos*," in *This Thing of Ours: Investigating* The Sopranos, ed. David Lavery (New York: Columbia University Press, 2002), p. 64.

2. In this context, see, as an instance of "viral marketing," www.jeffrey wernick.com, a "homepage of a fictional author and Mafia buff who supposedly leaks information about the Sopranos/DiMeo family." Mark C. Rogers, Michael Epstein, and Jimmie L. Reeves, "The Sopranos as HBO Brand Equity: The Art of Commerce in the Age of Digital Reproduction," in Lavery, *This Thing of Ours*, p. 54.

3. On the relation between the *Godfather* series and *The Sopranos*, see the appendix to Maurice Yacowar's The Sopranos *on the Couch: Analyzing Television's Greatest Series* (New York: Continuum, 2002), pp. 177–83.

4. Ken Tucker, "Goons and 'Toons," *Entertainment Weekly*, April 2, 1999, p. 74.

5. Ellen Willis, "Our Bodies, Ourselves," in Lavery, *This Thing of Ours*, p. 2.

6. Stephen Holden, "*The Sopranos*: An Introduction," in *The New York Times on* The Sopranos (New York: ibooks, 2000), p. xii.

7. Yacowar, introduction to The Sopranos *on the Couch*, p. 9. Chase himself, in the introduction to The Sopranos: *Selected Scripts from Three Seasons*, comments that *his* "personal goal [is] for the episodes to be stand-alone feature films." The Sopranos: *Selected Scripts* (New York: Warner Books, 2002), p. viii.

8. On Chase's status as an *auteur*, see Yacowar, "Author! Author!," in The Sopranos *on the Couch*, pp. 18–20; and David Lavery and Robert J. Thompson, "David Chase, *The Sopranos*, and Television Creativity," in Lavery, *This Thing of Ours*, pp. 18–25. For Chase on TV, see Allen Rucker, "An Interview with David Chase," in The Sopranos: *A Family History* (New York: New Amer-

ican Library, 2000), p. [2]. Since there are no page numbers for this book, the bracketed numbers refer only to the interview, the pages of which I have numbered consecutively.

9. Chase, in Rucker, The Sopranos: *A Family History*, p. [2]. Bill Carter, "He Engineered a Mob Hit, and Now It's Time to Pay," in *The New York Times on* The Sopranos, p. 157.

10. Chase, in Rucker, The Sopranos: *A Family History*, p. [4].

11. Ibid., p. [7].

12. Fred Gardaphé, "Fresh Garbage: The Gangster as Suburban Trickster," in *A Sitdown with* The Sopranos, ed. Regina Barreca (New York: Palgrave Macmillan, 2002), p. 99.

13. On the gangster or crime film, see, for example, Colin McArthur, *Underworld U.S.A.* (London: Secker and Warburg/BFI, 1972); Eugene Rosow, *Born to Lose: The Gangster Film in America* (New York: Oxford University Press, 1978); Carlos Clarens, *Crime Movies* (New York: Da Capo Press, 1997); and Jonathan Munby, *Public Enemies, Public Heroes* (Chicago: Chicago University Press, 1999).

14. The "sausage" discourse reappears in "The Legend of Tennessee Moltisanti" when Christopher, haunted by his killing of Kolar, suffers from a recurring nightmare where a "freezer" hand, presumably Kolar's, feeds sausage to his girlfriend, Adriana (Drea de Matteo), who, in turn, metamorphoses into Carmela. Later, Kolar, wrapped up in plastic like a mummy, asks Christopher, who's behind the counter in a blood-smeared butcher's apron, for a salami sub.

15. James Wolcott, "HBO's Singular Sensation," *Vanity Fair*, February 2000, p. 66.

16. On some of the intertextual connections between *The Sopranos* and the *Godfather* films, especially in relation to fish (e.g., "Luca Brasi sleeps with the fishes"), see Sara Lewis Dunne, "'The Brutality of Meat and the Abruptness of Seafood': Food, Family, and Violence in *The Sopranos*," in Lavery, *This Thing of Ours*, p. 224.

17. Christopher himself says, "My cousin's girlfriend, Amy—the one who works for Tarantino—said Mob stories are always hot." The relation between *The Sopranos* and Tarantino's films is too complex to take up here, but Glenn Creeber argues that "while Tony's 'traditional' sensibilities appear to represent Coppola's old 'film school' generation, Christopher clearly encapsulates the new priorities of Tarantino's 'video store' generation." "'TV Ruined the Movies': Television, Tarantino, and the Intimate World of *The Sopranos*," in Lavery, *This Thing of Ours*, p. 134.

18. Mike Flaherty and Mary Kaye Schilling, "Family Reunion," *Entertainment Weekly*, June 11, 1999, p. 22.

19. I am playing here on Andreas Huyssen's rendition of Löwenthal: "Löwenthal once put it this way: culture industry is psychoanalysis in reverse, referring of course to Freud's famous statement, 'Where Id is, Ego shall be.'" *After the Great Divide: Modernism, Mass Culture, Postmodernism* (Bloomington: Indiana University Press, 1986), p. 22. On the postmodern "loss of affect" or what Fredric Jameson calls a "new kind of flatness or depthlessness," see his *Postmodernism*,

Or, The Cultural Logic of Late Capitalism (Durham, NC: Duke University Press, 1991), pp. 9 and 156.

20. On satire and realism, see Jay Parini, "The Cultural Work of *The Sopranos*," in Barreca, *A Sitdown with* The Sopranos, p. 76.

21. Eventually, because Mr. Satriale cannot meet his debts, Johnny Boy comes to own Satriale's store; moreover, as we learn in "To Save Us All from Satan's Power" (III, 10), the annual Christmas party put on by the Soprano Family for the neighborhood children originates from the time of the death of Mr. Satriale, who committed suicide when he lost his store. In this context (that is, Tony's growing awareness of his "father's criminal life," as Melfi puts it), see also "Down Neck" where little Tony misses the school bus only to watch his father "whack the shit" out of Rocco Allitori for unpaid debts. In the same episode, Tony also remembers hiding out as a boy in the trunk of his father's Cadillac in order to go with Janice and him to the Rideland amusement park, then watches as Johnny Boy is arrested—along with Junior and a clown!—after having used Janice as a front for a stolen-goods racket.

22. Tucker, "Remade Men," *Entertainment Weekly*, March 2, 2001, p. 53.

23. On the depiction of psychoanalysis in *The Sopranos*, see Glenn O. Gabbard, *The Psychology of* The Sopranos: *Love, Desire, Death and Betrayal in America's Favorite Gang Family* (New York: Basic Books, 2002), pp. 1–21. I would only add that the cinematic appropriation of psychoanalysis has a long, illustrious history in Hollywood; in particular, the conceit of gangster and psychiatrist meeting cute can be traced back to Charles Vidor's 1939 *Blind Alley*.

24. See Jameson's remarks en passant on *Chinatown* in *Postmodernism*, p. 19.

25. On the operatic elements of the *Godfather* series, see Naomi Greene, "Family Ceremonies: Or, Opera in *The Godfather* Trilogy," *Francis Ford Coppola's* Godfather *Trilogy*, ed. Nick Browne (New York: Cambridge University Press, 2002), pp. 133–55.

26. Steven Hayward and Andrew Brio, "The Eighteenth Brumaire of Tony Soprano," in Lavery, *This Thing of Ours*, p. 211.

27. On *The Sopranos* and *GoodFellas*, see Pattie's "Martin Scorsese's Gangster Films," a subsection of "Mobbed Up," in Lavery, *This Thing of Ours*, pp. 141–44. For a comparison between Karen Hill (Lorraine Bracco) in *Good Fellas* and the various women in *The Sopranos*, see Donatelli and Alward, "'I Dread You'?," pp. 60–70.

28. David Chase is on record professing his admiration for *Public Enemy*; in The Sopranos: *Selected Scripts*, he notes that "originally, Tony was to be named Tommy Soprano—an homage to the character of Tom Powers (played by James Cagney) in one of my favorite films, *Public Enemy*" (p. vii). It's not surprising, then, that the "Proshai, Livushka" episode (III, 2) features Tony watching—in the wake of his mother's death—the emotionally charged conclusion to Wellman's film.

29. Akass and McCabe, "Beyond the Bada Bing!: Negotiating Female Narrative Authority in *The Sopranos*," in Lavery, *This Thing of Ours*, p. 160.

30. Mario Puzo, *The Godfather* (New York: New American Library, 2002). All citations from this text hereafter cited in parentheses.

31. Donatelli and Alward, "'I Dread You'?," p. 68.

32. Parini, "The Cultural Work of *The Sopranos*," p. 87.

33. See Akass and McCabe, "Beyond the Bada Bing!," pp. 146–60.

34. Donatelli and Alward, "'I Dread You'?," p. 60.

35. Ralphie's quotations from *Gladiator* are not restricted to, and in fact precede, the "University" episode. See, for example, "Another Toothpick" (III, 5) where he exclaims, "'In this world or the next, I shall have my revenge.'"

36. It should also be noted that in the "University" episode, Carmela bakes a "bun cake for AJ's fundraiser" and Silvio—during a lavish dinner party at Ralphie's attended by Tony and Carmela (one that contrasts with Tracee's lower-class life)—says admiringly to Rosalie Aprile (Sharon Angela), "Nice cake."

37. Akass and McCabe, "'I Dread You'?," p. 71.

38. In "Amour Fou," Patsy Parisi (Dan Grimaldi), warning Tony's ex-*goomah*, Gloria Trillo (Annabella Sciorra), to stay away from Tony and his family, says, "My face is the last one you'll see, not Tony's. It won't be cinematic."

39. See Laura Mulvey, "Visual Pleasure and Narrative Cinema" (1975), in *Visual and Other Pleasures* (Bloomington: Indiana University Press, 1989), pp. 14–26.

40. Kim Akass and Janet McCabe, "Beyond the Bada Bing!," p. 160.

41. Though I do not have space to discuss her character here, Caitlin's situation in "University," as the title of the episode suggests, parallels both Meadow's and Tracee's. On one hand, Caitlin's self-destructive hair-pulling visually rhymes with the scene outside Ralphie's where Silvio violently grabs Tracee by her hair; moreover, Caitlin, like Tracee, is the object of the abuse of male power (for example, Len Tannenbaum files a restraining order against Caitlin because she "caused" Noah to receive a C– on a paper). On the other hand, Caitlin's affluent, university life is not only diametrically opposed to Tracee's but links her economically to Meadow's. Yacowar, The Sopranos *on the Couch*, p. 146.

42. Donatelli and Alward, "'I Dread You'?," p. 71.

43. Akass and McCabe, "Beyond the Bada Bing!," p. 150. On this dynamic, where the "therapy sessions appear to fragment the series' narrative dynamic," see also Creeber, "'TV Ruined the Movies,'" pp. 132–33.

44. Donatelli and Alward, "'I Dread You'?," p. 65.

45. Ibid.

46. This sequence is preceded by another one slightly earlier in the episode where Tony explains why he "bitch-slapped" Ralphie: "He bashed that poor girl's brains in." Silvio's response (which is couched in an especially flat tonal register) is, as it were, paradigmatic: "It was a tragedy. The fact is, though, she wasn't related to you by blood or marriage. She wasn't your *goomah*." And in the succeeding sequence, set like its predecessor in a restaurant, Ralphie, enjoying a postprandial cigar in the company of made men, remarks, "I could see if it was his daughter or a niece of his. But all this over a dead whore." Finally, Ralphie, defending his bad behavior to Johnny Sack in the backyard of the latter's house, says, "A, she was a whore. B, she hit me. And that wasn't my kid she was carrying."

47. The name of the store WrapNation, which appears above the Employee of the Month picture of Jesus Rossi on the rear wall in this scene, would appear to be a pejorative pun on rap music. In this context, the diegetic music in this scene—Britney Spears' "Oops! . . . I Did It Again" (2000)—not only offers a generic musical counterpoint to the mise-en-scène but ironically underscores Melfi's reidentification of Rossi. Since Richard, Melfi's husband, has already commented, earlier in the episode, on Rossi's ethnicity (he's Hispanic but his name "sounds Italian"), I would only add that the signifier "WrapNation" provides one compact instance of the complex, if problematic, racial economy at work in *The Sopranos*.

48. Since the audio register of *The Sopranos* is a major part of its televisual appeal (for a sample, see The Sopranos: *Music from the HBO Original Series* [Sony, 1999]), I'd be remiss if I did not mention that in a scene set in her living room at home, we see Janice holding a guitar, practicing the opening chords of the Rolling Stones' "Satisfaction." Needless to say, neither Janice nor Melfi gets the sort of satisfaction—whether economic or emotional—that they're looking for.

49. The buried critical link between Tracee and Dr. Melfi is Tony's characterization of the latter as a "whore" in "The Legend of Tennessee Moltisanti." When Melfi informs Tony that she'll have to charge him for a missing appointment, Tony stands up, outraged, and starts throwing money at her (an act of real disrespect in his world): "This is what it's all about, right? Motherfuckin' cocksuckin' money. I don't appreciate feeling like I pour my heart out to a fuckin' callgirl."

Reprise: Tony Soprano, Meet Buffy the Vampire Slayer

1. Mario Machi, Allan May, and Charlie Molino, "Buffalo Crime Family," American Mafia.com, http://www.americanmafia.com/Cities/Buffalo.html.

2. Aaron M. Smith, "Stefano Magaddino," Gangsters Incorporated, http://www.gangstersinc.tripod.com/Magaddino.html.

3. Lisa Parks, "Brave New *Buffy*: Rethinking 'TV Violence,'" in *Quality Popular TV: Cult TV, The Industry and Fans*, ed. Mark Jancovich and James Lyons (London: BFI, 2003), p. 122. The soap-operatic aspects of *Buffy* have been much commented upon; see, for example, Roz Kaveney's "She Saved the World. A Lot," which argues that *Buffy*'s "emotional structures have more in common with soap opera relationships than with most genre series." *Reading the Vampire Slayer*, ed. Kaveney (London: I. B. Tauris, 2004), p. 5.

4. Parks, "Brave New *Buffy*," p. 122.

5. Patricia Pender, "'I'm Buffy and You're . . . History': The Postmodern Politics of *Buffy*," in *Fighting the Forces: What's at Stake in* Buffy the Vampire Slayer, ed. Rhonda Wilcox and David Lavery (Lanham, MD: Rowman & Littlefield, 2002), p. 43.

6. On Buffy's femininity as femme-inanity, see Pender, p. 38. On Buffy as warrior woman, see part 2, "*Buffy the Vampire Slayer*," in *Athena's Daughters: Television's New Warrior Women*, ed. Francis Early and Kathleen Kennedy (Syracuse, NY: Syracuse University Press, 2003), pp. 53–102; and Dawn Heinecken,

"*Buffy the Vampire Slayer* and the Body in Relation," in *Warrior Women of Television* (New York: Peter Lang, 2003), pp. 91–131.

7. Catherine Johnson, "*Buffy the Vampire Slayer*," in *The Television Genre Book*, ed. Glen Creeber (London: BFI, 2001), p. 42.

8. Micol Ostow, *Once More with Feeling*, ed. Ostow (New York: Simon Pulse, 2002), p. 62.

9. Joss Whedon, quoted in *Once More with Feeling*, p. 63.

10. On Whedon's practice of hosting informal Sunday-night readings of Shakespeare at his home, see *Once More with Feeling*, p. 63.

11. In another context (i.e., principal characters pretending to be a secondary character), see Ian Shuttleworth's discussion of *As You Like It* in "They Always Mistake Me for the Character I Play!: Transformation, Identity and Role-Playing in the *Buffy*verse," in Kaveney, *Reading the Vampire Slayer*, p. 235.

12. On the relation between "The Red Shoes" and "Once More with Feeling," see the sidebar "Walk through the Fire" in Ostow, *Once More with Feeling*, p. 73. "The Red Shoes" was, of course, adapted into a ballet and later into the celebrated color film by Michael Powell (1948).

13. For the source of Anya's riff about bunnies, see "Fear, Itself" (IV, 4).

14. On the depiction of Willow's addiction (which has been much criticized), see, for example, Kaveney, "She Saved the World," pp. 34–35.

15. This moment recollects the final scene of "New Moon Rising," in which Tara says, "I understand: you have to be with the person you love," and Willow responds, "I am." On this scene, see Shuttleworth, "They Always Mistake Me For the Character I Play!," p. 242.

16. Tara's dark "family romance," including her shift from her male-dominated biological family to that other "family" which is the Scooby gang, is played out in "Family" (V, 6).

17. On Lethe's Bramble, see the sidebar "Under Your Spell" in Ostow, *Once More with Feeling*, p. 79.

18. For the writer's take on Tara's death, see Stephen S. DeKnight's remarks on "Seeing Red" in "Writing the Vampire Slayer," interview conducted by Kaveney, in Kaveney, *Reading the Vampire Slayer*, p. 127.

19. On *Buffy* and the Columbine incident, see Parks, "Brave New *Buffy*," pp. 118–33.

20. Shuttleworth, "They Always Mistake Me for the Character I Play!," p. 253. For reminding me of, in the context, the perfectly appropriate demotic locution "Life sucks," thanks go to Laurence Rickels's *Vampire Lectures* (Minnesota: University of Minnesota Press, 1999), p. 314. Colin McArthur's citation of Geoffrey Block is pertinent here: "Just as Beethovenian ideals of thematic unity and organicism became increasingly applied to dramatic works (culminating in Wagner's musical dramas), Broadway musicals after . . . *Oklahoma* . . . would be evaluated on how convincingly they realized a new 'type,' the integrated musical." *Brigadoon, Braveheart and the Scots* (London: I. B. Tauris, 2003), p. 34.

21. In *Screen Couple Chemistry: The Power of 2*, Martha Nochimson mentions the "thematic couple" Buffy and Angel, but one can, I think, update this notation to include Buffy and Spike. (Austin: University of Texas Press, 2002, p. 287).

22. Karen Sayer, "This Was Our World and They Made it Theirs," in Kaveney, *Reading the Vampire Slayer*, p. 153.

23. On the association between California and the Frankfurt School critique of the culture industry, see Rickels, *The Case of California* (Baltimore: Johns Hopkins University Press, 1991), p. 1.

24. For this passage from Marx's *Capital*, see Rob Latham's sophisticated take on the relation between Marxism and vampirism as well as on the "dialectic of exploitation and empowerment" in contemporary youth culture, *Consuming Youth: Vampires, Cyborgs, and the Culture of Consumption* (Chicago: University of Chicago Press, 2002), p. 3.

25. Adorno and Horkheimer, *Dialectic of Enlightenment* (New York: Continuum, 1987), p. 124.

26. Jenny Bavidge, "Chosen Ones: Reading the Contemporary Teen Heroine," in *Teen TV: Genre, Consumption and Ideology*, ed. Glyn Davis and Kay Dickinson (London: BFI, 2004), p. 47. To be fair, Giles is not simply a "tweedy, English, literary mentor" (47) but, rather unlike Adorno, a proponent of popular and, especially, rock music (e.g., Cream's "Tales of Brave Ulysses" [1967]).

27. Ibid., p. 4.

28. Adorno and Horkheimer, *Dialectic of Enlightenment*, p. 135.

29. Ibid.

30. Chuck Berry, *The Autobiography* (New York: Harmony Books, 1987), p. 158.

31. On *Buffy*-related websites, fanzines, e-mail lists, and artwork, see Alan McKee, "*Buffy the Vampire Slayer*," in *Television Studies*, ed. Toby Miller (London: BFI, 2002), p. 69.

Bibliography

Abrams, Alexander, and David Lipsky. *Late Bloomers*. New York: Random House, 1994.

Adorno, Theodor. *Aesthetic Theory*. Trans. Christian Lenhardt. London: Routledge and Kegan Paul, 1984.

———. *Beethoven: The Philosophy of Music*. Ed. Rolf Tiedemann. Trans. Edmund Jephcott. Stanford: Stanford University Press, 1998.

———. "The Culture Industry Reconsidered." In *The Adorno Reader*, ed. Brian O'Connor and trans. Anson G. Rabinbach, 230–237. Oxford, UK: Blackwell, 2000.

———. *Essays on Music*. Ed. Richard Leppert. Berkeley: University of California Press, 2002.

———. "The Fetish Character in Music and the Regression in Listening." In *The Essential Frankfurt School Rea*der, ed. Andrew Arato and Eike Gebhardt, 270–299. New York: Urizen Books, 1978.

———. *Introduction to the Sociology of Music*. Trans. E. B. Ashton. New York: Seabury Press, 1976.

———. "On Popular Music." In *On Record: Rock, Pop, and the Written Word*, ed. Simon Frith and Andrew Goodwin, 301–314. New York: Pantheon, 1990.

———. *Philosophy of Modern Music*. Trans. Anne G. Mitchell and Wesley V. Blomster. New York: Seabury Press, 1973.

———. "Scientific Experiences of a European Scholar in America." In *Critical Models: Interventions and Catchwords*, trans. Henry W. Pickford, 215–42. New York: Columbia University Press, 1999.

———. "Television and Patterns of Mass Culture." In *Mass Culture: The Popular Arts in America*, ed. Bernard Rosenberg and David Manning White, 474–488. Glencoe, IL: Free Press, 1957.

Adorno, Theodor, and Hans Eisler. "Prejudices and Bad Habits." In *Movie Music: The Film Reader*, ed. Kay Dickinson, 25–36. New York: Routledge, 2003.

Adorno, Theodor, and Max Horkheimer. *Dialectic of Enlightenment*. New York: Continuum, 1987.

Adorno, Theodor, et al. *Aesthetics and Politics*. Trans. ed. Ronald Taylor. London: Verso, 1977.

Aglietta, Michel. *A Theory of Capitalist Regulation: The U.S. Experience*. Trans. David Fernbach. London: New Left Books, 1979.

Akass, Kim, and Janet McCabe. "Beyond the Bada Bing!: Negotiating Female Narrative Authority in *The Sopranos*." In *This Thing of Ours: Investigating The Sopranos*, ed. David Lavery, 146–161. New York: Columbia University Press, 2002.

Allen, Robert C., ed. Introduction to *To Be Continued . . . Soap Operas Around the World*. New York: Routledge, 1995.

———. *Speaking of Soap Operas*. Chapel Hill: University of North Carolina Press, 1985.

Altman, Rick, McGraw Jones, and Sonia Tatroe. "Inventing the Cinema Sound Track." In *Music and Cinema*, ed. James Buhler, Caryl Flinn, and James Neumeyer, 339–359. Hanover, NH: Wesleyan University Press, 2000.

Ang, Ien. *Living Room Wars*. New York: Routledge, 1996.

———. *Watching "Dallas": Television and the Melodramatic Imagination*. New York: Routledge, 1985.

Ang, Ien, and Jon Stratton. "The End of Civilization As We Know It." In *To Be Continued*, ed. Robert C. Allen, 234–255. New York: Routledge, 1995.

Baldwin, Kristen. "Classic Reruns: *Melrose Place*." *Entertainment Weekly*, August 2, 1996, 51.

Baldwin, Kristen, et al. "Fall TV Preview." *Entertainment Weekly*, September 13, 1996, 52ff.

Bangs, Lester. "The British Invasion." In *The Rolling Stone Illustrated History of Rock & Roll*, ed. Jim Miller, 169–176. New York: Random House/Rolling Stone Press, 1980.

Barenboim, Daniel, and Edward Said. *Parallels and Paradoxes: Explorations in Music and Society*. New York: Pantheon, 2002.

Barnard, Malcolm. *Fashion as Communication*. New York: Routledge, 1996.

Barnes, Alan, and Marcus Hearn, eds. *Tarantino, A to Zed: The Films of Quentin Tarantino*. London: B. T. Batsford, 1996.

Barthes, Roland. *The Fashion System*. Trans. Matthew Ward and Richard Howard. New York: Hill & Wang, 1983.

———. *Mythologies*. Trans. Annette Lavers. New York: Noonday Press, 1990.

Bauer, Erik. "The Mouth and the Method." *Sight and Sound* 8, no. 3 (March 1996): 8–12.

Bavidge, Jenny. "Chosen Ones: Reading the Contemporary Teen Heroine." In *Teen TV: Genre, Consumption and Ideology*, ed. Glyn Davis and Kay Dickinson, 41–53. London: BFI, 2004.

Bellafante, Gina. "Stop the Inanity!" *Time*, May 13, 1996, 85.

Berghan, Volker R. "European Elitism, American Money, and Popular Culture." In *The American Century in Europe*, ed. R. Laurence Moore and Maurizio Vaudagna, 117–130. Ithaca, NY: Cornell University Press, 2003.

Berry, Chuck. *The Autobiography*. New York: Harmony Books, 1987.

Bhabha, Homi. "The Other Question: The Stereotype and Colonial Discourse." In *The Sexual Subject: A* Screen *Reader in Sexuality*, 312–331. London: Routledge, 1992.

"The Billboard 200." *Billboard*, November 20, 1999, 132.

Bordwell, David. "Contemporary Film Studies." In *Post-Theory*, ed. David Bordwell and Noël Carroll, 3–36. Madison: University of Wisconsin Press, 1996.

———. *Making Meaning: Inference and Rhetoric in the Interpretation of Cinema*. Cambridge: Harvard University Press. 1991.

Botting, Fred, and Scott Wilson. *The Tarantinian Ethics*. London: Sage, 2001.

Bourdieu, Pierre. *Distinction*. Trans. Richard Nice. Cambridge: Harvard University Press, 1984.

Boyd, Todd. *The New H.N.I.C.: The Death of Civil Rights and the Rise of Hip Hop*. New York: New York University Press, 2002.

Bradby, Barbara. "Do-Talk and Don't-Talk: The Division of the Subject in Girl Group Music." In *On Record: Rock, Pop, and the Written Word*, ed. Simon Frith and Andrew Goodwin, 341–368. New York: Pantheon, 1990.

Bradley, Dick. *Understanding Rock 'n' Roll: Popular Music in Britain, 1955–1964*. Buckingham, UK: Open University Press, 1992.

Brunner, Rob. "Birth of Rap." *Entertainment Weekly*, January 9, 1998, 84.

———. "By George, He's Got It." *Entertainment Weekly*, December 19, 1997, 78.

———. "Winner of the Week." *Entertainment Weekly*, December 19, 1997, 79.

Buckland, Warren, and Thomas Elsaesser. "Oedipal Narratives and the Post-Oedipal." In *Studying Contemporary American Film: A Guide to Movie Analysis*, 220–247. London: Arnold, 2002.

Buhler, James. "Analytical and Interpretive Approaches to Film Music (II)." In *Film Music: Critical Approaches*, ed. J. K. Donnelly, 39–61. New York: Continuum, 2001.

Bull, Chris. "Acting Gay." *Advocate*, December 27, 1994, 46.

Burgess, Anthony. *A Clockwork Orange*. New York: Ballantine, 1963.

Caldwell, John Thornton. *Televisuality: Style, Crisis, and Authority in American Television*. New Brunswick, NJ: Rutgers University Press, 1995.

Campbell, Michael, and James Brody. *Rock and Roll: An Introduction*. New York: Schirmer Books, 1999.

Carroll, Noël. *Mystifying Movies: Fads and Fallacies in Film Theory*. New York: Columbia University Press, 1988.

———. *A Philosophy of Mass Art*. Oxford, UK: Clarendon, 1998.

Carter, Alan. "The Hard-Bodied Men of 'Melrose Place.'" *Entertainment Weekly*, May 20, 1994, 17.

Carter, Bill. "He Engineered a Mob Hit, and Now It's Time to Pay." In *The New York Times on* The Sopranos, 149–157. New York: ibooks, 2000.

———. "This Fall, The Barely Adult Set Is the Object of Network Desire." *New York Times*, September 10, 1992, sec. C, 17.

———. "Three Networks Frantically Seek Fountain of Youth and Profits." *New York Times*, August 3, 1992, sec. D, 8.

Casetti, Francesco. *Theories of Cinema, 1945–1995*. Trans. Francesca Chiostri, Elizabeth Gard Bartolini-Salimbeni, and Thomas Kelso. Austin: University of Texas Press, 1999.

Chandler, Raymond. *Farewell, My Lovely*. New York: Vintage Crime/Black Lizard, 1992.

"Change of Address." *Entertainment Weekly*, October 31, 1995, 98.

Chartier, Pierre. "The Americans Are Making Dark Films Too." 1946. In *Perspectives on Film Noir*, ed. R. Burton Palmer, 25–27. New York: G. K. Hall, 1996.

Chase, David. "An interview with David Chase." By Allen Rucker, in Rucker, *The Sopranos: A Family History*, [1–10]. New York: New American Library, 2000.

———. The Sopranos: *Selected Scripts from Three Seasons*. New York: Warner Books, 2002.

Chion, Michel. *Audio-Vision: Sound on Screen*. Ed. and Trans. Claudia Gorbman. New York: Columbia University Press, 1994.

Christgau, Robert. "The Rolling Stones." In *The Rolling Stone Illustrated History of Rock & Roll*, ed. Jim Miller, 190–200. New York: Random House/Rolling Stone Press, 1980.

Clarens, Carlos. *Crime Movies*. New York: Da Capo Press, 1997.

Clarke, Donald. *Wishing on the Moon: The Life and Times of Billie Holiday*. New York: Viking, 1994.

Cohn, Nick. "Classic Rock." In *The Penguin Book of Rock and Roll Writing*, ed. Clinton Heylin, 37–54. New York: Viking, 1992.

Collins, Jim, ed. "High Pop: An Introduction." In *High Pop: Making Culture into Mass Entertainment*, 1–31. Oxford: Blackwell, 2002.

Collis, John. *Chuck Berry: The Biography*. London: Arum Press, 2002.

Cooper, David. *Bernard Hermann's* Vertigo*: A Film Score Handbook*. Westport, CT: Greenwood Press, 2001.

Cooper, Henry. "On *Über Jazz*: Replaying Adorno with the Grain." *October* 75 (Winter 1996): 99–133.

Cowie, Elizabeth. *Representing the Woman: Cinema and Psychoanalysis*. Minneapolis: University of Minnesota Press, 1998.

Crane, Diana. *The Production of Culture: Media and the Urban Arts*. Thousand Oaks, CA: Sage, 1992.

Crease, Robert B. "Jazz and Dance." In *Cambridge Companion to Jazz*, ed. Mervyn Cooke and David Horn, 69–82. Cambridge: Cambridge University Press, 2002.

Creeber, Glenn. "'TV Ruined the Movies': Television, Tarantino, and the Intimate World of *The Sopranos*." In *This Thing of Ours: Investigating* The Sopranos, ed. David Lavery, 124–134. New York: Columbia University Press, 2002.

Cross, Brian. *It's Not About a Salary . . . : Rap, Race, Resistance and Los Angeles*. New York: Verso, 1993.

Daly, Steven, and David Kamp. "The Rock Snob Dictionary, Volume 3." *Vanity Fair*, November 2000, 297ff.

Davis, Angela Y. *Blues Legacies and Black Feminism*. New York: Pantheon, 1998.

Dayan, Daniel. "The Tutor-Code of Classical Cinema." *Film Quarterly* 28, no. 1 (Fall 1974): 22–31.

Denselow, Robin. *When the Music's Over: The Story of Political Pop*. London: Faber and Faber, 1989.

DeRosia, Margaret. "An Erotics of Violence: Violence and (Homo) Sexuality in Stanley Kubrick's *A Clockwork Orange*." In *Stanley Kubrick's* A Clockwork Orange, ed. Stuart Y. McDougal, 61–84. New York: Cambridge University Press, 2003.

De Vries, Hilary. "Quentin Tarantino: Master of Mayhem." In *Quentin Tarantino: Interviews*, ed. Gerald Peary, 115–123. Jackson: University of Mississippi Press, 1998.

Doane, Mary Ann. "Film and Masquerade: Theorizing the Female Spectator." 1982. In *The Sexual Subject: A* Screen *Reader in Sexuality*, 227–243. London: Routledge, 1992.

Donatelli, Cindy, and Sharon Alward. "'I Dread You'?: Married to the Mob in *The Godfather, GoodFellas*, and *The Sopranos*." In *This Thing of Ours: Investigating* The Sopranos, ed. David Lavery, 60–71. New York: Columbia University Press, 2002.

Dunne, Sara Lewis. "'The Brutality of Meat and the Abruptness of Seafood': Food, Family, and Violence in *The Sopranos*." In *This Thing of Ours: Investigating* The Sopranos, ed. David Lavery, 215–226. New York: Columbia University Press, 2002.

Dyer, Richard. "Don't Look Now: The Male Pin-Up." 1982. In *The Sexual Subject: A* Screen *Reader in Sexuality*, 265–276. London: Routledge, 1992.

Early, Francis, and Kathleen Kennedy, eds. *Athena's Daughters: Television's New Warrior Women*. Syracuse, NY: Syracuse University Press, 2003.

Edelman, Lee. *Homographesis: Essays on Gay Literary and Cultural Theory*. New York: Routledge, 1994.

Ehrenreich, Barbara. *Fear of Falling: The Inner Life of the Middle Class*. New York: Harper Perennial, 1989.

Ehrenreich, Barbara, and John Ehrenreich. *Between Labor and Capital*. Boston: South End Press, 1979.

Eliscu, Jenny. "2002's Music Biz Disaster." *Rolling Stone*, February 6, 2003, 11–12.

Falsetto, Mario. *Stanley Kubrick: A Narrative and Stylistic Analysis*. Westport, CT: Praeger, 2001.

Faurschou, Gail. "Fashion and the Cultural Logic of Postmodernity." In *Body Invaders: Panic Sex in America*, ed. Arthur and Marilouise Kroker, 78–93. New York: St. Martin's, 1987.

Feuer, Jane. *Seeing Through the Eighties*. Durham, NC: Duke University Press, 1995.

Finch, Mark. "Sex and Address in 'Dynasty.'" In *The Media Reader*, ed. Manuel Alvarado and John O. Thompson, 65–81. London: British Film Institute, 1990.

Fink, Robert. "Elvis Everywhere: Musicology and Popular Music Studies at the Twilight of the Canon." In *Rock Over the Edge: Transformations in Popular Music Culture*, ed. Roger Beebe, Denise Fulbrook, and Ben Saunders, 60–109. Durham, NC: Duke University Press, 2002.

Flaherty, Mike, and Mary Kaye Schilling. "Family Reunion." *Entertainment Weekly*, June 11, 1999, 22ff.

Flinn, Caryl. *Strains of Utopia: Gender, Nostalgia, Hollywood Film Music*. Princeton, NJ: Princeton University Press, 1992.

Frank, Nino. "The Crime Adventure Story: A New Kind of Detective Film." In *Perspectives on Film Noir*, ed. R. Burton Palmer, 21–24. New York: G. K. Hall, 1996.

Freeman, Mike. "Spelling Entertainment on a Roll Again." *Broadcasting and Cable* 122, no. 24 (June 8, 1992): 14.

———. "Spelling Pitches Prime-Time Block." *Broadcasting and Cable*, October 4, 1993, 16.

Fretts, Bruce. "Spelling Lessons." *Entertainment Weekly*, March 8, 1996, 50–52.

Friedlander, Paul. *Rock and Roll: A Social History*. Boulder, CO: Westview Press, 1996.

Friedlander, Paul, and Tim Brace. "Rock and Roll on the New Long March: Popular Music, Cultural Identity, and Political Opposition in the People's Republic of China." In *Rockin' the Boat: Mass Music and Mass Movements*, ed. Reebee Garofalo, 115–127. Boston: South End Press, 1992.

Frith, Simon. *Music for Pleasure: Essays in the Sociology of Pop*. New York: Routledge, 1988.

Gabbard, Glenn O. *The Psychology of* The Sopranos*: Love, Desire, Death and Betrayal in America's Favorite Gang Family*. New York: Basic Books, 2002.

Gabbard, Krin. *Jammin' at the Margins: Jazz and the American Cinema*. Chicago: University of Chicago Press, 1996.

Gabbard, Krin, and Shailja Sharma. "Stanley Kubrick and the Art of Cinema." In *Stanley Kubrick's* A Clockwork Orange, ed. Stuart Y. McDougal, 85–108. New York: Cambridge University Press, 2003.

Gans, Herbert J. *Popular and High Culture: An Analysis and Evaluation of Taste*. New York: Basic Books, 1999.

Gardaphé, Fred. "Fresh Garbage: The Gangster as Suburban Trickster." *A Sit-down with* The Sopranos, ed. Regina Barreca, 89–111. New York: Palgrave Macmillan, 2002.

Garner, Ken. "Would You Like to Hear Some Music?: In-and-Out-of-Control in the Films of Quentin Tarantino." In *Film Music: Critical Approaches*, ed. J. K. Donnelly, 188–205. New York: Continuum, 2001.

George, Nelson. *The Death of Rhythm and Blues*. New York: Pantheon, 1988.

———. *Hip Hop America*. New York: Viking, 1998.

Geraghty, Christine. *Women and Soap Opera: A Study of Prime-Time Soaps*. Cambridge: Polity Press, 1991.

Giddens, Gary. *Bing Crosby: A Pocketful of Dreams, The Early Years, 1903–1940*. Boston: Little, Brown & Co., 2001.

Gilbert, Jeremy, and Ewan Pearson. *Discographies: Dance Music Culture and the Politics of Sound*. London: Routledge, 1999.

Gill, John. *Queer Noises: Male and Female Homosexuality in Twentieth-Century Music*. Minneapolis: University of Minnesota Press, 1995.

Gillett, Charlie. *The Sound of the City*. London: Sphere Books Limited, 1971.

Gliatto, Tom, Tom Cunneff, and Craig Tomashoff. "Hot Property." *People Weekly*, February 21, 1994, 65.

Goodman, Fred. "The Most Dangerous Man in the Music Business." *Rolling Stone*, July 6–20, 2000, 42.

Gorbman, Claudia. *Unheard Melodies: Narrative Film Music*. Bloomington: Indiana University Press, 1987.

Gottlieb, Joanne, and Gayle Wald. "Smells Like Teen Spirit: Riot Grrrls, Revolution and Women in Independent Rock." In *Microphone Fiends: Youth Music and Youth Culture*, ed. Andrew Ross and Tricia Rose, 250–274. New York: Routledge, 1994.

Gracyk, Theodore. *Rhythm and Noise: An Aesthetics of Rock*. Durham, NC: Duke University Press, 1996.

Greenberg, Clement. "Avant-Garde and Kitsch." In *Mass Culture: The Popular Arts in America*, ed. Bernard Rosenberg and David Manning White, 98–110. Glencoe, IL: Free Press, 1957.

Greene, Naomi. "Family Ceremonies: Or, Opera in *The Godfather* Trilogy." In *Francis Ford Coppola's* Godfather *Trilogy*, ed. Nick Browne, 133–155. New York: Cambridge University Press, 2002.

Gripsrud, Jostein. *The Dynasty Years: Hollywood, Television, and Critical Media.* New York: Routledge, 1995.

Grossberg, Lawrence. *Bringing It All Back Home.* Durham, NC: Duke University Press, 1997.

———. *Dancing in Spite of Myself: Essays on Popular Culture.* Durham, NC: Duke University Press, 1997.

———. "Is Anybody Listening? Does Anybody Care? On 'The State of Rock.'" In *Microphone Fiends: Youth Music and Youth Culture,* ed. Andrew Ross and Tricia Rose, 41–58. New York: Routledge, 1994.

———. "Reflections of a Disappointed Popular Music Scholar." In *Rock Over the Edge: Transformations in Popular Music Culture,* ed. Roger Beebe, Denise Fulbrook, and Ben Saunders, 25–59. Durham, NC: Duke University Press, 2002.

———. *We Gotta Get Out of This Place.* New York: Routledge, 1992.

Guralnick, Peter. "Elvis Presley." In *Rolling Stone Illustrated History of Rock & Roll,* ed. Jim Miller, 19–34. New York: Random House/Rolling Stone Press, 1980.

Halberstam, Judith. *Female Masculinity.* Durham, NC: Duke University Press, 1998.

Handy, Bruce. "1600 Melrose Place." *Time,* May 30, 1994, 18.

Hanson, Ellis, ed. Introduction to *Out Takes: Essays on Queer Theory and Film.* Durham, NC: Duke University Press, 1999.

Harker, Dave. "Blood on the Tracks: Popular Music in the 1970s." In *The Arts in the 1970s: Cultural Closure?*, ed. Bart Moore-Gilbert, 240–258. New York: Routledge, 1994.

Harvey, David. *The Condition of Postmodernity.* Cambridge: Blackwell, 1989.

Hayward, Steven, and Andrew Brio. "The Eighteenth Brumaire of Tony Soprano." In *This Thing of Ours: Investigating* The Sopranos, ed. David Lavery, 203–214. New York: Columbia University Press, 2002.

Heath, Stephen. "Difference." In *The Sexual Subject: A* Screen *Reader in Sexuality,* 47–106. London: Routledge, 1992.

———. "Cinema and Psychoanalysis: Parallel Histories." In *Endless Night: Cinema and Psychoanalysis, Parallel Histories,* ed. Janet Bergstrom, 25–56. Berkeley: University of California Press, 1999.

———. "Notes on Suture." *Screen* 18, no. 4 (1977): 48–76.

———. *Questions of Cinema*. Bloomington: Indiana University Press, 1981.

Heinecken, Dawn. *Warrior Women of Television*. New York: Peter Lang, 2003.

Hiatt, Brian, and Evan Serpick. "The 99 Cent Solution." *Entertainment Weekly*, June 6, 2003, 12–13.

Hirsch, Foster. *Detours and Lost Highways: A Map of Neo-Noirs*. New York: Limelight, 1999.

Hobson, Dorothy. *Soap Opera*. London: Polity, 2003.

Holden, Stephen. "*The Sopranos*: An Introduction." In *The New York Times on The Sopranos*, xi–xix. New York: ibooks, 2000.

Holiday, Billie, with William Dufty. *Lady Sings the Blues*. New York: Penguin, 1956.

Holtz, Jeffrey. *Welcome to the Jungle: The Why Behind Generation X*. New York: St. Martin's, 1995.

hooks, bell. "Oppositional Gaze." In *Film and Theory*, ed. Robert Stam and Toby Miller, 510–523. New York: Blackwell, 2000.

———. *Reel to Real: Race, Sex and Class at the Movies*. New York: Routledge, 1996.

Horn, David. "The Identity of Jazz." In *Cambridge Companion to Jazz*, ed. Mervyn Cooke and David Horn, 9–32. Cambridge: Cambridge University Press, 2002.

Huyssen, Andreas. "Adorno in Reverse." In *Adorno: A Critical Reader*, ed. Nigel Gibson and Andrew Rubin, 29–56. Oxford: Blackwell, 2002.

———. *After the Great Divide: Modernism, Mass Culture, Postmodernism*. Bloomington: Indiana University Press, 1986.

Jameson, Fredric. *The Ideologies of Theory: Essays 1971–1986*. Minneapolis: University of Minnesota Press, 1988.

———. *Late Marxism, or the Persistence of the Dialectic*. London, Verso: 1990.

———. *Postmodernism, Or, The Cultural Logic of Late Capitalism*. Durham, NC: Duke University Press, 1991.

Jenkins, Henry, Tara McPherson, and Jane Shattuc. "Defining Popular Culture." In *Hop on Pop: The Politics and Pleasures of Popular Culture*, 26–42. Durham, NC: Duke University Press, 2003.

Johnson, Bruce. "The Jazz Diaspora." In *Cambridge Companion to Jazz*, ed. Mervyn Cooke and David Horn, 33–54. Cambridge: Cambridge University Press, 2002.

Johnson, Catherine. "*Buffy the Vampire Slayer.*" In *The Television Genre Book*, ed. Glen Creeber, 42. London: BFI, 2001.

Joyrich, Lynne. *Re-Viewing Reception: Television, Gender, and Postmodern Culture.* Bloomington: Indiana University Press, 1996.

Kalinak, Kathryn. "The Language of Music: A Brief Analysis of *Vertigo.*" In *Movie Music: The Film Reader*, ed. Kay Dickinson, 15–23. New York: Routledge, 2003.

Kaveney, Roz. "She Saved the World. A Lot." In *Reading the Vampire Slayer*, ed. Kaveney, 1–82. London: I. B. Tauris, 2004.

———. "Writing the Vampire Slayer." Interviews with Jane Espenson and Steven S. DeKnight." In *Reading the Vampire Slayer*, 100–131. London: I. B. Tauris, 2004.

Kellner, Douglas. "Television and the Frankfurt School (T. W. Adorno)." In *Television Studies*, ed. Toby Miller, 17–20. London: British Film Institute, 2002.

Kleinhans, Chuck. "*Ethnic Notions, Tongues Untied*: Mainstreams and Margins." *Jump Cut* (May 1991): 108–118.

Kreutzner, Gabriele, and Ellen Seiter. "Not All 'Soaps' Are Created Equal." In *To Be Continued . . . Soap Operas Around the World*, ed. Robert C. Allen, 122–144. New York: Routledge, 1995.

Kubrick, Stanley. "Kubrick Country." 1971. Interview by Penelope Houston. In *Stanley Kubrick: Interviews*, ed. Gene D. Phillips, 110–115. Jackson: University of Mississippi Press, 2001.

———. "Modern Times: An Interview with Stanley Kubrick." 1972. By Philip Strick and Penelope Houston. In *Stanley Kubrick: Interviews*, ed. Gene D. Phillips, 126–139. Jackson: University of Mississippi Press, 2001.

Lacan, Jacques. *The Four Fundamental Concepts of Psycho-Analysis.* Trans. Alan Sheridan. New York: Norton, 1981.

Laclau, Ernesto, and Chantal Mouffe. *Hegemony and Socialist Strategy: Towards a Radical Democratic Politics.* London: Verso, 1985.

Lang, Robert. "Looking for the 'Great Whatzit': *Kiss Me Deadly* and Film Noir." In *Perspectives on Film Noir*, ed. R. Burton Palmer, 171–184. New York: G. K. Hall, 1996.

Latham, Rob. *Consuming Youth: Vampires, Cyborgs, and the Culture of Consumption.* Chicago: University of Chicago Press, 2002.

Latifah, Queen, with Karen Hunter. *Ladies First: Revelations of a Strong Woman.* New York: William Morrow, 1999.

Lavery, David, and Robert J. Thompson. "David Chase, *The Sopranos*, and Television Creativity." In *This Thing of Ours: Investigating* The Sopranos, ed. David Lavery, 18–25. New York: Columbia University Press, 2002.

Lee, Martyn J. *Consumer Culture Reborn*. New York: Routledge, 1993.

Lehmann, Chris. *Revolt of the Masscult*. Chicago: Prickly Paradigm Press, 2003.

Leonard, Elmore. *Rum Punch*. New York: Delacorte, 1992.

Leppert, Richard. "Commentary: Music and Mass Culture." In *Essays on Music*, ed. Leppert, 327–372. Berkeley: University of California Press, 2002.

Lockett, Andrew. "Cultural Studies and Television." In *Television Studies*, ed. Toby Miller, 24–27. London: British Film Institute, 2002.

López, Humberto Manduley. "Rock in Cuba: History of a Wayward Son." In "Bridging Enigmas: Cubans on Cuba," ed. Ambrosio Fornet, *South Atlantic Quarterly* 96, no. 1 (Winter 1997): 135–141.

Macdonald, Dwight. *Against the American Grain*. New York: Random House, 1962.

———. "A Theory of Mass Culture." In *Mass Culture: The Popular Arts in America*, ed. Bernard Rosenberg and David Manning White, 59–73. Glencoe, IL: Free Press, 1957.

Machi, Mario, Allan May, and Charlie Molino. "Buffalo Crime Family." American Mafia.com, http://www.americanmafia.com/Cities/Buffalo.html.

Marc, David, and Robert J. Thompson. *Prime Time, Prime Movers*. Boston: Little, Brown, 1992.

Marcus, Greil. "The Girl Groups." In *Rolling Stone Illustrated History of Rock & Roll*, ed. Jim Miller, 160–161. New York: Random House/Rolling Stone Press, 1980.

———. *Ranters & Crowd Pleasers: Punk in Pop Music, 1977–92*. New York: Anchor, 1994.

Marin, Rick. "TV Tour Guide to the New LA." *New York Times*, August 23, 1992, sec. 9, 8.

Martin, Denis-Constant. "Music beyond Apartheid?" Trans. Val Morrison. In *Rockin' the Boat: Mass Music and Mass Movements*, ed. Reebee Garofalo, 195–207. Boston: South End Press, 1992.

Martin, Russell. *Beethoven's Hair*. New York: Broadway Books, 2000.

Marx, Karl. *Karl Marx: Selected Writings*. Ed. David McLellan. Oxford: Oxford University Press, 1985.

McArthur, Colin. Brigadoon, Braveheart *and the Scots*. London: I. B. Tauris, 2003.

———. *Underworld U.S.A.* London: Secker and Warburg/BFI, 1972.

McClary, Susan, and Robert Walser. "Start Making Sense! Musicology Wrestles with Rock." In *On Record: Rock, Pop, and the Written Word*, ed. Simon Frith and Andrew Goodwin, 277–292. New York: Pantheon, 1990.

McDonnell, Evelyn. "Rebel Girls." In *Trouble Girls: The Rolling Stone Book of Women in Rock*, ed. Barbara O'Dair, 453–463. New York: Random House/Rolling Stone Press, 1997.

McHugh, Kathleen. "Women in Traffic: LA Autobiography." In "Psycho-Marxism: Marxism and Psychoanalysis Late in the Twentieth Century," ed. Robert Miklitsch, special issue, *South Atlantic Quarterly* 97, no. 2 (Spring 1998): 391–412.

McKee, Alan. "*Buffy the Vampire Slayer*." In *Television Studies*, ed. Toby Miller, 69. London: BFI, 2002.

———. "Fandom." In *Television Studies*, ed. Toby Miller, 66–69. London: British Film Institute, 2002.

McRobbie, Angela. "Settling Accounts with Subcultures: A Feminist Critique." 1981. In *On Record: Rock, Pop, and the Written Word*, ed. Simon Frith and Andrew Goodwin, 66–80. New York: Pantheon, 1990.

Meisler, Andy. "A 'Soap' Mogul with an Eye for the 90's." *New York Times*, August 29, 1993, sec. 2, 29.

Menand, Louis. "Culture Club: The Short, Happy Life of an American Highbrow." *New Yorker*, October 15, 2000, 210ff.

Mercer, Kobena. "Dark and Lovely Too: Black Gay Men in Independent Film." In *Queer Looks: Perspectives on Lesbian and Gay Film and Video*, ed. Martha Gever, Pratibha Parmar, and John Greyson, 257–274. New York: Routledge, 1993.

Metz, Christian. *The Imaginary Signifier: Psychoanalysis and the Cinema*. Trans. Celia Britton, Annwyl Williams, Ben Brewster, and Alfred Guzzetti. Bloomington: Indiana University Press, 1982.

Middleton, Richard. *Studying Popular Music*. Buckingham, UK: Open University Press, 1990.

Miklitsch, Robert. *From Hegel to Madonna: Towards a General Economy of "Commodity Fetishism"*. Albany: State University of New York Press, 1998.

Miller, D. A. "Visual Pleasure in 1959." In *Out Takes: Essays on Queer Theory and Film*, ed. Ellis Hanson, 97–128. Durham, NC: Duke University Press, 1999.

Miller, Jacques-Alain. "La suture." *Cahiers pour l'analyse* 1 (1966): 39–51.

———. "Suture: Elements of the Logic of the Signifier." Trans. Jacqueline Rose. *Screen* 18, no. 4 (1977): 35–47.

Miller, James. *Flowers in the Dustbin: The Rise of Rock and Roll, 1947–1987.* New York: Simon and Schuster, 1999.

Miller, Toby. *Avengers.* London: British Film Institute, 1997.

Morley, David, with Roger Silverstone. *Television, Audiences, and Cultural Studies.* New York: Routledge, 1992.

Morris, Meaghan. *Too Soon, Too Late: History in Popular Culture.* Bloomington: Indiana University Press, 1998.

"MP Art: Art by the GALA Committee as Seen on Melrose Place." http://www. arts.ucsb/projects/mpart/about/about.html.

Mulvey, Laura. "Visual Pleasure and Narrative Cinema." In *Visual and Other Pleasures*, 14–26. Bloomington: Indiana University Press, 1989.

———. "Visual Pleasure and Narrative Cinema." In *The Sexual Subject: A* Screen *Reader in Sexuality*, 22–34. London: Routledge, 1992.

Munby, Jonathan. *Public Enemies, Public Heroes.* Chicago: Chicago University Press, 1999.

"Music Services Ready for Business." *USA Today*, December 3, 2001, sec. D, 3.

Neale, Steve. "Masculinity as Spectacle." 1983. In *The Sexual Subject: A* Screen *Reader in Sexuality*, 277–294. London: Routledge, 1992.

Negus, Keith. *Popular Music in Theory.* Hanover, NH: Wesleyan/University Press of New England, 1997.

———. *Producing Pop: Culture and Conflict in the Popular Music Industry.* London: Edward Arnold, 1992.

Nehring, Neil. *Flowers in the Dustbin: Culture, Anarchy, and Postwar England.* Ann Arbor: University of Michigan Press, 1993.

———. *Popular Music, Gender, and Postmodernism: Anger Is an Energy.* Thousand Oaks, CA: Sage, 1997.

Nelson, Rob, and Jon Cowan. *Revolution X: A Survival Guide for Our Generation.* New York: Penguin, 1994.

Nelson, Thomas Allen. *Kubrick: Inside a Film Artist's Maze.* Bloomington: Indiana University Press, 2000.

Nicholson, Stuart. *Billie Holiday.* Boston: Northeastern University Press, 1995.

Nightingale, Virginia. *Studying Audiences: The Shock of the Real*. New York: Routledge, 1996.

Nochimson, Martha. *Screen Couple Chemistry: The Power of 2*. Austin: University of Texas Press, 2002.

O'Connor, Brian. Introduction to *The Adorno Reader*, ed. O'Connor. Oxford, UK: Blackwell, 2000.

O'Connor, John. "An Emotional Subtext in the Sexy New Shows." *New York Times*, August 9, 1992, sec. 2, 28.

———. "Once More unto the Pool, Hunks." *New York Times*, July 15, 1992, sec. C, 15.

———. "TV's Midterm Grade." *New York Times*, November 1, 1992, sec. 2, 1.

Ostow, Micol, ed. *Once More with Feeling*. New York: Simon Pulse, 2002.

Oudart, Jean-Pierre. "Cinema and Suture." Trans. Kari Hanet. *Screen* 18, no. 44 (1977): 35–47.

———. "La suture." *Cahiers du cinéma* 211/212 (1969): 36–55.

Owen, Rob. *Gen X TV*. Syracuse, NY: Syracuse University Press, 1997.

Paddison, Max. *Adorno's Aesthetics of Music*. Cambridge: Cambridge University Press, 1993.

Palmer, Robert. "Rock Begins." In *The Rolling Stone Illustrated History of Rock & Roll*, ed. Jim Miller, 3–14. New York: Random House/Rolling Stone Press, 1980.

Parini, Jay. "The Cultural Work of *The Sopranos*." In *A Sitdown with* The Sopranos, ed. Regina Barreca, 75–87. New York: Palgrave Macmillan, 2002.

Parks, Lisa. "Brave New *Buffy*: Rethinking 'TV Violence.'" In *Quality Popular TV: Cult TV, The Industry and Fans*, ed. Mark Jancovich and James Lyons, 118–133. London: BFI, 2003.

Pattie, David. "Mobbed Up: *The Sopranos* and The Modern Gangster Film." In *This Thing of Ours: Investigating* The Sopranos, ed. David Lavery, 135–145. New York: Columbia University Press, 2002.

Pegg, Bruce. *Brown Eyed Handsome Man: The Life and Hard Times of Chuck Berry*. New York: Routledge, 2002.

Pender, Patricia. "'I'm Buffy and You're . . . History': The Postmodern Politics of *Buffy*." In *Fighting the Forces: What's at Stake in Buffy the Vampire Slayer*, ed. Rhonda Wilcox and David Lavery, 35–44. Lanham, MD: Rowman & Littlefield, 2002.

Perkins, William Eric. "The Rap Attack." In *Droppin' Science: Critical Essays on Rap Music and Hip Hop Culture*, ed. Perkins, 1–47. Philadelphia: Temple University Press, 1996.

Peterson, Richard. *The Production of Culture*. Thousand Oaks, CA: Sage, 1976.

Pfeil, Fred. *Another Tale to Tell*. London: Verso, 1990.

Polan, Dana. *Pulp Fiction*. London: British Film Institute, 2000.

Porter, Dennis. "Soap Time: Thoughts on a Commodity Art Form." 1977. In *Television: The Critical View*, ed. Horace Newcomb, 94–98. New York: Oxford University Press, 1979.

Puzo, Mario. *The Godfather*. New York: New American Library, 2002.

Rabinowitz, Peter. "'A Bird of Like Rarest Spun Heavenmetal': Music in *A Clockwork Orange*." In *Stanley Kubrick's* A Clockwork Orange, ed. Stuart Y. McDougal, 109–130. New York: Cambridge University Press, 2003.

Ramet, Sabrina Petra, ed. *Rocking the State*. Boulder, CO: Westview, 1994.

"Ranks for the Memories." *Entertainment Weekly*, June 7, 1996, 23.

Rapping, Elayne. "That Jane Austen Thing." *Progressive* 60, no. 7 (July 1996): 38ff.

———. "The Year of the Young." *The Progressive* (February 1993): 37ff.

Rasmussen, Randy. *Stanley Kubrick: Seven Films Analyzed*. Jefferson, NC: McFarland, 2001.

Richards, Keith. "Glimmer of Youth." Interview by David Browne. *Entertainment Weekly*, October 3, 1997, 31.

Rickels, Laurence. *The Case of California*. Baltimore: Johns Hopkins University Press, 1991.

———. *Vampire Lectures*. Minneapolis: University of Minnesota Press, 1999.

Riggs, Marlon. "*Tongues Untied*: An Interview with Marlon Riggs." Interview by Ron Simmons. In *Brother to Brother: Collected Writings by Black Gay Men*, ed. Essex Hemphill, 253–257. Los Angeles: Alyson Books, 1991.

Ritchie, Karen. *Marketing to Generation X*. New York: Lexington Books, 1995.

Ro, Ronin. *Gangsta: Merchandising the Rhymes of Violence*. New York: St. Martin's Press, 1996.

Robinson, Deanna Campbell, Elizabeth B. Buck, and Marlene Cuthbert, eds. *Music at the Margins: Popular Music and Global Diversity*. Newbury Park, CA: Sage, 1991.

Rogers, Mark C., Michael Epstein, and Jimmie L. Reeves. "*The Sopranos* as HBO Brand Equity: The Art of Commerce in the Age of Digital Reproduction." In *This Thing of Ours: Investigating* The Sopranos, ed. David Lavery, 42–57. New York: Columbia University Press, 2002.

"Rolling Stone Music Awards." *Rolling Stone*, January 20, 2000, 49.

Rose, Tricia. *Black Noise: Rap Music and Black Culture in Contemporary America.* Hanover, NH: Wesleyan/New England University Press, 1994.

———. "One Queen, One Tribe, One Destiny." In *Rock She Wrote*, ed. Evelyn McDonnell and Ann Powers, 312–317. New York: Delta, 1995.

Rosen, Philip, ed. *Narrative, Apparatus, Ideology: A Film Theory Reader.* New York: Columbia University Press, 1986.

Rosow, Eugene. *Born to Lose: The Gangster Film in America.* New York: Oxford University Press, 1978.

Ross, Alex. "Listen to This." *New Yorker*, February 16 and 23, 2004, 150–155.

———. "Pop 101: Academia Tunes In." *New Yorker*, July 14 and 21, 2003, 93–97.

Ross, Andrew. *Real Love: In Pursuit of Cultural Justice.* New York: New York University Press, 1998.

———. "This Bridge Called My Pussy." In *Madonnarama*, ed. Lisa Frank and Paul Smith, 47–54. Pittsburgh, PA: Cleis Press, 1993.

Rothman, William. "Against 'The System of the Suture.'" *Film Quarterly* 29, no. 1 (1975): 45–50.

Rothwell, Fred. *Long Distance Information: Chuck Berry's Recorded Legacy.* York, UK: Music Mentor Press, 2001.

Ryback, Timothy W. *Rock Around the Bloc: A History of Rock Music in Eastern Europe and the Soviet Union.* New York: Oxford University Press, 1990.

Salt, Barry. "Film Style and Technology in the Forties." *Film Quarterly* 31 (Fall 1977): 46–57.

Saunders, Francis Stonor. *The Cultural Cold War: The CIA and the World of Arts and Letters.* New York: New Press, 2000.

Sayer, Karen. "This Was Our World and They Made It Theirs." In *Reading the Vampire Slayer*, ed. Roz Kaveney, 132–155. London: I.B. Tauris, 2004.

Schwarzbaum, Lisa. "Spielberg." *Entertainment Weekly*, August 8, 2003, 54.

Seabrook, John. "The Money Note: Can the Record Business Survive?" *New Yorker*, July 7, 2003, 42–55.

Shadoian, Jack. *Dreams and Dead Ends: The American Gangster/Crime Film*. Cambridge, MA: MIT Press, 1977.

Sharkey, Betsy. "Grant Show: The Blue-Collar Sex Symbol of 'Melrose Place.'" *New York Times*, July 26, 1992, sec. 2, 23.

Shier, Steven E. *After the Boom: The Politics of Generation X*. Lanham, MD: Rowman and Littlefield, 1997.

Shuttleworth, Ian. "They Always Mistake Me for the Character I Play!: Transformation, Identity and Role-Playing in the *Buffy*verse." In *Reading the Vampire Slayer*, ed. Roz Kaveney, 233–276. London: I. B. Tauris, 2004.

Silver, Alain. "*Kiss Me Deadly*: Evidence of a Style." In *Film Noir Reader*, ed. Silver and James Ursini, 209–235. New York: Limelight Editions, 2000.

Silverman, Kaja. *Male Subjectivity at the Margins*. New York: Routledge, 1992.

———. *The Subject of Semiotics*. New York: Oxford University Press, 1983.

Smith, Aaron M. "Stefano Magaddino." Gangsters Incorporated. http://gangstersinc.tripod.com/Magaddino.html.

Smith, Jeff. *The Sounds of Commerce*. New York: Columbia University Press, 1998.

———. "Unheard Melodies: A Critique." In *Post-Theory*, ed. David Bordwell and Noël Carroll, 230–247. Madison: University of Wisconsin Press, 1996.

Smith, Valerie. *Not Just Race, Not Just Gender*. New York: Routledge, 1998.

Soja, Edward. *Postmodern Geographies: The Reassertion of Space in Critical Social Theory*. London: Verso, 1988.

Spelling, Aaron. *Aaron Spelling: A Prime-Time Life*. New York: St. Martin's, 1995.

Stacey, Jackie. "Desperately Seeking Difference." In *The Sexual Subject: A Screen Reader in Sexuality*, 244–264. London: Routledge, 1992.

Staiger, Janet. *Perverse Spectators: The Practices of Film Reception*. New York: New York University Press, 2000.

Steinert, Heinz. *Culture Industry*. Trans. Sally-Ann Spencer. Malden, MA: Polity, 2003.

Storey, John. "'Expecting Rain': Opera as Popular Culture?" In *High Pop: Making Culture into Mass Entertainment*, ed. Jim Collins, 32–55. Oxford, UK: Blackwell, 2002.

Sullivan, Andrew. "Washington Diarist." *New Republic*, December 12, 1994, 43.

Tarantino, Quentin. "Blaxploitation: What It Is, What It Was!" In *The Film Geek Files*, ed. Paul A. Woods, 138–143. London: Plexus, 2000.

————. "Interview." 1998. By Adrian Wootton. http://film.guardian.co.uk/ Guardian_NFT/interview.

————. "Interview with Quentin Tarantino." 1994. By Joshua Mooney. In *Quentin Tarantino: Interviews*, ed. Gerald Peary, 70–79. Jackson: University of Mississippi Press, 1998.

————. *Jackie Brown: A Screenplay*. New York: Hyperion, 1997.

————. "Press Conference on *Jackie Brown*." 1997. In *Quentin Tarantino: Interviews*, ed. Gerald Peary, 198–203. Jackson: University of Mississippi Press, 1998.

Taylor, Timothy D. *Global Pop: World Music, World Markets*. New York: Routledge, 1997.

————. "His Name Was in Lights: Chuck Berry's 'Johhny B. Goode.'" In *Reading Pop*, ed. Richard Middleton, 165–182. New York: Oxford University Press, 2000.

Toop, David. *Rap Attack 2: African Rap and Global Hip Hop*. London: Serpent's Tail, 1991.

Torres, Sasha. "Melodrama, Masculinity, and the Family: *thirtysomething* as Therapy." In *Male Trouble*, ed. Constance Penley and Sharon Willis, 283–302. Minneapolis: University of Minnesota Press, 1993.

Tropiano, Stephen. *Prime Time Closet: A History of Gays and Lesbians on TV*. New York: Applause, 2002.

Tucker, Ken. "Goons and Toons." *Entertainment Weekly*, April 2, 1999, 74ff.

————. "Remade Men." *Entertainment Weekly*, March 2, 2001, 53ff.

Tyrnauer, Matthew. "Star Power!" *Vanity Fair*, May 1995, 173ff.

Van Leer, David. "Visible Silence: Spectatorship in Black Gay and Lesbian Film." In *Representing Blackness: Issues in Film and Video*, ed. Valerie Smith, 157–181. New Brunswick, NJ: Rutgers University Press, 1997.

Vila, Pablo. "*Rock Nacional* and Dictatorship in Argentina." In *Rockin' the Boat: Mass Music and Mass Movements*, ed. Reebee Garofalo, 209–229. Boston: South End Press, 1992.

Walker, Alexander. *Stanley Kubrick: Director*. New York: Norton, 1999.

Walser, Robert. *Running with the Devil: Power, Gender, and Madness in Heavy Metal Music*. Hanover, NH: Wesleyan/University Press of New England, 1993.

Washington, Booker T. *Up From Slavery*. New York: Signet, 2000.

White, Emily. "Revolution Girl Style Now." In *Rock She Wrote*, ed. Evelyn McDonnell and Ann Powers, 396–408. New York: Delta, 1995.

Whiteley, Shiela. *The Space Between the Notes: Rock and the Counter-Culture*. New York: Routledge, 1992.

Wicke, Peter. *Rock Music: Culture, Aesthetics, and Sociology*. Trans. Rachel Fogg. Cambridge: Cambridge University Press, 1990.

Wild, David. "*Melrose Place* Is a Really Good Show." *Rolling Stone*, May 19, 1994, 50ff.

Willeman, Paul. *Looks and Frictions: Essays in Cultural Studies and Film Theory*. Bloomington: Indiana University Press, 1994.

Williams, Raymond. *Marxism and Literature*. London: Oxford University Press, 1977.

———. *Politics and Letters: Interviews with New Left Review*. London: Verso, 1979.

Willis, Ellen. "Our Bodies, Ourselves." In *This Thing of Ours: Investigating* The Sopranos, ed. David Lavery, 2–9. New York: Columbia University Press, 2002.

Willis, Sharon. *High Contrast: Race and Gender in Contemporary Hollywood Film*. Durham, NC: Duke University Press, 1997.

Willman, Chris. "Addicted to the 'Place.'" *New York Times*, March 16, 1994, sec. F, 1.

———. "Beautiful South." *Entertainment Weekly*, January 17, 2003, 77ff.

Wolcott, James. "HBO's Singular Sensation." *Vanity Fair*, February 2000, 66ff.

Wreszin, Michael. Introduction to *Interviews with Dwight Macdonald*. Jackson: University of Mississippi Press, 2003.

Yacowar, Maurice. The Sopranos *on the Couch: Analyzing Television's Greatest Series*. New York: Continuum, 2002.

Žižek, Slavoj. *The Fright of Real Tears*. London: British Film Institute, 2000.

———. "Looking Awry." In *Film and Theory*, ed. Robert Stam and Toby Miller, 524–538. New York: Blackwell, 2000.

Zoglin, Richard. "The Young and the Senseless." *Time*, March 28, 1994, 69.

Index